The K Club Cookbook

The K Club Cookbook

Producer to Plate

Celebrating 25 Years

ATRIUM

First published by Atrium
Atrium is an imprint of Cork University Press
Youngline Industrial Estate, Pouladuff Road, Togher, Cork, Ireland

British Library Cataloguing in Publication Data

A CIP catalogue record for this book is available from the British Library.

ISBN 978-1-78205-151-0

Recipes	Finbarr Higgins
Editor	Lizzie Gore-Grimes
Photography	Hugh McElveen
Book design and typesetting	Anú Design, Tara
Cover design and illustrations	Orlagh Murphy
Wine Pairing notes	Lisa O'Doherty
Wine & Bar copy	Aoife Carrigy
Printed by	Gutenberg Press, Malta

Photograph of Dr Smurfit on page xiii by Justin MacInnes. Photograph of Finbarr Higgins on page xiv by Anthony Woods.

Irish linen featured in the book is by bespoke Irish linen company 31 Chapel Lane, www.31chapellane.com.

CONTENTS

SPRING SUMMER RECIPES

STARTER

MAIN COURSE

MAIN COURSE

DESSERT

Portrait. Attributed to FRANS HALS, b. c.1580 ; d. 1666 Dutch School

A word from Dr Michael Smurfit

I'm delighted and very proud to introduce to you *The K Club Cookbook* in celebration of our 25th anniversary.

One of the many things that I am most proud of here at The K Club is our food. Since opening first as a luxury hotel in 1991 we were Ireland's first AA Five Red Star Property. To this day we continue to deliver the very highest levels of service and standards and nowhere is this more apparent than in our food and beverage offerings.

Food has always played a very important role here at The K Club. For the last twenty-five years we have hosted heads of state, celebrities, sports personalities and stars from the large and small screen. These people and many others who have dined with us have all enjoyed our food and our legendary hospitality.

I hope that you will enjoy reading this book and it just remains for me to say a huge thank you to Finbarr Higgins and his team who make dining here at The K Club such a wonderful experience.

Dr M.W.J Smurfit
September 2015

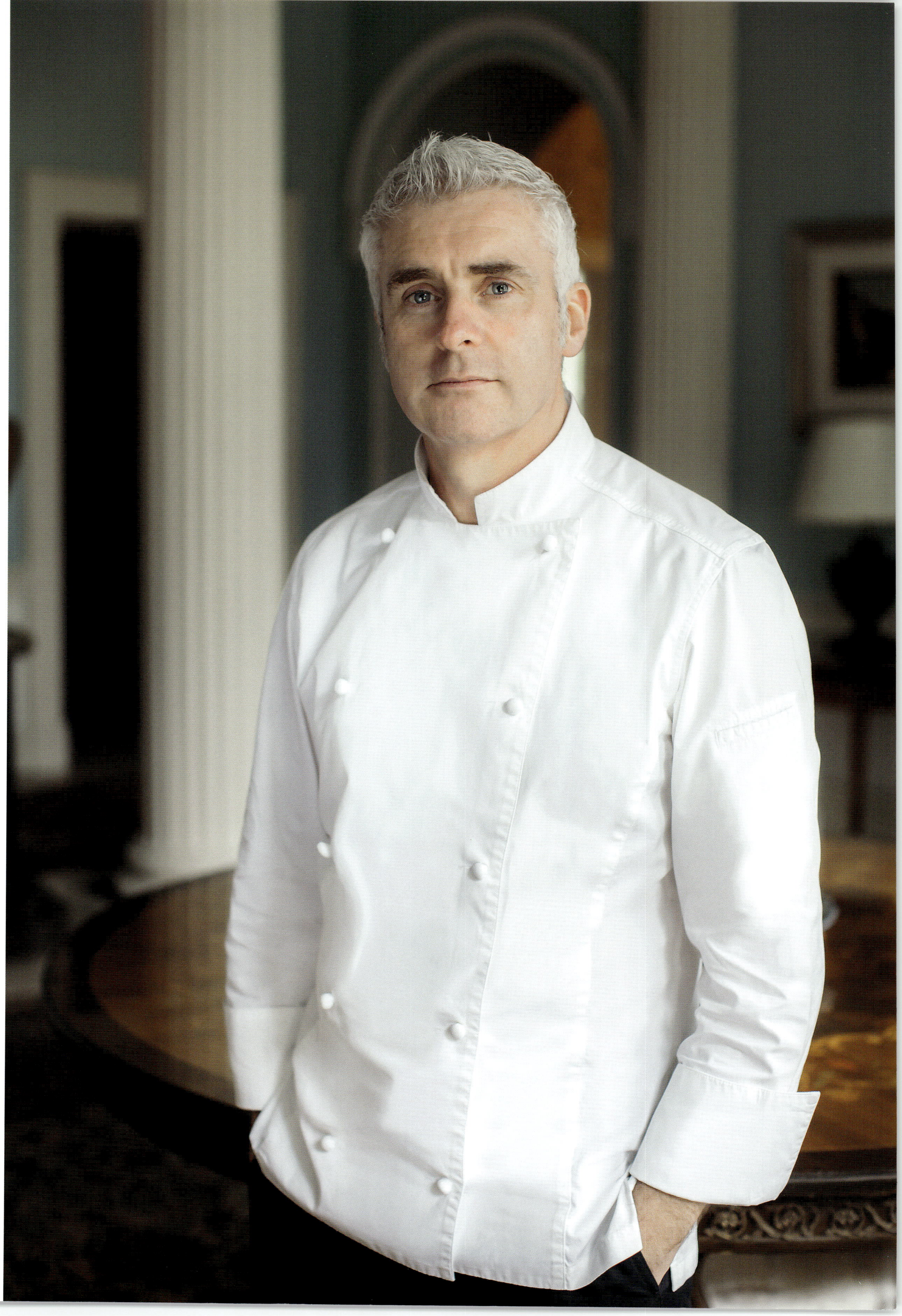

An introduction from Finbarr Higgins

We have been planning this book and talking about it for so many years that I can't believe it's actually here now, in our hands. To see it in print has been immensely rewarding. I have been working here at The K Club for twenty-three years and this tome documents half of my life. The book's transformation from concept to concrete form has been an extended one – and one that simply could not have happened without the support and contribution of the great team of chefs working here in the kitchen – and indeed the hundreds of talented people who have passed through these doors over the years. I am also very grateful for the trust bestowed on me by the owner and management at The K Club who gave me free rein to produce this book. It has been a memorable, if challenging, experience and I hope that the end result does justice to that trust.

When I first arrived at The K Club, I planned to be here for about two years … somehow that changed into twenty-three! I believe it's a testament to the business that I am only one of many staff who have been here for over a quarter of a century and more. Over the years I have seen the resort evolve and grow. When I started working at the The K Club it was a small hotel with thirty-nine guest bedrooms and one restaurant – The Byerley Turk. Today, The K Club is a world-renowned international destination with over 140 guest bedrooms, an award-winning spa, two world-class golf courses, six restaurants and a private property for exclusive use.

The business model has changed dynamically over the last twenty-five years but one thing has remained steadfast over the decades, and that is our abiding food philosophy. When I began working at the K Club there was a very straightforward premise in place when it came to sourcing produce – we simply sought out the best in season and local produce, and then set out to combine them elegantly on the plate, without over complicating the flavours. And this is how we continue to do things today; the only real difference is that we are now more vocal about it. There is such a wealth of stellar indigenous produce on our doorstep, it makes us proud to stand behind the quality of the ingredients that we use and therefore the resulting dishes on our menu.

As the business has expanded and evolved I too feel that I have changed. Needless to say the challenges that I faced when I started out as Head Chef of a single restaurant, managing a team of twelve, are very different to the challenges that I tackle today as Executive Chef over the entire resort, responsible for over thirty staff. But there is a great sense of working together. We really value our staff here and I am proud to run a collaborative kitchen.

One of my first jobs was in The Savoy kitchen in London, working under über-chef Anton Edelmann. He was a brilliant chef and it was an amazing place in which to work, but it was such an aggressive, volatile environment – fuelled on frenzy and competitive stress. Over the years I have learned that you get a better result when you run a quiet, controlled kitchen.

I am happy to say that there is no place for ego or ego-led histrionics in my kitchen and as a result we have quite a remarkable staff retention rate; I've lost count of the number of chefs who came for six months and ended up staying six years. It is their collective blood, sweat and tears that have enabled The K Club to maintain its high level of service and award-winning food. Every day we have to fight to maintain that standard; as a chef you can never sit back and take your foot off the pedal. I think the day that you stop feeling that little frisson of fear, that a customer will come away unhappy with your food is the day that you need to pack it all in.

I'll admit that putting this book out there has been the greatest frisson of all. I can only hope that it acts as an adequate tribute to all of the people over the last twenty-five years who have helped to make the food experience at The K Club what it is today.

Finbarr Higgins
September 2015

10
HONDA
The MAYFLY Ultra

Acknowledgements

First and foremost I would like to thank The K Club team of chefs for all their hard work and diligence in helping to make this book a reality. I would also like to acknowledge the wider K Club food and beverage teams for their vital contribution and indeed the multitude of chefs past and present who have passed through the kitchen here at The K Club for their input and professionalism.

I would like to thank the management team for their support of the book and for their patience and understanding during the process. Thanks also to Dr Smurfit for his belief in me and for giving me the opportunity to head up his kitchen.

This book is also dedicated to the producers that have supported us over the last 25 years and helped us achieve our goal to produce food that we are all endlessly proud of.

I would also like to thank the book's team leader Lizzie Gore-Grimes for all her extremely helpful input, advice, editing skills and relentless deadline keeping. And huge thanks to Hugh McElveen for his creative expertise, endless patience and stunning photography.

And last but most definitely not least – to Sandra, Caoimhe and Oisin for supporting and understanding their chef husband and Dad.

Finbarr Higgins
September 2015

SPRING / SUMMER

New season green asparagus tips with fresh morels, baby artichokes and mushroom foam

We used to grow our own asparagus in the Victorian Garden on the estate here, but sadly the crop died off. We now source it from the Rye Valley in England, where they produce very good asparagus. Once the asparagus and morels come into season, that's spring on a plate for me.

WINE PAIRING

Seresin Sauvignon Blanc, Marlborough, New Zealand

The combination of the slight herby quality of this wine with the asparagus is sublime.

FOR THE MOREL DRESSING

50ml (2fl oz) morel stock (see page 270)
5ml (¼fl oz) hazelnut oil
10ml (½fl oz) peanut oil
10ml (½fl oz) groundnut oil
10ml (½fl oz) extra virgin first-press olive oil
½ tsp truffle vinegar
salt and milled white pepper

FOR THE FRESH MORELS

25gm (1oz) unsalted Avonmore butter
15gm (½oz) chopped shallots
200gm (7oz) fresh morels
25ml (1fl oz) fresh chicken stock (see page 270)

FOR THE MUSHROOM FOAM

30gm (1oz) unsalted Avonmore butter
20gm (¾oz) chopped leek
10gm (½oz) chopped celery
20gm (¾oz) chopped onion
½ garlic clove
200gm (7oz) fresh wild mushroom trimmings or 50gm (2oz) dried mushrooms
400ml (14fl oz) chicken stock (see page 270)
10 coriander seeds
1 small sprig of fresh thyme
1 tsp xanthan gum

FOR THE GREEN ASPARAGUS TIPS

12 green asparagus tips
10ml (½fl oz) Newgrange Gold rapeseed oil
salt and freshly milled white pepper

TO SERVE

4 preserved baby artichokes (see page 274)
micro-coriander, to garnish

SERVES 4

MOREL DRESSING

Place the morel stock in a bowl. Slowly whisk in the oils one by one and then whisk in the vinegar. Season with salt and white pepper to taste.

FRESH MORELS

Melt the unsalted butter in a pan over a medium heat. Add the shallots and cook over a low heat until they are soft and translucent. Add the fresh morels, followed by the chicken stock and lightly poach the morels until soft. Set aside to keep warm.

MUSHROOM FOAM

Melt the butter in a pot, add the chopped vegetables and mushrooms and sweat gently over a low heat until soft but not coloured. Add the stock and the coriander and thyme and bring to the boil, then reduce to simmer for 1 hour. Pass the stock through a fine sieve and measure out the liquid. You will need to add 2gm (1 tsp) of xanthan gum per 200ml (7fl oz) of stock. Transfer the liquid back to the pot, add the correct amount of xanthan gum and bring back up to the boil. Then pour into a siphon bottle and add 2 ISI gas chargers. Shake very well.

GREEN ASPARAGUS TIPS

Trim the bottoms from the asparagus tips and remove any excess leaves with a knife. Cook the asparagus in boiling, salted water until al dente. Toss in a little oil and season with salt and freshly milled white pepper.

TO SERVE

Remove the artichokes from the fridge 30 minutes before serving. Drain the artichokes and toss them in a little Manodori balsamic vinegar and rapeseed oil with salt and milled white peppercorn. Place 1 artichoke on a warm plate. Cut the asparagus tips in half at an angle and place 3 on the plate, as pictured. Add the morels and finish with a drizzle of morel dressing. Sprinkle with micro-coriander and siphon on the foam last.

Summer carrot plate with fennel seed oil and cumin-spiced crumble

This is a really light vegetarian starter. The delicate spicing of the cumin works beautifully to bring out the natural earthy sweetness of the carrot.

WINE PAIRING

Colombette Pinot Noir

This is a light, fruity Pinot from the south of France. A good New Zealand example would also work well.

FOR THE FENNEL SEED OIL

25gm (1oz) fennel seeds
50ml (2fl oz) Newgrange Gold rapeseed oil

FOR THE DEHYDRATED CARROT STICK

1 large carrot

FOR THE CARROT EMULSION

125ml (4fl oz) organic carrot juice
¼ tsp xanthan gum

FOR THE CARROT PARFAIT

750ml (26fl oz) organic carrot juice
350ml (12fl oz) Avonmore cream, whipped
7 leaves of gelatine, soaked in water

FOR THE CUMIN-SPICED CRUMBLE

15gm (½oz) unsalted Avonmore butter
¾ tsp ground cumin
85gm (3oz) caster sugar
25ml (1fl oz) olive oil
60gm (2oz) pear purée
35gm (1¼oz) strong flour

FOR THE SPICED CARROT JELLY

¼ tsp ground cumin powder
125ml (4½fl oz) organic carrot juice
3 leaves of gelatine, soaked in water
salt and freshly milled black pepper

FOR THE WHITE CARROT PURÉE

10g (½oz) unsalted Avonmore butter
¼ shallot, finely chopped
¼ small garlic clove, chopped
1 small sprig of fresh thyme
100g (3½oz) peeled and chopped white carrot
150ml (5.3fl oz) vegetable stock (see page 271)
salt and freshly milled black pepper

FOR THE BABY CARROTS

10 baby carrots
20ml (¾fl oz) Newgrange Gold rapeseed oil
salt and freshly milled white pepper

TO SERVE

Carrick Farm micro-carrot

SERVES 10

FENNEL SEED OIL

Toast the fennel seeds in a dry pan over a medium heat to release the flavour. Add rapeseed oil and heat to 160°C, then set aside to cool. Leave the oil to infuse for 2 days before use.

DEHYDRATED CARROT STICK

Slice the carrot lengthwise into very fine ribbon strips (no thicker than 2mm/1/10in). Place in the dehydrator for 4 hours at 125°C. Remove when crisp and dry.

CARROT EMULSION

Place the juice in a pot and boil until reduced to 80ml (3fl oz). Whisk in the xanthan gum. Pass through a fine chinois or sieve and leave to cool.

CARROT PARFAIT

Place the carrot juice in a pot and reduce by two-thirds to 250ml. Squeeze the excess water out of the gelatine leaves and add them to the warm carrot juice reduction. Allow to cool slightly. Fold in the whipped cream, a little at a time, until the parfait is completely mixed. Pour immediately into ten 7cm x 3cm (3in x 1in) rectangular moulds and allow to set. Once set, remove the carrot parfait from the moulds and set aside in the fridge for serving.

CUMIN-SPICED CRUMBLE

Melt the butter in a pan and mix in the ground cumin and caster sugar until the sugar is dissolved. Pour in the olive oil and mix for 1 minute at approximately 150°C. Add the pear purée and flour and mix until smooth. Spread the mixture very thinly on to a baking sheet and cook in an oven preheated to 160°C until golden brown. Remove and leave to cool, then crush into small pieces.

SPICED CARROT JELLY

Place the cumin in a dry pot over a medium heat and cook for 1–2 minutes to release the flavour. Pour in the carrot juice and bring up to the boil. Squeeze the excess water out of the gelatine leaves and then add them to the juice. Remove from the heat and whisk until the gelatine dissolves. Season to taste and pass through a fine chinois or sieve. Place in a mould to set and then cut up into dice as required.

WHITE CARROT PURÉE

Place the unsalted butter, shallot, garlic and thyme in a pot and cook over a low heat until soft. Add the chopped carrot and vegetable stock and cook until the carrot is cooked through. Blitz in a HotmixPRO blender (or similar) and season to taste. Keep warm.

BABY CARROTS

Cook the baby carrots in salted water until al dente. Toss the carrots in rapeseed oil and season to taste with salt and freshly milled white pepper.

TO SERVE

Add a dollop of warm white carrot purée to the side of a plate and drag a spoon through it. Place the parfait in the centre of the plate. Put 3 dots of carrot emulsion to the side. Place the crumble in a neat line. Pile some jelly half on, half off the parfait. Stand the baby carrot against the parfait and finish with the dehydrated carrot. Drizzle over a little fennel seed oil and add micro-carrot to garnish.

Macroom Irish buffalo bocconcini mozzarella, Bloody Mary jelly, Newgrange Gold rapeseed oil and apple balsamic vinegar

This dish is all about the merging of three beautiful Irish artisan products – I simply present them on a plate for people to enjoy. I love the combination of Carrick Farm peppery micro-rocket, the nutty Newgrange Gold rapeseed oil and the sharpness of the balsamic pearls cutting through the creamy, sweet Macroom Irish buffalo mozzarella.

WINE PAIRING

Santa Sofia Pinot Grigio

If you serve Italian wine with Italian food, you won't go wrong. The fruity pear flavours in this Pinot Grigio work beautifully with the creamy mozzarella.

FOR THE DEHYDRATED SHALLOT TUILE

1 shallot

FOR THE APPLE BALSAMIC PEARLS

50gm (2oz) apple balsamic vinegar
50gm (2oz) water
½ tsp agar-agar
5 litres (9 pints) of vegetable oil, chilled to 2°C

FOR THE BLOODY MARY JELLY

220ml (8fl oz) tomato juice
36ml (1¼fl oz) vodka
4 dashes Worcestershire sauce
4 dashes Tabasco
generous pinch of salt and freshly milled black pepper
12 leaves of gelatine, soaked in water

FOR THE BASIL CUSTARD

40gm (1½oz) egg yolk
pinch of salt
pinch of sugar
15gm (½oz) fresh basil leaves
125ml (4fl oz) Avonmore cream
½ leaf of gelatine, soaked in water

TO SERVE

18 pieces of Macroom Dairy bocconcini mozzarella (3 per portion), room temperature
80ml (3fl oz) Newgrange Gold rapeseed oil
20ml (¾fl oz) apple balsamic vinegar
micro-rocket

SERVES 6

DEHYDRATED SHALLOT TUILE

Peel the shallot, leaving a little of the root on. Slice the shallot lengthwise into 2mm-thick slices. Place in a dehydrator, set to 125°C, for 4 hours until crisp. Set aside ready to use.

APPLE BALSAMIC PEARLS

Place the vinegar and water in a pot and bring to the boil. Add the agar-agar and whisk until combined. Pour into a disposable piping bag and snip a tiny cut at the tip of the bag to allow a very small amount to leak out. Pipe the full bag into the container of chilled oil; small apple balsamic pearls will form and set as they sink in the oil. Pass the oil through a sieve to extract the pearls and wash off the excess oil with cold water. Set aside ready to use.

BLOODY MARY JELLY

Mix all the ingredients together in a pot and place over a gentle heat to warm. Squeeze the excess water from the gelatine leaves and add to the pot. Whisk until the gelatine is completely dissolved. Remove from the heat and allow to cool. Pour into a shallow mould and leave to set in the fridge. Once set, cut the jelly into 10cm (4in) wide and 5mm-thick circles.

BASIL CUSTARD

Place the egg yolks in a bowl with the sugar and salt and whisk lightly to combine. In a separate pot add the cream and basil leaves and heat gently over a low heat to infuse for 20 minutes. Remove from the heat, pass through a fine sieve or chinois and allow to cool. Then whisk the warm cream into the egg yolk mix. Place the combined mixture back over the heat for about 1 minute. Squeeze the excess water out of the gelatine leaf and add it to the pot. Whisk until the gelatine is completely dissolved and then remove from the heat and allow to cool.

TO SERVE

Place the jelly (straight from the fridge) into the centre of a wide-rimmed bowl with a lip. Pour in enough rapeseed oil to surround the jelly, then place the mozzarella on top. Dress the micro-rocket with a little apple balsamic vinegar and oil and place on top. Finish with the dehydrated shallot tuile. Draw a line of basil custard on the plate and garnish with a pile of apple balsamic pearls.

Kerry prawn tails in garlic and flat-leaf parsley butter

On a number of occasions I tried to remove this dish from the menu to make way for a new one, but we were met with such resistance that it's now a permanent feature. Some dishes are so simple and yet so good. Of course, the success of this dish is all down to the quality of the prawns. You need to source the absolute best you can lay your hands on.

WINE PAIRING

Hubert Brochard Sancerre

You need acidity here to match the richness of the garlic butter. Any good Sancerre will do.

6 Kerry prawn tails or langoustines (5–7 per kg grade)
salt and freshly milled white pepper
20gm (¾oz) plain flour
10ml (½fl oz) Newgrange Gold rapeseed oil
10ml (½fl oz) clarified butter (see page 272)
1 tsp garlic purée
100gm (3½oz) Avonmore unsalted butter
5ml (¼fl oz) freshly squeezed lemon juice
1 tbsp chopped flat-leaf parsley

SERVES 1

Season the prawns with a little salt and white pepper, then roll them in the flour, patting off any excess flour. Add the rapeseed oil and clarified butter to a hot pan and fry off the prawns until golden brown on each side. Drain off any excess cooking oil and then add the garlic purée, unsalted butter and lemon juice. Add the parsley at the last minute. Taste, and adjust the seasoning. Serve directly from the pan into warm bowls.

Rock of native shellfish and sea air

This dish is all about showcasing my three favourite Irish shellfish – crab, lobster and prawn. I like serving this dish on a rock, to enhance the sense of eating the shellfish in its freshest form, as if just pulled from the sea. The Kerry prawn and cocktail sauce combination is a classic, obviously, and one I never tire of. The tangy mango and vanilla chutney works brilliantly with the naturally creamy, sweet lobster. I have to admit, the rocks are hard work for the serving staff, but there is always an audible gasp when they arrive at the table, which makes it worth it.

WINE PAIRING

Domaine Mosnier Chablis

There is nothing better than the combination of Chablis and seafood. Grown on fossilised oyster shells left over from the ice age, this wine is flinty and dry but with an essence of the sea.

FOR THE MANGO AND VANILLA CHUTNEY

2 ripe mangoes, peeled and diced
30ml (1fl oz) malt vinegar
15gm (½oz) sugar
¼ fresh vanilla pod, cut in half and seeds removed

FOR THE PLUM TOMATO CORIANDER SALSA

50gm (2oz) fresh plum tomatoes, peeled, deseeded and chopped
30ml (1fl oz) Newgrange Gold rapeseed oil
5gm (¼oz) finely chopped shallot
½ red chilli, chopped
½ tsp chopped fresh coriander
squeeze of fresh lemon juice

FOR THE IRISH ATLANTIC LOBSTER

1 fresh lobster (about 750gm/1lb 10oz)
1 tbsp olive oil
1 tsp fresh lemon juice
salt and freshly milled black pepper

FOR THE POACHED KERRY PRAWN TAIL WITH PIPETTE OF COCKTAIL SAUCE

5 native prawns or langoustines (5–7 per kilo grade)
1 tbsp Newgrange Gold rapeseed oil
5ml (¼fl oz) freshly squeezed lemon juice
salt and freshly milled black pepper
100ml (3½fl oz) fresh mayonnaise (see page 272)
40gm (1½oz) fresh tomato chutney (see page 274)
½ tsp Worcestershire sauce
1 drop Tabasco sauce
small pinch cayenne pepper
1 tbsp Armagnac

FOR THE TRALEE BAY CRAB

100gm (3½oz) Tralee Bay crab meat
35gm (1¼oz) crème fraîche
zest of ½ lime
salt and freshly milled black pepper

FOR THE SEA AIR

3 fresh Clarinbridge oysters
200ml (7fl oz) Avonmore low-fat milk
squeeze of fresh lemon juice
1 level tsp lecithin powder
2ml (¼fl oz) balsamic vinegar

FOR THE SEAWEED SALAD

20gm (¾oz) dried seaweed
5gm (¼oz) shallot, finely chopped
10gm (½oz) sesame seeds, toasted
¼ red chilli, chopped
50ml (2fl oz) curry oil (see page xxx)
5ml (¼fl oz) rapeseed oil
½ clove garlic, crushed
50ml (2fl oz) rice wine vinegar

TO SERVE

orange pearls, to garnish (see page 24, smoked salmon starter)
citrus dressing, to garnish (see page 272)

SERVES 5

MANGO AND VANILLA CHUTNEY

To make the chutney, place the sugar in a small pot and cook to a light caramel. Add the malt vinegar, mix to combine and then add the vanilla. Next add the mango and cook until the mixture softens and forms a chutney consistency. Transfer to a sterilised Kilner jar and transfer to a steamer for 15 minutes to seal. Preserve for at least 1 month before using.

PLUM TOMATO CORIANDER SALSA

Mix all the ingredients together in a container with a lid and then cover and chill overnight to allow the flavours to infuse.

IRISH ATLANTIC LOBSTER

For detailed instructions on preparing and cooking the lobster, please see page 277. Place the claws and knuckles in a small bowl and slice the tail into 4 equal pieces. Place the tail, claws and knuckles in a small bowl and pour over the rapeseed oil and lemon juice. Toss gently and season to taste. Set aside.

POACHED KERRY PRAWN TAIL WITH PIPETTE OF COCKTAIL SAUCE

To prepare the prawns, peel the tails from the shells and discard. Using a small knife, remove the back vein running down the middle of the prawn. Place the prawns in simmering salted water for 1 minute and then immediately transfer to a bowl of iced water to cool. When cold, remove, drain and dry. Toss the cooked prawns in a bowl with the rapeseed oil, squeeze of lemon juice and salt and pepper to taste. To make the cocktail sauce, whisk all the remaining ingredients together and fill 5 pipettes with the sauce.

TRALEE BAY CRAB

Pick through the crab meat very carefully and remove any cartilage or small bits of shell. Mix in the lime zest and crème fraîche and season to taste.

SEA AIR

Remove the oyster meat and juice from the shell and place in a blender. Add the lemon juice, milk and balsamic vinegar. Blend for 1 minute and then pass through a fine sieve. Transfer into a rectangular container (you need this shape to form a good foam). Add the lecithin powder and, using a stick blender, whizz until the liquid starts to foam up. Leave to settle a little and scoop up the air bubbles.

SEAWEED SALAD

Soak the dried seaweed in cold water for 10 minutes and drain. Mix all the rest of the ingredients together in a bowl to make the dressing. Place the seaweed in a bowl and mix well in the dressing.

TO SERVE

Fill a 5cm (2in) ring mould with crab. Place it on the rock (or a long rectangular plate) and put a spoonful of the tomato salsa on top. Place a pile of seaweed salad in the middle of the rock (or plate) and top with a prawn. Quenelle the mango chutney on the rock (or plate) and lean the lobster against it. Place a few orange pearls on the prawn. Add a few dots of citrus dressing and scoop some bubbles of sea air over just before serving.

Seared Castletownbere scallops with curried pineapple and fennel cannelloni, cauliflower purée and beetroot ice cream

We have been using the king scallops from this part of Cork for the best part of twenty years. They are large, sweet and meaty and really stand out in quality. The beetroot ice cream lends an earthiness to the dish, which really complements the scallops, and the cauliflower and curry elements naturally work very well together.

WINE PAIRING

Butterfly Sauvignon Blanc, Loire Valley

This is one of the new crop of fruit-driven French wines that play slightly outside the rules. Crisp dry and fruity, it is perfect with creamy scallops.

FOR THE BEETROOT PAINT

100ml (3½fl oz) beetroot juice
20ml (¾fl oz) sunflower oil

FOR THE PINEAPPLE JELLY

50ml (2fl oz) fresh pineapple juice
¼ tsp agar-agar

FOR THE BEETROOT ICE CREAM (MAKES 20 PORTIONS)

500ml (17fl oz) fresh beetroot juice
75gm (2½oz) caster sugar
4 free-range egg yolks
20gm (¾oz) trimoline

FOR THE BEETROOT CRISPS

1 whole beetroot, cleaned

FOR THE CURRIED PINEAPPLE CANNELLONI

¼ tsp Madras curry powder
50ml (2fl oz) water
15gm (½oz) caster sugar
100gm (3½oz) fresh pineapple, cut into 2mm (1/10in)-thick slices

FOR THE CANNELLONI FILLING

50gm (2oz) pineapple, finely diced
50gm (2oz) fennel bulb, finely diced
¼ tsp chopped fresh coriander
50ml (2fl oz) curry oil (see page 273)

FOR THE CAULIFLOWER PURÉE

100gm (3½oz) cauliflower, finely chopped
150ml (5fl oz) Avonmore cream
fresh thyme
salt and freshly milled white pepper, to taste

FOR THE SCALLOPS

6 large Castletownbere king scallops
1 tbsp Newgrange Gold rapeseed oil
salt and freshly milled white pepper, to taste

TO SERVE

6 leaves of red chard, to serve

SERVES 4

BEETROOT PAINT

Pour the beetroot juice into a pot, bring to the boil and boil until reduced by 80%. Add the oil and, using a hand blender, blitz until emulsified. Store in an airtight container.

PINEAPPLE JELLY

Bring the pineapple juice to the boil and then whisk in the agar-agar. Pour into a mould, cover and transfer to the fridge to set. Once set, cut into 1cm (½in)-square cubes.

BEETROOT ICE CREAM

Bring the beetroot juice to the boil. In a separate bowl whisk the egg yolks and caster sugar together. Pour the hot beetroot juice and trimoline into the egg yolk mixture and whisk well, then transfer back to the pot and continue to cook for 2 minutes over a low heat. Remove from the heat and allow to cool. Place in a Taurus Rowzer beaker and freeze. Then blitz when required. Alternatively, place in an ice cream machine and churn for 20 minutes and then freeze.

BEETROOT CRISPS

Slice the beetroot into 1mm (1/10in)-thick slices, then trim each slice into a triangle shape. Place in the dehydrator for 3½ hours at 125°C until crisp.

CURRIED PINEAPPLE CANNELLONI

Heat the curry powder in a dry non-stick pan to extract the flavour. Add the water and caster sugar and continue to cook until the sugar is dissolved. Allow to cool. Place the pineapple slices in the syrup in a bowl and refrigerate overnight.

CANNELLONI FILLING

Mix the diced pineapple, fennel bulb and chopped coriander with the curry oil. Remove the pineapple slices from the curry syrup and pat dry. Trim the edges to form rectangles of pineapple (about 6cm/2½in wide). Place a spoonful of the diced pineapple mix at one end of the pineapple slice and roll it up tightly to form a cylinder shape.

CAULIFLOWER PURÉE

Place the ingredients into a HotmixPRO blender (or similar) and cook at 80°C for 15 minutes or until just soft, then blend on high until it forms a smooth purée. Check and adjust seasoning.

SCALLOPS

Remove the roe and sac from each scallop, just leaving the white meat, and stand the scallop on its side and cut in half. Season with salt and pepper. Heat a pan until very hot, add the oil and then seal the scallops very quickly until golden brown on each side and medium rare in the middle.

TO SERVE

Using a 2cm (¾in) brush, paint a stripe of beetroot on to the plate and place a red chard leaf on top. Put a cube of jelly at one end of the beetroot paint stripe and place the pineapple cannelloni at the opposite end. Dollop and drag the warm cauliflower purée. Place a scoop of ice cream on the red chard leaf and top with the triangle of dehydrated beetroot. Finally, place the very hot scallops against the cannelloni, add five dots of curry oil and serve.

Slow-poached terrine of foie gras, home-preserved mirabelle plums, Coteaux du Layon jelly and pear tuile

Mirabelle plums come in to us in July and we preserve them for use in winter. We used to prepare the slow-poached terrine the traditional way – by cooking it in duck fat – but now we use the modern water-bath technology, which gives a purer result.

WINE PAIRING

Château la Roulerie Coteaux du Layon

This is a no-brainer: match this wine with this dish and you've found perfection. It was a challenge to find this wine but it works perfectly.

FOR THE FOIE GRAS

1 x 600gm (1lb 5oz) foie gras lobe
6gm (¼oz) salt
½ tsp caster sugar
¾ tsp freshly milled black pepper
¾ tsp five spice
30ml (1fl oz) Madeira
30ml (1fl oz) Armagnac
30ml (1fl oz) ruby port

FOR THE COTEAUX DU LAYON JELLY

100ml (3½fl oz) water
80gm (3oz) caster sugar
juice of ½ lemon
375ml (13fl oz) Coteaux du Layon
8 gelatine leaves, soaked in water

FOR THE TRUFFLE CUSTARD

40gm (1½oz) free-range egg yolk
pinch of salt
pinch of caster sugar
125ml (4fl oz) Avonmore cream
½ leaf gelatine, soaked in water
10ml (½fl oz) white truffle oil

FOR THE PEAR TUILE

15gm (½oz) unsalted Avonmore butter
85gm (3oz) caster sugar
25ml (1fl oz) olive oil
60gm (2oz) pear purée (we use Boiron or Ravifruit)
35gm (1¼oz) strong flour

TO SERVE

preserved mirabelle plums, see page 274
smoked sea salt

SERVES 8

FOIE GRAS

Leave the foie gras lobe at room temperature until extremely soft. Separate the lobe into its two natural pieces. Spread each piece apart gently with your fingers, until you find the large veins. Remove each vein without damaging the lobe and leaving the lobes flat. Mix the salt, sugar and spices together and sprinkle over the foie gras. Transfer into a vacuum-pack bag and sprinkle in the alcohol. Seal and set aside for 24 hours in the fridge.

The next day, remove the foie gras from the fridge and remove it from the bag. Allow it to come back up to room temperature. Lay it out on a sheet of fine muslin cloth and roll up tightly. Transfer to a vacuum-pack bag and return to the fridge to firm up fully. Once firm, place in a waterbath set to 56°C and cook for 10 minutes. Remove and cool immediately in a bowl of heavily iced water. Once firm, place again in the waterbath at a temperature of 60°C for 14 minutes. Once again, remove and cool immediately in a bowl of heavily iced water. Remove from the vacuum-pack bag, roll tightly in cling film and allow to set in the fridge.

COTEAUX DE LAYON JELLY

Place the water, lemon juice and sugar in a pot and bring to the boil. Squeeze the excess water out of the gelatine leaves and add to the pot with the wine. Whisk until the gelatine is completely dissolved. Remove from the heat. Pour into a mould lined with cling film and leave to set. Once set, dice into 5mm (¼in) cubes.

TRUFFLE CUSTARD

Place the egg yolks in a bowl with the pinch of salt and sugar. Heat the cream gently in a pot and, when warm, whisk into the egg yolk mix and then return to the pot to cook for 1 minute over a low heat. Squeeze any excess water from the gelatine, add it to the custard and mix until dissolved. Finally add the white truffle oil, mix to combine and then remove from the heat and leave to cool. Transfer into a squeezy bottle.

PEAR TUILE

Preheat the oven to 160°C. Melt the butter in a pan and mix in the caster sugar. Add the olive oil and combine for 1 minute at approximately 150°C – check with a thermometer if needed. Add the pear purée and flour and mix until smooth. Spread the mixture very thinly on to a baking sheet and transfer to the preheated oven. Bake until golden brown. Remove from the oven and, while still warm, cut the tuile into eight 7cm x 2cm (3in x 1in) strips. Leave to cool.

TO SERVE

Remove the foie gras from the fridge. Cut into 2cm (¾in) slices per portion (should make 10-12 slices). Let it sit for at least 10 minutes before serving to allow it to come up to room temperature. Pipe a line of truffle custard on to the plate. Place 3 mirabelle plums across the top of the line. Place a pear tuile on top of the plums. Cut a slice of foie gras in half and position on the plate as pictured. Arrange cubes of jelly to the side of the foie gras. Add a pinch of smoked sea salt to the plate to garnish and serve with some fresh brioche on the side.

THE
AMERICAN
CYCLOPÆDIA
VOL V
CODE-DEM
VOL XIV
PRI - SHO

Roulade of McConnell's Irish oak-smoked salmon with citrus dressing, warm blini and orange pearls

McConnell's produce the best smoked salmon in the country as far as I am concerned. It is lovely with this lightly horseradish-scented cream and fresh citrus dressing. When this dish is on the menu, we sell twenty or more in a night – as soon as one leaves the kitchen, we get a slew of orders for it.

WINE PAIRING

Pierre Vessigaud Pouilly-Fuissé

This old-vine Chardonnay from Mâconnais is our favourite. Smoked salmon is a difficult dish to match with wine, but remember, smoke loves oak.

FOR THE SMOKED SALMON ROULADE

50gm (2oz) McConnell's Irish oak-smoked salmon
150ml (5fl oz) Avonmore cream
¼ tsp fresh horseradish
pinch cayenne pepper
4 gelatine leaves, soaked in water
150gm (5oz) whipped Avonmore cream
½ tsp chopped fresh chives
150gm (5oz) smoked salmon, to assemble
salt and freshly milled black pepper, to taste
30 grapefruit segments, to garnish

FOR THE CITRUS EMULSION

juice of 2 oranges
juice of 1 grapefruit
juice of ½ lemon
juice of ½ lime
½ tsp Dijon mustard
70ml (2½fl oz) sunflower oil
25ml (1fl oz) olive oil
2ml (1/10fl oz) walnut oil
salt and freshly milled black pepper, to taste

FOR THE ORANGE PEARLS

100ml (3½fl oz) fresh orange juice
50ml (2fl oz) Champagne
¼ tsp agar-agar
5 litres (10½pints) vegetable oil, chilled to 2°C

FOR THE BLINIS

120ml (4fl oz) Avonmore milk
10gm (½oz) fresh yeast
90gm (3oz) strong flour
2 free-range egg yolks
2 free-range egg whites

TO SERVE

Carrick Farm micro-mesclun salad, to garnish
citrus dressing (see page 272)

SERVES 6

SMOKED SALMON ROULADE

Put the cream, smoked salmon, grated horseradish and cayenne pepper into a pot and bring to the boil, then remove from the heat and transfer to a HotmixPRO blender (or similar) and blitz. Check and adjust the seasoning and then pass the mixture through a chinois or sieve. Transfer the mixture to a bowl. Squeeze any excess water out of the gelatine leaves and add them to the mix. Allow to cool slightly. Quickly fold in the chopped chives and whipped cream. Transfer the mixture to a piping bag and leave to set in the fridge for 30 minutes. To assemble the roulades, on a bench lay out two lengths of cling film, each 40cm (16in) long. On each one lay 3 long strips of sliced smoked salmon to cover a 30cm (12in) length of cling film. Pipe a length of cooled salmon cream mix (about 2cm/1in thick) along the centre of each strip of salmon. Picking up the edge of the cling film, roll the salmon into a tight roll and tie each end tightly with string (like a Christmas cracker). Place the rolls in the freezer and, when set, cut each one into three 10cm (4in) lengths and defrost for use.

CITRUS EMULSION

Pour the juice of the citrus fruit into a pot and bring to the boil. Reduce the heat and cook until reduced by 80%. Pass the juice through a chinois or fine sieve. Place the juice and Dijon mustard in a blender and slowly add the oil as you blitz the mix on a high setting. Once blended, check the seasoning and leave to cool.

ORANGE PEARLS

Place the orange juice in a pot, bring to the boil, reduce the heat and cook until reduced by 50%. Whisk in the agar-agar and Champagne, then remove from the heat and allow to cool to 54°C. Place in a disposable piping bag. Nip a tiny cut at the tip of the bag to allow a very small amount to leak out. Pipe the full bag of liquid into the container of chilled oil and you will see the little orange pearls form and set as they sink to the bottom in the oil. Pass the oil through a sieve to extract the pearls and wash off the excess oil with cold water. Set the pearls aside, ready for use.

PEARL MAKING

BLINIS

Add the milk and yeast to a small pot and heat to 70°C. In a separate bowl, mix the strong flour and egg yolks together and then add the warm milk and yeast. Whisk to combine and pass through a sieve to remove any lumps if required. In a separate bowl, whisk the egg whites until stiff and then fold into the mix. Pour the batter into a siphon gun, add one charger of ISI gas and shake the bottle well. To make the blinis you are going to release the batter mix directly from the siphon gun on to a heated non-stick pan. Once the pan has come up to temperature, squeeze out four 3cm (1in) discs of batter, each one directly below the other, to form one rectangular-shaped blini. Cook until golden brown on each side and set aside to keep warm. Repeat to make 6 blinis.

TO SERVE

Place 5 segments of grapefuit on the plate and then layer a warm blini on top. Place 7 dots of citrus emulsion to the side. Dress the salad leaves with a little citrus dressing and pinch the leaves into a neat pile on the plate with a small mound of orange pearls. Place the piece of salmon roulade on top of the blini and serve.

DAVID HANLEY AND KEITH PLUNKETT |

CATERWAY

Two well-established fruit and vegetable suppliers, the Fitzpatrick family and the Hanley family, both on the go since the 1940s, came together to form Caterway in 1998. This Irish-owned family business now employs over fifty people from their base in Dublin 7, in the heart of the city's fruit and vegetable market. 'The business has developed in many ways over the years,' explains David Hanley, one of the company's four directors. 'But one of the new areas we are most excited about at the moment is our focus on sea vegetables. Only recently we harvested the first samphire in Ireland under glasshouse conditions. Under the label Wildway we will be cultivating an array of seashore crops such as samphire, sea beet, salsola, monk's beard and others. Finbarr has always been a great supporter of ours, so we are looking forward to seeing how he works his magic on this new range.'

www.caterway.ie

Loin of wild Kildare rabbit with pulled, braised leg, home-smoked prune purée, crab apple and jus

The flavour of the lightly smoked prune purée complements the rabbit superbly – prepared both ways. The trick here is to make sure you get a little of each on your fork – prune purée, cauliflower, rabbit and jus – and boom, brilliant flavour!

WINE PAIRING

Château de Fleurie Beaujolais

A light Beaujolais is good with anything, but this one has a richness that beguiles.

FOR THE RABBIT

2 wild Kildare rabbits, skinned only
salt and freshly milled black pepper
2 sprigs of fresh thyme
20ml (¾fl oz) Newgrange Gold rapeseed oil

FOR THE STOCK

2 rabbit carcasses and all the trimmings, from above
2 litres (3½ pints) brown chicken stock (see page 270)

FOR THE PULLED LEGS

4 rabbit legs, from above
salt and freshly milled black pepper
20ml (¾fl oz) vegetable oil
rabbit stock, from above
30gm (1oz) chopped onion
30gm (1oz) chopped leek
20gm (¾oz) chopped celery
30gm (1oz) peeled and chopped carrot
1 garlic clove
10 crushed black peppercorns
1 small sprig of fresh sage and thyme
1 small bay leaf

FOR THE SMOKED PRUNE PURÉE

50gm (2oz) seasoned oak chippings
100gm (3½oz) dried prunes
250ml (9fl oz) prune juice

FOR THE CAULIFLOWER PURÉE

100gm (3½oz) cauliflower, finely chopped
150ml (5fl oz) Avonmore cream
pinch of fresh thyme
salt and freshly milled white pepper

FOR THE CRAB APPLE AND JUS

4 crab apples
100ml (3½fl oz) light sugar syrup (see page 271)
100ml (3½fl oz) rabbit jus
salt

FOR THE CABBAGE

2 savoy cabbage leaves
10gm (½oz) Avonmore unsalted butter

SERVES 8

TO PREPARE THE RABBIT

Before you start to prepare the rabbit, it is very important to note that all the meat trimmings and bones you remove in the process are kept aside to help make the stock for the sauce later. To begin preparing the rabbit, remove the front legs, double rack, whole saddle and the back legs. Chop the front legs and the remaining carcass into small chunks.

Next remove any excess trim from the double saddles and place the saddles in a vacuum-pack bag. Season with a little milled black pepper and salt, add the remaining sprig of thyme and 10ml (½fl oz) of the rapeseed oil and seal the bag. Place a fine needle probe in the centre of one of the saddles and transfer to a waterbath, set to 58°C, and cook until the needle probe reaches 52°C. Remove from the bag and set aside.

THE STOCK

Preheat the oven to 160°C. Chop the rabbit carcasses into small pieces. Place on a baking tray and transfer to the oven for about 20 minutes, or until golden brown. Drain off the excess fat and place the bones in a saucepan with the brown chicken stock. Bring to the boil, then reduce to a low simmer for 4 hours. Skim off the fat as it rises to the top to keep the stock clear. Check for a good strong flavour before passing the stock through a fine sieve. If the flavour has not developed enough, leave it to simmer for as long as is needed until the flavour is right.

THE PULLED LEGS

Preheat the oven to 110°C. Season the legs with salt and freshly milled black pepper. Pour the oil into a hot ovenproof pan and seal the legs until golden brown. Turn them over and quickly seal the other side, then remove the legs from the pan and set aside. Add the mirepoix (chopped vegetables and herbs) to the pan and cook until golden. Deglaze the pan with a little rabbit stock, put the rabbit legs back in the pot and pour over just enough stock to cover them. Cover with a disc of parchment paper and transfer to the oven to cook for 4 hours, or until the legs are nice and tender. Remove the legs from the stock and, while still warm, pull the meat off the bone; the meat should come away easily. Pass the cooking liquor from the legs through a fine sieve and muslin cloth and set aside 100ml (3½fl oz) to use as the finished jus. Boil the remaining cooking liquor until it has reduced by 70% and is nice and sticky, then add some of this to the pulled leg meat (just enough to bind and moisten the meat). Line a 2cm-deep (1in) rectangular mould with cling film, press the mixture into the mould and cover. Refrigerate overnight to set. Once set, remove the meat from the mould and cut into rectangular pieces (about 7cm x 2.5cm; 3in x 1in).

SMOKED PRUNE PURÉE

Place the oak chips in the base of a steamer and cover with a perforated steamer tray and lid. Place the pot over a high heat for 2–3 minutes. When a sufficient amount of smoke has built up, turn the heat off and allow the smoker to stand for 2 minutes. Place the prunes on the perforated tray, cover with the lid and leave to smoke for just 1 minute – no longer, or the flavour will be very harsh. Place the smoked prunes in a HotmixPRO blender (or similar) and add the prune juice. Blitz on high until very smooth.

CAULIFLOWER PURÉE

Place all the ingredients in a HotmixPRO blender (or similar) and cook at 80°C for 15 minutes, or until just soft. Blend on high to produce a smooth purée. Check and adjust the seasoning. Transfer to a squeezy bottle and set aside.

CRAB APPLE AND JUS

Peel and slice the crab apple into 3mm (1⁄10in)-thick slices, then cut into small dice. Place the sugar syrup in a small saucepan over a medium heat and bring to a simmer. Blanch the crab apple for 10 seconds in the simmering sugar syrup. Remove the crab apple, drain and cool immediately. Heat the 100ml (3½fl oz) of rabbit jus (from the leg cooking liquor) in a small saucepan, add the blanched crab apple dice, check the seasoning and then set aside.

CABBAGE

Blanch the savoy cabbage leaves in boiling, salted water. Cut the leaves into 12cm x 2.5cm (4½in x 1in) strips. Melt the unsalted butter in a pan and toss the cabbage strips in the butter with a little salt and milled black pepper.

TO SERVE

Put the pulled leg meat on a plate, cover with cling film and place in a steamer for 6–7 minutes to reheat. Seal the saddles in a hot pan for a few minutes until golden brown. Remove the loins from the saddle and cut each loin lengthways into 4 pieces. Place a spoonful of the smoked prune purée in the centre of a warmed plate. Arrange the warm pulled leg meat on the plate and lay the cabbage leaf strip on top, allowing it to overrun the edge of the plate. Then top with the loin of rabbit. Pour the rabbit and crab apple jus around the edge, squeeze a line of cauliflower purée on the edge of the plate and serve.

PRESERVE CAGE

Carpaccio of Ballyheigue Kerry Head lobster tail and claw with vanilla and mango chutney, raw oyster mousse, mango leather and lobster oil

The lobster carpaccio here is so pure in flavour, so clean and unadulterated, that it's hard to beat. But when you marinate it in fresh lime juice and lobster oil you take things up another notch. The mango leather adds a wonderful tangy, sweet, sour, chewy counterpart. I feel like a kid when I eat it. However, the raw oyster mousse might still be my favourite element, as one mouthful transports you straight to the ocean.

WINE PAIRING

Barton & Guestier Vouvray

This wine impressed me at a tasting recently as it went so well with everything. The slight off-dry nature of the wine compliments the intense flavours of this dish without overpowering it.

FOR THE LOBSTER

2 x 600gm (1lb 5oz) live lobsters

FOR THE LOBSTER TAIL CARPACCIO

2 Ballyheigue Kerry Head lobster tails
zest and juice of 1 lime
40ml (1½fl oz) lobster oil

FOR THE LOBSTER CLAWS

4 Ballyheigue Kerry Head lobster claws

FOR THE LOBSTER OIL

lobster shells, from above
100ml (3½fl oz) Newgrange Gold rapeseed oil

FOR THE RAW OYSTER MOUSSE

4 Clarinbridge oysters
2 drops balsamic vinegar
3 drops fresh lemon juice
140ml (5fl oz) Avonmore cream
1 leaf gelatine, pre-soaked in a little water
1 pinch cayenne pepper

FOR THE MANGO LEATHER

250ml (9fl oz) mango purée (we use Boiron or Ravifruit)

FOR THE MANGO CRISPS

1 ripe mango, peeled

TO SERVE

mango and vanilla chutney, see page 274

LOBSTER TAIL CARPACCIO

For detailed instructions on preparing the lobster tails, please turn to page 277. Add half the lime zest to the lobster oil, then add the juice and mix to combine. Slice each lobster tail into 6 slices and lay these flat on a tray. Pour over the lime marinade or cure mix, turn the pieces over and leave for 4 minutes, then remove from the cure and set aside.

LOBSTER CLAWS

For detailed instructions on preparing and cooking the lobster claws, please see page 277.

LOBSTER OIL

Preheat the oven to 160°C. Crush the lobster shells with a mallet, place on a tray and roast in the preheated oven for 20 minutes. Add the rapeseed oil and return to the oven for 10 minutes. Set aside for 24 hours to let the oil cool and infuse. Pass the shells and oil through a fine chinois or sieve and then a muslin cloth, then retain the oil for service. This recipe will give you more oil than you will need, but you can use it to garnish soups and a host of other dishes.

RAW OYSTER MOUSSE

Open the oysters and place the flesh and all the juice into a HotmixPRO blender (or similar). Add the fresh lemon juice and balsamic vinegar with 100ml (3½fl oz) of the cream and blitz. This oyster sauce does not need any additional salt, as the oysters naturally provide this. Place the remaining cream in a pot over a gentle heat, add the softened gelatine and allow to dissolve fully. Add this cream mixture to the oyster sauce. Pass through a fine sieve or chinois into a bowl, adjust the seasoning with a little cayenne pepper and allow to set. Once set, whisk the mousse very quickly until smooth and transfer it to a disposable piping bag for service.

MANGO LEATHER

Spread the mango purée on a tray lined with a Silpat or similar non-stick mat and place in the dehydrator at 54°C for about 8–12 hours, or until just dry and pliable. Cut the leather into long strips (4cm x 12cm; 1½in x 4½in).

MANGO CRISPS

Cut the mango into 2mm (1/10in)-thick strips. Cut out twelve 4cm (1½in) discs and then place them on a tray in the dehydrator, set to 54°C, for 10 hours, until dry and crisp. Store in an airtight container until required.

TO SERVE

Place a rectangle of mango chutney on a plate using an 8cm x 3cm (3in x 1in) template. Lay the lobster claw on top of the mango rectangle. Lay a piece of mango leather on the plate, pipe a 1cm (½in)-thick line of oyster mousse the length of the leather and place 3 slices of the lobster tail carpaccio on top. Garnish with mango crisps and some micro-chard leaves. Finish the plate with a drizzle of lobster oil and a sprinkle of grated lime zest.

PAT CLARKE | GROWER

For three generations the Carrick family have been growing and selling vegetables from their farm in North County Dublin. As a relatively small family business – they run a 24-acre farm – they have had to work hard to stay afloat in a highly competitive market, but Carrick Farm's location along the relatively frost-free, sandy Fingal coast allows them to supply much-sought-after young vegetables. Moving with the times, they now specialise in growing a range of micro-veg and micro-herbs and enjoy working closely with chefs to seek out innovative new lines to develop .

www.carrickfarmfresh.ie

Ballyheigue Kerry Head lobster trifle with smoked cod roe custard and velvet crab jelly

This dish is a shellfish lover's dream. There is quite a bit of work involved in pulling this starter together, but it's so worth it. The depth of flavour is something else. The combination of velvet crab, lobster and smoked cod roe offset by the sesame-infused seaweed is a master match.

WINE PAIRING

Boyer-Martenot Meursault

Burgundy

This dish needs a wine with a slight oaky edge to stand up to the smoked roe but something delicate enough not to overpower the star of the dish.

FOR THE SMOKED COD ROE CUSTARD

500ml (17fl oz) Avonmore cream
160gm (5½oz) free-range egg yolks
230gm (8oz) smoked cod roe
2½ leaves gelatine, pre-soaked in a little water
salt and cayenne pepper, to taste

FOR THE VELVET CRAB JELLY

650g (1lb 6oz) velvet crab
1.6 litre (2¾ pints) fish stock (see page 270)
160ml (5½fl oz) white wine
¼ leek, chopped
1 stick of celery, chopped
1 medium carrot, peeled and chopped
½ fresh bay leaf
1 garlic clove
½ star anise
salt and freshly milled white pepper
2 leaves gelatine, pre-soaked in a little water

FOR THE LOBSTER

800gm (1lb 12oz) whole Ballyheigue Kerry Head lobster
1 tbsp fresh lemon juice
salt and freshly milled white pepper

FOR THE SMOKED COD FILLET

300gm (10½oz) natural smoked cod fillet
500ml (17½fl oz) Avonmore milk
1 bay leaf
1 sprig of fresh thyme
1 garlic clove, smashed
10ml (½fl oz) fresh lemon juice

FOR THE SESAME MINI-BAGUETTES

250gm (9oz) strong white flour
5gm (¼oz) salt
30ml (1fl oz) Newgrange Gold rapeseed oil
180ml (6fl oz) water
5gm (¼oz) fast-action yeast
egg wash
5gm (¼oz) sesame seeds

FOR THE SEAWEED SALAD

20gm (¾oz) dried seaweed
5gm (¼oz) shallot, finely chopped
10gm (½oz) sesame seeds, toasted
¼ red chilli, chopped
50ml (2fl oz) curry oil (see page 273)
5ml (¼fl oz) rapeseed oil
½ clove garlic, crushed
50ml (2fl oz) rice wine vinegar

SERVES 6

SMOKED COD ROE CUSTARD

Put the cream in a saucepan and heat until just under boiling point. Pour some of the cream on to the egg yolks and whisk well, then pour the egg mixture back into the pot with the remaining cream. Continue to cook gently over a low heat until it thickens slightly. Split the amount of cod roe in half and scrape one half into the cream. Cook over a low heat for 2 minutes to infuse. Squeeze out the excess water from the gelatine leaves before adding them to the cream and allowing them to dissolve. Pass the custard through a fine chinois or sieve to remove any lumps of roe left in the custard. Season with salt and cayenne pepper and allow to cool. Store in a squeezy bottle for service.

FINBARR HIGGINS | EXECUTIVE CHEF

VELVET CRAB JELLY

Put the live velvet crabs in the freezer for 1 hour to render them insensible, then sever their hind and front nerve centre to kill them instantly and humanely. Preheat the oven to 160°C. Place the crabs in a gastronorm tray and crush them with a heavy mallet. Add the chopped leek, carrot, celery, garlic, bay leaf and star anise. Put the tray in the preheated oven for 20–25 minutes, stirring occasionally, until the crabs are nicely roasted. Transfer the crab to a saucepan. Place the tray on top of the stove over a gentle heat and deglaze it with the white wine, then pour the deglazed juices and wine over the crab in the pot. Place the saucepan with the crab over the heat and simmer until the liquid has been reduced by 25%. Add the fish stock, bring up to just under boiling and then reduce to simmer for about 1 hour. Remove any fat residue that may rise to the top as it simmers. Do not boil the stock, as this will make it cloudy. Pass the stock through a muslin cloth and fine chinois. Squeeze the excess water from the gelatine leaves. While the stock is still warm, add the gelatine and stir until it has dissolved. Season with salt and milled white peppercorn if required and then leave to cool.

LOBSTER

See page 277 for detailed instructions on preparing and cooking the lobster tails and claws. Once cooked, cut the tail into 12 slices and chop the claw and knuckle meat into 1cm (½in) pieces. Season with the salt, milled white pepper and fresh lemon juice to taste.

SMOKED COD FILLET

Place the smoked cod fillet and the rest of the ingredients (except the lemon juice) in a pot over the heat and bring up to a simmer for about 4 minutes, until the cod is just cooked. Remove the smoked cod from the milk and flake into small pieces while it is still warm. Season with the lemon juice and leave to cool.

SESAME MINI-BAGUETTES

Place the flour, salt, rapeseed oil and 150ml (5fl oz) of water in a mixer with a dough hook attached. Start to mix on a slow speed and add in the yeast. Gradually add the rest of the water until you have a smooth dough – this should take about 5 minutes. Tip the dough into a lightly oiled bowl, cover with cling film and leave to prove for 2 hours. Put the dough on to an oiled surface and cut it into 15gm (½oz) pieces. Knock back the rolls and stretch and fold them into baguette-shaped pieces. Place the mini-baguettes on a baking tray lined with a Silpat or similar non-stick mat. Cover with cling film and leave to prove until they have doubled in size. Preheat an oven to 200°C. Brush the mini-baguettes with egg wash and sprinkle with the sesame seeds. Bake in the hot oven for 8 minutes, or until they are golden brown with a slight sheen to them.

SEAWEED SALAD

Soak the dried seaweed in cold water for 10 minutes and drain. Mix all the rest of the ingredients together in a bowl to make the dressing. Place the seaweed in a bowl and mix well in the dressing.

TO SERVE

Divide the lobster meat evenly between 6 glasses. Pour over enough velvet crab stock to cover the lobster meat in each glass and refrigerate for 3–4 hours, or until the jelly is set. Remove from the fridge 10 minutes before serving to allow the dish to come up to room temperature. Add a layer of seaweed salad and then top with a layer of cod roe custard. Finish with a small heap of smoked cod fillet. Garnish with a few strands of seaweed salad. Place a warm mini-baguette on the edge of each glass and serve.

Rod-caught wild Straffan estate brown trout, wild spring nettle purée, fresh morels and Carrick Farm pea shoots

This dish is an ode to March. This month marks the beginning of our river trout season and also heralds the arrival of our fresh morels and nettles. We pick the nettles down by the banks of the River Liffey, which flows through The K Club estate, so I feel they have a natural affinity with the rod-caught fish. And Dublin-grown pea shoots are simply spring in a mouthful.

WINE PAIRING

Seresin Sauvignon Blanc, Marlborough, New Zealand

New Zealand Sauvignon Blanc has taken the world by storm and with this example it is easy to see why. The freshness of the wine matches the peas and nettle purée here perfectly.

FOR THE FRESH FENNEL JUICE FOAM

300ml (10fl oz) freshly pressed fennel bulb juice
¾ tsp xanthan gum

FOR THE CRISPY NETTLE LEAVES

12 nettle leaves
10ml (½fl oz) vegetable oil
pinch of salt

FOR THE SPRING NETTLE PURÉE

20ml (¾fl oz) Newgrange Gold rapeseed oil
1 shallot, finely chopped
60gm (2oz) fresh fennel bulb, finely chopped
1 garlic clove, chopped
200gm (7oz) spring nettles, thoroughly washed
40ml (1½fl oz) rapeseed oil

FOR THE FRESH MORELS

30gm (1oz) unsalted Avonmore butter
150gm (5oz) fresh morels
15gm (½oz) chopped shallots
40ml (1½fl oz) chicken stock (see page 270)

FOR THE PEAS AND BROAD BEANS

100gm (3½oz) pea pods, shelled
80gm (3oz) broad beans, shelled
10gm (½oz) Avonmore unsalted butter
salt and freshly milled white pepper

FOR THE TROUT

4 fillets of wild brown trout
200ml (7fl oz) water
20gm (¾oz) salt
10ml (½fl oz) Newgrange Gold rapeseed oil
1 mint leaf

TO SERVE

16 Carrick Farm pea shoots

SERVES 4

FENNEL JUICE FOAM

Boil the freshly pressed fennel bulb juice in a pot. Add the xanthan gum and pass through a fine sieve. Pour into a siphon gun and charge with two ISI gas chargers. Shake very well and refrigerate.

CRISPY NETTLE LEAVES

Wrap a plate tightly in cling film. Brush the nettle leaves with a little oil on each side, place on the cling-film-wrapped plate and season with a pinch of salt. Cover tightly with cling film and cook in the microwave for 1 minute on high. Remove immediately from the cling film and place on kitchen paper to remove any excess oil. Store the leaves in an airtight container until required.

SPRING NETTLE PURÉE

Heat the oil in a pan and add the shallot, fennel and garlic and cover with a lid. Cook over a low heat until the shallot has become soft and translucent but not coloured. Add the spring nettle leaves and cook gently until wilted. Remove from the heat. Transfer the nettle mix into a HotmixPRO blender (or similar) and blitz on high for 3 minutes until smooth and glossy. Slowly add the rapeseed oil, blitzing gently as you go. Season with salt and milled white pepper to taste. Transfer to a bowl and store in the fridge.

FRESH MORELS

Melt the unsalted butter in a pan over a medium heat. Add the shallots and cook over a low heat until soft and translucent but not coloured. Add the fresh morels and chicken stock and lightly poach the morels until soft. Set aside.

PEAS AND BROAD BEANS

Bring a saucepan of salted water to the boil, add the broad beans and cook for 30 seconds. Remove the beans and place in iced water immediately. Drain the broad beans, pop them out of their skins and set aside. Using the same pot of boiling, salted water, cook the peas for 1 minute and then add the shelled broad beans for 30 seconds. Drain the peas and beans. In a separate pot, melt the unsalted butter over a medium heat, add the peas and broad beans and toss together. Season with salt and milled white pepper to taste.

TROUT

Dissolve the salt in the water to make a brine. Soak the fillets of trout in the brine for 5 minutes. This will prevent protein albumin leaching out of the fish and coagulating on the surface. Once the trout has been brined, rinse with cold water and pat dry. Vacuum pack the trout fillets with the rapeseed oil and mint leaf. Cook the trout in a waterbath, set to 52°C, for 7 minutes.

TO SERVE

Spoon enough nettle purée into the centre of a warmed plate to form a pool about 6cm (2½in) in diameter. Place the fresh morels, peas and broad beans on top of the nettle purée and then place the trout on top. Garnish with pea shoots and a few crispy nettle leaves. Finish with the fennel foam and a pinch of smoked sea salt.

Wild Atlantic black sole with west coast mussel, tomato and caper dressing

I love cooking Sole Meunière, basting the sole in the frothy nutty butter, inhaling all those wonderful cooking smells. Traditionally you might serve it with a bisque or a rich sauce, but I like to pair it with pickled mussels and capers, where the light acidity of the dressing cuts through the butter-basted fish perfectly.

WINE PAIRING

Baron de Ladoucette

Such a majestic dish demands a majestic wine. This is one of the best the Loire produces. It is expensive, but a lesser Pouilly-Fumé with a flinty edge would work too.

FOR THE SOLE

4 Wild Atlantic black sole (about 700g/1lb 8oz each), skinned, head and roe removed
30gm (1oz) plain flour
salt and freshly milled white pepper
80ml (3fl oz) Newgrange Gold rapeseed oil
80gm (3oz) Avonmore unsalted butter

FOR THE MUSSEL DRESSING

32 fresh west coast mussels, cleaned
200ml (7fl oz) white wine
20gm (¾oz) baby capers
1 banana shallot, peeled and finely diced
4 large plum vine tomatoes, skinned, seeded and finely diced
50ml (2fl oz) Newgrange Gold rapeseed oil
juice of 1 lemon
5gm (¼oz) finely chopped chives

SERVES 4

SOLE

Using a sharp knife, cut along the outside of the sole fillets on both sides, getting in between the fillet and the skirt without cutting through the bone. This will allow for easy removal of the fillets from the bone once the fish is cooked. Place the flour on a tray and season well with salt and freshly milled white pepper. Lay the sole flat and coat each side with the seasoned flour, dusting off any excess flour. Pour 20ml (¾fl oz) of oil into a hot frying pan (oval-shaped if you can), add a sole and fry until golden brown on each side. Add 20gm (¾oz) of unsalted butter, allow it to froth up, then baste the fish continually on each side for about 8 minutes, or until the sole is a little bit soft. The fish is cooked when the flesh will pull away from the bone at the head end. Set aside to keep warm and repeat this process for each sole fillet.

MUSSEL DRESSING

On the hob, heat a medium-sized pot with a lid until extremely hot. Add the mussels with the wine and cover immediately with the lid. Cook until the mussels open – this should only take a few minutes. Discard any mussels that do not open. Pass directly through a fine sieve. Remove the mussels from the shells. In a small bowl combine the baby capers, finely diced shallot, tomatoes and steamed mussels. Add the rapeseed oil and half of the lemon juice and season to taste.

TO SERVE

Remove one of the fillets from the topside of each sole and then turn it over to expose the underside of the flesh (as pictured). Place on a warm plate or elegant copper presentation pan to serve. Add the chives to the mussel dressing just before serving in order to keep their colour. Check the seasoning and add more lemon juice if desired. Lay the mussel dressing along the exposed bone.

Wild Atlantic cod fillet, baby spinach and almond purée, fresh fennel juice foam and wild flaxseed oil sphere

This is a very modern dish for us – the flaxseed oil sphere and raw fennel juice foam are a nod to modern cooking techniques, but what really matters for me is the marriage of flavours. The freshness of the foam against the pure flavour of the cod, the nutty almond and spinach purée, all work brilliantly together.

WINE PAIRING

Saint-Aubin Premier Cru Le Charmois

This dish needs a nutty flavour in the wine and this elegant Burgundy fits the bill.

FOR THE FLAXSEED OIL SPHERES

80ml (3fl oz) Newgrange Gold wild flaxseed oil
2 star anise
50gm (2oz) cocoa butter

FOR THE COD

1 side fresh wild Atlantic cod
salt and freshly milled white pepper
½ tsp fennel seeds
½ tsp coriander seeds

FOR THE BABY SPINACH AND ALMOND PURÉE

15gm (½oz) Avonmore unsalted butter
1 shallot, finely chopped
60gm (2oz) finely chopped fresh fennel bulb
1 garlic clove, smashed
300gm (10½oz) baby spinach
20ml (¾fl oz) almond oil

FOR THE FRESH FENNEL JUICE FOAM

300ml (10fl oz) freshly pressed fennel bulb juice
3gm (⅔ tsp) xanthan gum

FOR THE BRAISED FENNEL BULB

1 fennel bulb, cut into 8 pieces
150ml (5fl oz) fish stock (see page 270)
½ tsp fennel seeds
sprig of fresh thyme
½ fresh bay leaf

FOR THE CHAPELURE

50gm (2oz) panko breadcrumbs or fresh breadcrumbs
25gm (1oz) Avonmore unsalted butter

TO SERVE

flaxseed oil

SERVES 4

FLAXSEED OIL SPHERES

Pour the flaxseed oil into a 3cm (1in) semi-sphere rubber mould tray and freeze – fill at least 12 semi-circles so that you will have spare spheres. In a pot, warm the cocoa butter and add the whole star anise. Leave to infuse for an hour somewhere warm so that the cocoa butter does not solidify. Once the flaxseed oil spheres are frozen, remove from the freezer and stick each half together to form a series of balls. Dip each ball in the infused cocoa butter, ensuring that there are no holes in the outer shell, and store in the fridge for service.

THE COD

Preheat the oven to 150°C. Remove the skin from the fillet and cut it into 5cm (2in) strips. Line a baking tray with greaseproof paper. Lay the skin out evenly on the paper and season with salt and freshly milled white pepper. Lay another sheet of paper on top and then another tray. Place in the preheated oven and cook until golden and crispy. Take the side of cod and trim the thicker end off (it should be about 2cm/1in thick). Turn this piece over and place at the tail end to make an even and level rectangular shape. Roll the fillet up very tightly in cling film and then slice it into 12cm (4.½in) rolls. Place the wrapped rolls in a vacuum-pack bag with the fennel and coriander seeds and season with a little salt and freshly milled white pepper. Cook in a waterbath set to 61°C for about 40 minutes, or until firm and cooked through.

BABY SPINACH AND ALMOND PURÉE

Place the butter, shallot, fennel and garlic in a pot and cover with a lid. Cook over a low heat until soft but not coloured. Add the baby spinach leaves and wilt them down. Transfer to a HotmixPRO blender (or similar) and blitz on high for 3 minutes until smooth. Slowly add in the almond oil and blitz gently to combine. Season with salt and freshly milled white pepper to taste. Leave to cool.

FENNEL JUICE FOAM

Boil the freshly pressed fennel bulb juice in a pot. Add the xanthan gum and pass through a fine sieve. Pour into a siphon gun and charge with two ISI gas chargers. Shake very well and refrigerate.

BRAISED FENNEL BULB

Place the fennel bulb in a vacuum-pack bag with the remaining ingredients. Seal and cook in a steamer for 30 minutes.

CHAPELURE

Blitz the panko breadcrumbs until fine. Melt the butter in a pot, add the breadcrumbs and cook until golden brown. Set aside.

TO SERVE

Remove the flaxseed spheres from the fridge 5 minutes before service to allow the oil inside the sphere to become liquid – you want it to flow out of the shell once broken. Place a pile of chapelure on the side of a warm plate and rest a flaxseed oil sphere on top. Pool the spinach purée in the centre of the plate. Place a piece of braised fennel to the side. Position the cod next and top with the crispy skin. Drizzle a little flaxseed oil around the fish and finish with 2 lines of fennel foam.

JENNY YOUNG | CHEESEMAKER

Cheesemaker and organic farmer Jenny Young started out in PR but threw it in seventeen years ago to become a full-time farmer, her true passion. Today she produces eggs, cheese, beef, honey, apple juice and vegetables on her fully certified organic farm and folk flock from far and wide to buy direct from Jenny's well-stocked farmshop. The truckle she holds in her hand here is the raw milk Castlefarm gouda style cheese, which she launched in 2009 at the Taste of Kildare festival held at The K Club. It has remained on our menu ever since.

www.castlefarmshop.ie

Wild lemon sole, ravioli of baby spinach and garlic, lobster sauce and lemon and vanilla glaze

For me, the most important part of this dish is the lemon and vanilla glaze that we brush over the fish. It lends the sole an extra depth of almost woody flavour, without overpowering the subtle taste of the fish itself. The velvety smooth bisque then tops it off.

WINE PAIRING

Sunny Grüner Veltliner,
Laurenz, Austria

This is a very versatile wine. It is crisp and aromatic and will match the lemon glaze here perfectly.

FOR THE LEMON SOLE

8 lemon sole fillets, skin removed

FOR THE PASTA

250gm (9oz) strong flour
3 free-range egg yolks
2 whole free-range eggs
salt
Newgrange Gold rapeseed oil
extra flour for dusting

FOR THE GARLIC CONFIT

8 large garlic cloves, peeled
sprig of fresh thyme
Newgrange Gold rapeseed oil (enough to cover the garlic)
pinch of sea salt

FOR THE SPINACH FILLING

5gm (¼oz) Avonmore unsalted butter
500gm (17oz) spinach, washed and dried
garlic confit (from above)
salt and freshly milled white pepper

FOR RAVIOLI ASSEMBLY

flour, for dusting
beaten egg yolk
spinach filling (from above)

FOR THE LEMON AND VANILLA GLAZE

250gm (9oz) dark brown sugar
1 vanilla pod, split in half lengthwise and seeds scraped out and retained
5gm (¼oz) Chinese five spice powder
25ml (1fl oz) cider vinegar
5gm (¼oz) fresh ginger, chopped
juice of ½ lime
2 lemons, peeled, chopped and juice squeezed out

FOR THE LOBSTER AND VANILLA SAUCE

500gm (17oz) lobster shells
200ml (7fl oz) Armagnac
250gm (9oz) mirepoix (vegetables washed, peeled and chopped the same size, to include carrots, celery, white onion, leeks and fennel)
150gm (5oz) fresh plum vine tomatoes and stalks, roughly chopped
150gm (5oz) tomato paste
300ml (10fl oz) fish stock (see page 270)
600ml (21fl oz) Avonmore double cream
2 vanilla pods, split in half lengthwise and seeds scraped out and retained

TO SERVE

1 courgette, cut into long thin strips and blanched
200gm (7oz) remaining spinach and garlic filling, from above
5 crayfish tails, chopped
½ tsp lecithin powder
1 vanilla pod, cut into shards, to garnish

SERVES 4

LEMON SOLE

Roll each fillet tightly, lengthwise, in cling film and chill in the fridge for 1 hour.

PASTA

Place the flour, egg yolks and whole eggs in a food processor and pulse until the mixture resembles fine breadcrumbs. Season with a little salt. Add enough oil just to bring the crumbs together. Transfer to a bowl and bring together by hand. Turn out on to a floured surface and knead for 1 minute. Divide the mixture into two, cover each piece with cling film and rest in the fridge for 30 minutes.

GARLIC CONFIT

Preheat the oven to 100°C. Put all the ingredients into a small pan, place in the preheated oven and cook until the garlic is soft and tender but still holding its shape. Strain, and purée the garlic with a hand blender.

SPINACH FILLING

Add the butter to a hot pan and sauté the spinach. Add the garlic confit and season. Strain through a muslin cloth and leave to hang for 1 hour to ensure that all excess liquid is removed. Reserve 80gm (3oz) of the cooked spinach and keep warm for service.

RAVIOLI ASSEMBLY

Remove the pasta dough from the fridge and dust lightly with flour. Using a pasta machine, roll out the pasta dough as thinly as possible, starting at the highest number on the dial and moving down a notch each time until you reach 1. Using a 10cm (4in) cutter, cut out 2 discs of the same size from the sheet of pasta – this will make 1 ravioli. Take a large spoonful of the spinach mixture and place it in the centre of the pasta disc. Brush the edges of the other pasta disc with the beaten egg yolk and press the two pieces together to form a flying saucer shape. Squeeze out any air trapped between the two discs as you go. Repeat this process 4 times. Arrange the four ravioli on a sheet of parchment paper and set aside.

LEMON AND VANILLA GLAZE

Place the sugar, vanilla pod, vanilla seeds, five spice powder, cider vinegar and ginger in a pan over a low heat and leave to cook, without stirring, until the sugar melts and forms a dark caramel. Once the caramel is ready, remove from the heat and slowly and carefully add the fresh lime juice and chopped lemon and juice. Return the pan to the heat and cook until the liquid is reduced by half. Strain through a fine sieve or chinois to remove any lumps and set aside.

LOBSTER AND VANILLA SAUCE

Preheat the oven to 170°C. Roast the lobster shells in the preheated oven for 30 minutes. Deglaze the roasting tray with the Armagnac and add the roasted shells to a large pot with the Armagnac. Add the mirepoix and sweat off the vegetables. Add the tomato paste and chopped fresh tomatoes and mix to combine. Add the fish stock and double cream. Add the vanilla pod and seeds and bring to the boil, then reduce the heat to a simmer and allow the sauce to reduce and thicken. Strain the sauce through a fine sieve and then strain again through a muslin cloth to ensure a silky smooth sauce. Set aside.

TO SERVE

Bring a large pot of salted water to the boil and add in the sheet of parchment paper with the ravioli on it (to prevent the risk of bursting the ravioli if you remove them from the paper). Cook the ravioli for 4 minutes until al dente. Remove from the heat and drain. Toss the ravioli in rapeseed oil and season with salt and milled pepper. Place the wrapped lemon sole fillets in a vacuum-pack bag and cook in a waterbath, set to 55°C, for 11–14 minutes (depending on thickness of the fillets) until firm and cooked through. Once cooked, remove the fillets from the bag and discard the cling film wrapping. Brush each one with the citrus glaze and set aside to keep warm. Using a hand blender, add 2gm of lecithin powder to 200ml (7fl oz) of the lobster sauce and blitz until bubbles form on the surface, then allow to stand for 30 seconds before using. Using a ring mould, arrange a circle of courgette in the centre of a warm plate. Fill with warm spinach mix and then remove the ring mould. Carefully pour lobster sauce around and dot pieces of crayfish tail in the sauce. Put 2 lemon sole fillets across the top of the spinach and place a ravioli on top. Spoon lobster bubbles over the ravioli and garnish with a vanilla stick. Brush the edge of the bowl with citrus glaze and serve.

GRZEGORZ PIEKAR | RESTAURANT MANAGER

East coast mackerel fillet with barigoule of vegetables with Crinnaughtaun apple juice and Newgrange Gold rapeseed oil

A 'barigoule' is a traditional French method of cooking vegetables in white wine and olive oil. In my version, I have replaced the white wine with Judith Keane's Crinnaughtaun apple juice from County Waterford and the olive oil with rapeseed oil from County Meath. The resulting dish is very simple and light but really refreshing.

WINE PAIRING

Thomas Barton Medoc

I know many would disagree but I think fish can take red wine (sometimes) and mackerel is one of those fish. The age of this wine has really softened the tannin, and the oak suits the oily fish.

FOR THE MACKEREL

4 fillets of fresh Irish mackerel
salt and freshly milled white peppercorn

FOR THE BARIGOULE

100ml (3.5fl oz) Crinnaughtaun apple juice
5ml (¼fl oz) cider vinegar
small bouquet garni (thyme, coriander stalks and bayleaf)
50ml (2fl oz) Newgrange Gold rapeseed oil
salt and freshly milled white peppercorn
100gm (3½oz) baby onions, peeled
100gm (3½oz) baby artichokes, peeled
50gm (2oz) girolle mushrooms
100gm (3½oz) baby carrots, peeled
2 garlic cloves, peeled
5gm (¼oz) coriander seeds
1 courgette

FOR THE APPLE AIR

200ml (7fl oz) Crinnaughtaun apple juice
½ tsp lecithin powder

TO SERVE

2–3 Granny Smith apples, peeled and cored and flesh scooped into small balls with a solfrino cutter
10 leaves fresh coriander, finely chopped
pinch of smoked sea salt

SERVES 4

THE MACKEREL

Preheat the oven to 120°C. Remove the pin bones very carefully from each mackerel fillet. Season the mackerel fillets with salt and milled white peppercorn. Add the seasoned fillets to a pan and pour over enough cooking liquid from the barigoule to just cover them. Set the pan over a low heat and cook for about 4 minutes, or until the fillets are soft and flaking.

THE BARIGOULE

Place the apple juice in a pot and boil to reduce to 60ml (2fl oz). Add the cider vinegar, bouquet garni and rapeseed oil. Season with salt and milled white peppercorn. Add the vegetables, garlic and coriander seeds and bring gently up to just under the boil. Then immediately remove from the heat, place a parchment paper lid on top and transfer to the preheated oven for about 20–25 minutes, or until the vegetables are just tender. Once the vegetables are cooked, remove from the oven. Cut the courgette into 4 equal lengths and cut each length into 4 wedges. Turn each wedge into a barrel shape. Blanch them in boiling, salted water for 30 seconds, then add into the barigoule.

THE APPLE AIR

Place the lecithin powder and the apple juice in a rectangular-shaped container and blitz together with a hand blender until bubbles appear.

TO SERVE

Add the apple balls and chopped coriander to the barigoule. Spoon some barigoule mixture into the centre of each warm plate, dividing the vegetables evenly between them. Lay a mackerel fillet on top and spoon on some apple air. Sprinkle a little smoked sea salt over the fish to serve.

Wild sea bass with estate wild garlic, red pepper confit, cod brandade and anchovy cream

Wild garlic is spring in a bud to me. We have a half-acre patch of wild garlic growing in the woods on the estate here and I wanted to create a recipe for it on my menu. This is a real fish lover's dish, with the strong flavour of the wild sea bass and the anchovy cream coming through. However, the fish flavour is balanced by the sweetness of the red pepper and the comfort of the brandade.

WINE PAIRING

Giaconda Nantua Les Deux Chardonnay, Australia

This dish is no shrinking violet. It has lots of big flavours so calls for a big wine. This is one of Australia's best wines, with full, rich flavour and a hint of spice.

FOR THE ANCHOVY CREAM

100gm (3½oz) tinned anchovies
50ml (2fl oz) Avonmore cream

FOR THE WILD GARLIC CRISP

6 stalks wild garlic
10ml (½fl oz) vegetable oil
pinch of salt

FOR THE RED PEPPER CANNELLONI

6 red peppers
20ml (¾fl oz) Newgrange Gold rapeseed oil
salt and freshly milled white pepper
6 anchovy fillets
3 leaves wild garlic

FOR THE BRANDADE

200gm (7oz) salted cod, soaked overnight in water
160gm (5½oz) peeled and diced potatoes
500ml (17fl oz) Avonmore milk
50ml (2fl oz) Avonmore cream
1 garlic clove, bashed
50ml (2fl oz) Newgrange Gold rapeseed oil
1 sprig of fresh thyme
1 small bayleaf
10ml (½fl oz) lemon juice
salt and freshly milled white pepper, to taste

FOR THE SEA BASS

6 portions wild sea bass (180gm/6oz each), descaled and pin bones removed
salt and freshly milled white pepper
30ml (1fl oz) olive oil

TO SERVE

120ml (4fl oz) Newgrange Gold rapeseed oil
60ml (2fl oz) 12-year-old Villa Manodori balsamic vinegar
40 wild garlic flowers

SERVES 6

ANCHOVY CREAM

Place the anchovy fillets in a HotmixPRO blender (or similar) and blitz for a few seconds, then slowly add the cream, a little at a time (to prevent it splitting), as you continue to blitz. Pass through a fine sieve and set aside in a squeezy bottle ready for service.

WILD GARLIC CRISP

Wrap a plate tightly in cling film. Brush the wild garlic with a little oil on each side. Place the oiled garlic on top of the cling film and season with a pinch of salt. Cover tightly with cling film and cook in the microwave for 2 minutes on high. Remove immediately from the cling film and place on kitchen paper to remove any excess oil. Store in an airtight container until required.

RED PEPPER CANNELLONI

Preheat the oven to 150°C. Cut the top off the red peppers and tap on a chopping board to remove the seeds. Pour the rapeseed oil on a baking tray and place the red peppers on the tray, rubbing them in the oil. Season with salt and milled white pepper and transfer to the preheated oven for 35–40 minutes, or until the skin is charred and blistered. Place the cooked peppers in a bowl, cover with cling film, and leave for 20 minutes. Carefully remove the skin from the peppers and cut each one into 3 even-sized pieces. Place half an anchovy fillet and a small piece of wild garlic on top of each strip of pepper and roll into a cylinder shape. Place the red pepper cannelloni on a baking tray, drizzle with some rapeseed oil, season with salt and milled white pepper and set aside for service.

BRANDADE

Rinse the cod in cold water. Place the potatoes in a pot, cover with cold water, add a pinch of salt and bring to the boil, then reduce the heat and simmer until tender. Drain, pass the potatoes through a fine sieve and set aside to keep warm. Place the milk, cream, garlic, bay leaf and thyme in a large pot and bring to the boil, then reduce the heat and simmer for 5 minutes. Remove the pot from the heat and allow the flavours to infuse for 30 minutes. Place the pot back on the heat and bring

the liquid to just below the boil. Reduce the heat to a simmer, add the cod and gently poach for 4–5 minutes, depending on the thickness of the cod fillet. Be careful not to overcook the fish. Once cooked, remove the cod and strain the cooking liquid. Place the mash into the pot and flake in the cooked cod. Beat in the rapeseed oil and add just enough of the cooking liquid to achieve a very smooth mash consistency. Finish with a little lemon juice and season with salt and milled white pepper to taste.

SEA BASS

Preheat the oven to 160°C. Season the sea bass fillets with salt and pepper. Place a non-stick, ovenproof pan over a medium-high heat. Add the oil and, once hot, add the fillets, skin-side down, and seal until golden brown. Turn the fish over and transfer to the preheated oven for 3–4 minutes, depending on the thickness of the fillets.

TO SERVE

Transfer the baking tray of red pepper cannelloni to the steam oven for 6 minutes to heat through. Stencil a triangle of anchovy cream in the centre of a warm plate and place three red pepper cannelloni in the centre. Quenelle a spoon of cod brandade to one side and lay the wild garlic crisp on top. Fill the gap between the anchovy cream and cannelloni with rapeseed oil and drizzle over a little balsamic vinegar. Place the sea bass on top of the cannelloni and serve. Draw a line of anchovy cream along the edge of the plate and finish with wild garlic flowers.

Poached free-range Irish chicken with locally grown baby vegetables and morel sauce

Morels herald the beginning of spring for me – but early spring, when there's still a nip in the air. This dish captures that mid-season moment perfectly, with its fresh spring flavours but comfort food undertone. The earthy truffle is a nod to the winter just gone.

WINE PAIRING

Original Organic Merlot, France

Poached chicken is delicate, but the morel sauce demands a fuller wine. This organic little gem is ripe and gluggable.

FOR THE CHICKEN

1 whole free-range Irish chicken
12 slices black Périgord truffle
6 litres (10½ pints) clear brown chicken stock (see page 270)
2 large carrots, peeled and chopped into chunky pieces
1 leek, washed and chopped into chunky pieces
3 celery sticks, chopped into chunky pieces
1 onion, peeled and chopped into chunky pieces
bouquet garni (1 bayleaf, 1 sprig of fresh thyme, 1 sprig of sage, 2 garlic cloves, 20 coriander seeds, 10 whole black peppercorns)

FOR THE SPRING VEGETABLES

8 baby carrots, peeled
6 baby leeks or spring onions
6 baby white turnips
12 baby onions
10 baby potatoes, pared into barrel shapes
20 broad beans, blanched and peeled
20gm (¾oz) fresh peas, podded
1 litre (1¾ pints) fresh chicken stock, from above

FOR THE FRESH MORELS

10gm (½oz) unsalted Avonmore butter
5gm (¼oz) chopped shallots
50gm (2oz) fresh morels
10ml (½fl oz) fresh chicken stock, from above

FOR THE MOREL SAUCE

20gm (¾oz) Avonmore unsalted butter
10gm (½oz) dried morels
30gm (1oz) shallots, finely chopped
½ garlic clove
10 black peppercorns, crushed
125ml (4½fl oz) white wine
250ml (9fl oz) Avonmore cream
salt
cooked fresh morels, from above

SERVES 2–4

CHICKEN

Remove the wishbone from the chicken. Work your fingers into the space between the skin and the breast to form a pocket and slide 6 slices of truffle under the skin on each breast. Truss the bird with butcher's string. Place the chicken and the rest of the ingredients in a saucepan with the clear stock and bring to the boil. It is important to keep the vegetables nice and chunky for this stock, so that they don't overcook and taint the flavour of the chicken stock. Simmer the bird for 1½ hours, or until the meat reaches 74°C on a meat probe. Set the chicken aside to keep warm. Retain the stock for cooking the vegetables and the morels.

SPRING VEGETABLES

Put a litre of the chicken stock in a saucepan and bring up to a simmer. Cook each variety of vegetable separately, to prevent over-cooking. Cook the vegetables until tender and just cooked through. Drain and set aside.

FRESH MORELS

Melt the unsalted butter in a warm pan. Add the shallots and cook on a low heat until soft. Add the fresh morels, followed by the chicken stock, and lightly poach the morels until soft.

MOREL SAUCE

Melt the butter in a saucepan and add the dried morels, shallots, garlic and peppercorns. Cover with a lid and cook on a low heat to sweat the vegetables without colouring for about 20 minutes, or until soft. Add the white wine and reduce by 80%. Add the cream and reduce until the liquid reaches a sauce consistency. Pass the sauce through a fine sieve or chinois, pushing the pulp through to extract all the flavour. Season with salt to taste. Add the cooked fresh morels and serve.

TO SERVE

Place the pot of stock over the heat and bring to the boil. Place the spring vegetables in the hot stock until heated through. Remove the legs from the chicken and separate the drumstick from the thigh. Remove both breasts and cut each one in half. Place a piece of the breast and a leg in each warm bowl. Arrange the vegetables neatly around the chicken and pour the hot stock over. Serve the morel sauce on the side.

Roast Thornhill duck with citrus glaze, celeriac gratin and Grand Marnier sauce

This dish is a nod to the old ways – with the crispy bird presented on the trolley and carved at the table for the diner. Once the breast has been carved and served, the legs are returned to the kichen to be finished and re-presented as a zesty salad. Accompanied by the gratin and the smooth orange sauce, this is a classic duck dish in every sense of the word.

WINE PAIRING

Baron de Ley Rioja Reserva

Rioja and duck are great together. The oakiness and spiciness of the wine complement this dish perfectly.

FOR THE CITRUS GLAZE

200ml (7fl oz) fresh orange juice
100ml (3½fl oz) fresh lemon juice
40ml (1½fl oz) Jane Sellers honey
½ tsp ground cloves
¼ tsp ground cinnamon

FOR THE CELERIAC GRATIN

400ml (14fl oz) Avonmore cream
½ tsp garlic purée
1 sprig of fresh thyme
600gm (1lb 5oz) potatoes, peeled and sliced into 2mm (1/10in)-thick slices
300gm (10oz) celeriac, peeled and sliced into 2mm (1/10in)-thick slices
grated nutmeg
salt and freshly milled white pepper

FOR THE DUCK

1 whole Thornhill duck
20ml (¾fl oz) vegetable oil
40gm (1½oz) Avonmore unsalted butter
1 sprig of fresh thyme
3 garlic cloves
salt and freshly milled black pepper

FOR THE GRAND MARNIER SAUCE

1 whole orange, peeled and chopped
40gm (1½oz) caster sugar
35ml (1¼fl oz) champagne vinegar
360ml (13fl oz) fresh orange juice
30ml (1fl oz) Grand Marnier
16 orange segments
pinch of salt

FOR THE SPICY VINAIGRETTE FOR THE DUCK LEG SALAD

100gm (3½oz) caster sugar
100ml (3½fl oz) water
100ml (3½fl oz) white wine vinegar
½ red Thai chilli
handful Carrick Farm mesclun leaves

SERVES 4

CITRUS GLAZE

Place the citrus juices and honey in a pot and boil gently until the liquid is reduced by 50%, then add the spices and reduce further until the liquid turns into a very thick syrup. Remove from the heat and set aside to cool. Store in a jar with a lid.

CELERIAC GRATIN

Preheat the oven to 115°C. Add the cream, garlic and thyme to a large heavy-bottomed pot and bring to the boil. Add the sliced potatoes and celeriac and add 2–3 grates of nutmeg. Cook over a medium heat for 10 minutes, stirring occasionally to prevent the starchy vegetables sticking to the bottom of the pot. Season with salt and pepper to taste, then spread the mixture evenly in a rectangular dish, about 30cm x 15cm (12in x 6in). Cook in the preheated oven for about 1 hour, or until the potatoes and celeriac are soft and cooked through and the top is golden brown.

DUCK

Remove the wishbone from the bird. Place a clean tea towel flat on a bench and lay two sheets of greaseproof paper on top to cover it. Place the duck, breast facing down, on the paper and towel and roll up tightly. Tie each end tight with kitchen twine, like a Christmas cracker. Blanch in a large pot of boiling salted water for 20 minutes. Remove the duck and place it in a large basin of iced water to cool. Once cool, remove the duck from the towel and paper wrapping. Season the bird with salt and pepper.

To roast the duck, place the oil in a large pan or tray to heat. Season the duck with salt and pepper and place it in the pan on its side. Seal off until nicely golden brown and then turn over and repeat on the other side. Finally, turn the duck breast-side-down and repeat the process. Add the butter, garlic and thyme and allow the butter to foam up, then flip the duck on to its back until golden brown. Transfer to a preheated oven set to 160°C. Baste the bird with butter, after 6 and 12 minutes approximately. After 16 minutes remove the duck from the oven, paint it with the citrus glaze and return it to the hot oven to cook for a further 4–10 minutes. The bird should be in the oven for a total of 20–25 minutes. The duck breast should be served pink. Check to see if the duck is ready by using a meat probe – the temperature should be 60°C.

GRAND MARNIER SAUCE

Place the chopped orange, sugar and champagne vinegar in a pot, bring to the boil and then reduce to simmer over a medium heat for 15 minutes. Add the orange juice and half the Grand Marnier and continue to reduce the liquid until you achieve a nice sauce consistency. Pass the sauce through a fine sieve and season with a pinch of salt to taste. Finally, add the orange segments and remaining Grand Marnier.

SPICY VINAIGRETTE FOR THE DUCK LEG SALAD

Add the sugar, water and vinegar to a small pot and bring to the boil. Remove from the heat and allow to cool. Pour into a blender, add the red Thai chilli and blitz. Set aside to serve.

TO SERVE

Brush the duck with glaze and place on the trolley or board with the sauce and gratin in dishes to the side. Carve the bird at the table, carving the breast on to warm plates with celeriac gratin and sauce. Remove both legs from the carcass and return them to the kitchen. Cut the meat from the bone into small slices and flash fry in rapeseed oil until crispy. Dress a pile of mesclun leaves with the spicy vinaigrette and sprinkle the crispy leg meat on top. Serve in a bowl.

ADRIAN SWEENEY | FISH SMOKER

When it comes to smoked fish, McConnell's is a name with a rich heritage dating back to 1928, when the name was emblazoned over a fish shop on Dublin's eminent Grafton Street. The family built up an enviable reputation over the years for selling the finest smoked salmon available. Today, the brand has developed into McConnell's Gourmet Smoked Foods, no longer based on Grafton Street but still in County Dublin. 'The only ingredients you'll find in our smoked salmon,' explains Adrian Sweeney, 'are salmon, salt, oak, smoke and time. Our smoking process is not something that can be rushed. We buy the salmon in fresh and whole (any McConnell's smoked salmon you eat today, will have been in the water a week ago), then fillet it and salt it by hand and finally smoke it on-site.' You'll find McConnell's superior smoked salmon on the menu at The K Club.

Glazed rack of suckling pig, slow-cooked Hardyman's belly pork, crispy crackling, devils on horseback and Granny Smith sorbet

This dish has become the most popular dish on our menu. Interestingly, about ten years ago a critic slated it in a national newspaper, but I believed in it. Over the years I have tweaked it a little, but I always knew it was a good dish. As a chef you need to believe in what you are doing and not let criticism cloud your judgement.

WINE PAIRING

Portia Prima Ribera del Duero

We love Spanish wine and this big full-bodied red from Ribera does the job. Rich, intense, but still aged and supple.

FOR THE GRANNY SMITH SORBET

100ml (3½fl oz) Granny Smith purée
60ml (2fl oz) sugar syrup (see page 271)
60ml (2fl oz) water
25g (¾oz) sorbitol
15ml (½fl oz) Mickey Finn Apple Whiskey Liquor

FOR THE CRAB APPLE GLAZE

250ml (9fl oz) crab apple juice
50g (2oz) Jane Sellers honey
½ tsp ground cloves
¼ tsp ground cinnamon

FOR THE CRISPY SAGE LEAVES

10 fresh sage leaves
20ml (¾fl oz) vegetable oil
salt and freshly milled white peppercorn

FOR THE CARAMELISED APPLE PURÉE

3 Granny Smith apples
125g (4½oz) caster sugar
125ml (4½fl oz) Crinnaugthaun apple Juice
5ml (¼fl oz) cider vinegar

FOR THE CRISPY CRACKLING

skin from the 2 racks of suckling pig, below
20ml (¾fl oz) crab apple jelly, from above, to glaze

FOR THE RACK OF SUCKLING PIG

2 racks of suckling pig, skin removed but retained and bone cleaned
salt and freshly milled black pepper
20gm (¾oz) Avonmore unsalted butter
60ml (2fl oz) crab apple jelly, from above

FOR THE PORK BELLY

250g (9oz) Hardyman's pork belly
salt and milled black pepper
½ tsp chopped fresh sage
½ tsp chopped fresh thyme
20gm (¾oz) Avonmore unsalted butter
20ml (¾fl oz) crab apple jelly, from above

FOR THE DEVILS ON HORSEBACK

for the prunes

8 dried prunes
100ml (3½fl oz) ruby port
zest of ¼ lemon
zest of ¼ orange
100ml (3½fl oz) water
10gm (½oz) caster sugar

to finish

8 slices belly bacon
1 tbsp olive oil
knob of butter

FOR THE SAGE OIL

50g (2oz) fresh sage leaves
35ml (1fl oz) sunflower oil

FOR THE CRISP APPLE TUILE

1 Granny Smith apple
300ml (10fl oz) light sugar syrup (see page 271)

FOR THE APPLE CHUTNEY

see page 274

GRANNY SMITH SORBET

Mix all the ingredients together and place in a Taurus Rowzer beaker and freeze. Then blitz when required. Alternatively, place in an ice cream machine and churn for 20 minutes and then freeze.

CRAB APPLE GLAZE

Place all the ingredients in a pot and bring to the boil. Continue to boil until the juice forms a light syrup. Remove from the heat and leave to cool.

CRISPY SAGE LEAVES

Wrap a plate tightly with cling film. Dip the sage leaves in the oil one by one, allow the excess oil to drip off, then place each leaf on the cling-film-covered plate. Season with salt and milled pepper to taste. Cover the sage leaves with another sheet of cling film, pulling tightly to secure the film around the plate. Place in the microwave for 2 minutes. Remove immediately from the cling film and place on a sheet of kitchen paper to remove the oil. Store in an airtight container until required.

CARAMELISED APPLE PURÉE

Peel, core and slice the apples. Place the sugar in a pot and lightly caramelise. Add in the apple juice, cider vinegar and sliced apple. Cook until the apples are soft and there is still a little liquid. Pour the mixture into a HotmixPRO blender (or similar) and blend until smooth. Refrigerate for service.

CRISPY CRACKLING

Preheat the oven to 140°C. Trim the skin to remove any excess meat or fat. Cut into 2cm (¾in) strips. Place the strips on a non-stick baking sheet, leaving space between each strip, and then place another non-stick backing sheet on top. Transfer to the oven and cook for 3 hours. Remove and allow to cool. Brush the crackling with crab apple glaze before serving.

RACK OF SUCKLING PIG

Season the racks with salt and milled black pepper and then vacuum pack the racks in one bag. Insert the fine needle probe directly into the middle of one rack and transfer to a waterbath, set to 70°C. When the probe reaches 67°C, remove the racks from the waterbath and then from the bag. Season again with salt and milled black pepper and set aside.

PORK BELLY

Season the pork belly with salt and pepper and vacuum pack in a bag with the fresh sage and thyme. Transfer to the waterbath, set to 70°C, and cook for 12 hours. Remove the pork from the bath and then from the bag and season again with salt and pepper.

DEVILS ON HORSEBACK

Place all the ingredients, except the bacon, in a pot and bring up to the boil, then reduce the heat and simmer for 20 minutes. Remove from the heat and allow to cool. Cover and transfer to the fridge to marinate for 24 hours minimum. Lay the bacon slices side by side on a board. Place a marinated prune at the bottom of each slice. Roll them up tightly and push a cocktail stick through each one to hold them firmly in place.

SAGE OIL

Blanch the sage leaves in a pot of boiling, salted water for 10 seconds, then remove and transfer to a bowl of iced water for 10 seconds. Remove the leaves and place in a dry cloth, squeezing gently to remove any excess water. Put the leaves and the oil into a blender and blend on high for 5 minutes. Pass the mixture through a fine sieve and set aside.

CRISP APPLE TUILE

Preheat the oven to 85°C. Thinly slice the apple widthways on a slicer, about 1mm (1⁄20 in) thick. Place the slices in a bowl and pour over the cold stock syrup. Leave to infuse for 10 minutes. Remove the apple from the syrup and lay out 4 lines of 3 slices on non-stick baking parchment, ensuring that each apple slice overlaps the next slightly. Transfer to the preheated oven for 40 minutes or until crisp. Remove from the oven and, while still warm, roll the apple over four 6cm (2½in) rings to form complete circles. Set aside to cool and set.

TO SERVE

Heat a large pan over a medium heat and add in the butter. Once the butter is foaming, add the racks and quickly seal them; this will take about 1 minute per side. Remove the racks from the heat and, using a pastry brush, glaze the ribs with crab apple jelly. Place under a hot grill or salamander until lightly caramelised. For the belly, heat a large pan over a medium heat and add the butter. Once the butter is foaming, add the pork belly and sauté until golden brown on both sides. Remove from the heat, brush with the crab apple glaze and place under a hot grill or salamander until lightly caramelised. For the devils on horseback, heat a large non-stick pan, add the oil and sauté the devils until golden. Add the butter and baste until slightly crispy. (You can do all of the above in the same pan.) Place the tuile on the plate, half-fill it with the apple chutney and top with 2 scoops of sorbet. Drag the caramelised apple purée across the plate, place the belly on the purée and top with the sage leaf. Place the rack and 2 devils on horseback to the side. Position the crackling up against the tuile and dot the plate with sage oil.

Caor Acla Blackface Achill Island lamb, Chulchoill goat's cheese fondue, fresh mint paint and estate wild garlic oil

Lamb and goat's cheese are natural bedfellows, perhaps because both animals graze in the same way. The lamb shoulder here is cooked slowly until beautifully tender and then topped with crunchy fines herbes to provide a contrast in texture. The wild garlic grows in great swathes here on the estate. We pick it in spring and preserve it as a flavoured oil to use in season. See page 273 for our flavoured oil recipes.

WINE PAIRING

Château du Cauze
Saint-Émilion Grand Cru 2001

Lamb and **Saint-Émilion** are a match made in heaven. The slightly minty finish sits perfectly with the lamb. Try and source an aged one.

FOR THE SLOW-COOKED SHOULDER

1 shoulder of Caor Acla Blackface Achill Island lamb, deboned
1 garlic clove
1 small sprig of fresh thyme
1 sprig of fresh rosemary
salt and freshly milled black pepper

FOR THE MINT PAINT

60gm (2oz) fresh mint leaves
80gm (3oz) Jane Sellers honey

FOR THE MINTED BREADCRUMBS

30gm (1oz) panko Japanese breadcrumbs
10gm (½oz) fresh mint leaves

FOR THE WILD GARLIC OIL

15gm (½oz) wild garlic leaf
5gm (¼oz) flat-leaf parsley
40gm (1½oz) sunflower oil
pinch salt

FOR THE CHULCHOILL GOAT'S CHEESE FONDUE

30ml (1fl oz) Avonmore fresh cream
60gm (2oz) Chulchoill goat's cheese, chopped
salt and freshly milled white pepper, to taste

FOR THE VEGETABLE TIAN

for the filling

50ml (2fl oz) Newgrange Gold rapeseed oil
1 shallot, finely chopped
1 red pepper, peeled and chopped
½ garlic clove, crushed
1 sprig of fresh thyme, finely chopped
1 small sprig of rosemary, finely chopped
½ courgette, finely diced
½ aubergine, finely diced
1 plum tomato, peeled and chopped
4 fresh basil leaves, finely sliced
salt and freshly milled white pepper, to taste

for the top

2 red peppers
10ml (½fl oz) olive oil

for the courgette ribbons

2 courgettes

FOR THE LAMB

2 racks of French-trimmed Caor Acla Blackface Achill Island lamb
salt and freshly milled black pepper

FOR THE SWEETBREADS

200ml (7fl oz) chicken stock (see page 270)
20gm (¾oz) chopped shallot
20gm (¾oz) chopped carrot
20gm (¾oz) chopped leek
10gm (½oz) chopped celery
1 sprig fresh thyme
10 whole white peppercorns
10 whole coriander seeds
pinch salt
6 fresh lamb sweetbreads
20gm (¾oz) plain flour
salt and freshly milled black pepper
10ml (½fl oz) vegetable oil
30gm (1oz) Avonmore unsalted butter

SERVES 6

SLOW-COOKED SHOULDER

Place the lamb in a vacuum-pack bag with the garlic and herbs and then season and seal the bag. Place in a waterbath set to 70°C and cook for 12 hours. Transfer the bag into ice-cold water to cool quickly. Once cold and set, cut the lamb into rectangular shapes and place in a vacuum-pack bag and seal.

MINT PAINT

Warm the honey in a HotmixPRO blender (or similar) to 45°C. Add the fresh mint leaves and blend until smooth. Transfer to a container and leave to cool.

MINTED BREADCRUMBS

Blend the crumbs and mint leaves in a blender on high until you have very fine, green crumbs.

WILD GARLIC OIL

Blanch the wild garlic and parsley in salted boiling water for 10 seconds. Drain and transfer directly to ice-cold water to cool. Drain and squeeze out any excess water. Place the blanched herbs and oil in a blender and blitz until smooth and green. Pass the oil through a fine muslin cloth and then transfer to a squeezy bottle.

CHULCHOILL GOAT'S CHEESE FONDUE

Place the cream in a pot and bring to the boil. Add the goat's cheese and whisk until smooth and runny. Season to taste. Transfer to a squeezy bottle and keep warm to serve.

VEGETABLE TIAN

To make the filling, place the oil in a pan, add the shallots, red peppers, garlic, herbs and a little salt and cook on a low heat until soft. Add the aubergine and courgette, cook for 3 minutes, then add the tomato and basil and season to taste. Set aside to cool.

To make the top, preheat the oven to 145°C. Place the whole red peppers in a roasting tray and cook in the preheated oven for 30 minutes. Remove from the oven, wrap in cling film and leave to cool. Peel off the skin, remove the seeds and cut into disc shapes (about 5cm/2in diameter).

To make the courgette ribbons, finely slice the courgette lengthwise on a mandolin, about 2mm (1/10in)-thick. Blanch in a pot of boiling salted water for 20 seconds. Transfer directly to a bowl of iced water to cool and then drain and pat dry.

To assemble the tian, grease the inside of 6 stainless steel rings (5cm/2in) with a little olive oil. Line each ring with 2 strips of courgette ribbon, then fill each ring with the vegetable filling and place the roasted red pepper disc on top.

THE LAMB

Place the racks in a vacuum-pack bag with a little salt and pepper and seal. Place in a waterbath set to 62°C. Insert the needle probe into the centre of the rack and cook until the meat has reached 56°C. Remove the lamb from the waterbath and from the bag and set aside.

THE SWEETBREADS

Place the stock, vegetables, fresh thyme, peppercorns and coriander seeds in a small pot and bring to the boil; season with a little salt and reduce the heat to simmer for 20 minutes. Add the lamb sweetbreads and cook for about 5 minutes until they are slightly firm. Remove the sweetbreads from the cooking liquid and set aside to cool.

TO SERVE

Place the shoulder back in the waterbath, set to 65°C, for 15 minutes. Remove and season with salt and pepper, seal it quickly in a hot pan with a little oil to colour it slightly and then brush it with mint paint and dip it in the minted breadcrumbs. Meanwhile, transfer the tians to a steamer to heat through for 10 minutes. Seal the racks in a hot pan with a little oil until golden brown on all sides. Season and brush with the mint paint. Roll the sweetbreads in seasoned flour. Pat off excess flour and add the oil to a hot frying pan, then seal the sweetbreads until golden brown. Add the unsalted butter and let it foam up, then baste the sweetbreads in the nut-brown butter for 4 minutes. Place 2 lines of fondue on a warm plate. Paint on 2–3 lines of the mint paint using a 4cm (1½in)-wide brush. Place the vegetable tian and a piece of the lamb shoulder on the plate. Cut the racks into double-boned cutlets, and six 2cm (¾in)-thick slices. Place a cutlet and a slice of lamb on the plate with the sweetbread on top of the slice. Drizzle over with wild garlic oil and serve.

AUDREY BROPHY | HOTEL MANAGER

BROCHAN AND JOSEPH COCOMAN |

DAIRY FARMERS

The Cocoman family have been Avonmore dairy farmers since 1978, although the picturesque County Kildare farm has been in Brochan's family since 1939. Today the Cocoman farm boasts a dairy herd of 100 pedigree Canadian Holstein cows, producing one million litres of magnificent-quality Irish milk a year. In 2009 he was awarded the inaugural National Dairy Council's Quality Milk award.

www.avonmore.ie

740

Crispy cannelloni of wild sweet cicely and liquorice mousse, coconut sorbet and spiral

Sweet cicely grows on the estate here. I love the intense aniseedy, liquorice flavour of it. The creamy flavour of the coconut sorbet then mellows it out and cleans the taste buds, ready for the next burst of cicely. This is a dessert which always draws the camera out for a snapshot.

FOR THE SWEET CICELY MOUSSE

250gm (9oz) coconut purée (we use Boiron or Ravifruit)
40gm (1½oz) chopped sweet cicely
1 stick liquorice, grated
5gm (¼oz) gelatine leaves, soaked in water
300ml (10fl oz) Avonmore cream, whipped

FOR THE COCONUT SORBET

500gm (17oz) coconut purée
225ml (8fl oz) sugar syrup (see page 271)
50ml (2fl oz) fresh lime juice
10gm (½oz) trimolene or sorbitol
125ml (4½fl oz) coconut milk
35ml (1¼fl oz) coconut liqueur

FOR THE CANNELLONI TUBE TUILES

200gm (7oz) Jane Sellers honey
200gm (7oz) caster sugar
65gm (2½oz) Avonmore unsalted butter
65gm (2½oz) plain flour

FOR THE COCONUT SPONGE

20gm (¾oz) Avonmore unsalted butter
50gm (2oz) caster sugar
125gm (4½oz) coconut purée
50gm (2oz) plain flour
½ tsp baking powder
35gm (1¼oz) eggs

FOR THE ISOMALT SPIRALS

100gm (3½oz) isomalt
green food colouring

FOR THE GUAVA PURÉE

100ml (3½fl oz) guava purée (we use Boiron or Ravifruit)
5ml (¼fl oz) freshly squeezed lime juice

TO SERVE

10 chocolate sticks (see page 275), to garnish

MAKES 10

SWEET CICELY MOUSSE

Add the coconut purée, sweet cicely and grated liquorice to a pot and bring to the boil. Remove from the heat. Squeeze any excess water out of the gelatine and add the leaves to the mix. Stir until dissolved. Transfer to a covered bowl and leave to refrigerate overnight.
To finish the sweet cicely mousse, remove it from the fridge and mix well with a whisk until soft and lump-free. Fold in the whipped cream and mix to combine. Place the mousse into a piping bag and refrigerate it for at least an hour before needed.

COCONUT SORBET

Mix all the ingredients together and place in a Taurus Rowzer beaker and freeze. Then blitz when required. Alternatively, place in an ice cream machine and churn for 20 minutes and then freeze.

CANNELLONI TUBE TUILES

Preheat the oven to 160°C. Place the honey, sugar and butter in a pot and heat until melted. Add the flour and whisk together, off the heat, until it forms a paste. Roll out the paste between 2 pieces of parchment paper to form a sheet no more than 2mm (1/10in) thick. Place on a flat baking tray and cook in the preheated oven for 18 minutes. Remove from the oven and, while still warm, cut the dough into ten 12cm x 12cm (5in x 5in) squares. Mould each square over a 4cm (1½in)-diameter plastic tube and seal along the joining line to form a complete tube. Store in a sealed container, away from moisture and heat, until ready to serve.

COCONUT SPONGE

Preheat the oven to 160°C. Beat the butter and sugar briefly together in a mixer and then add the coconut purée. Mix to combine. Add the flour and baking powder, followed by the eggs, and mix well. Spread the mix out (about 5mm/¼in thick) on a baking tray lined with parchment paper and cook in the preheated oven for 15 minutes. Remove from the oven and transfer to a cooling rack. Once cool, cut into ten 7cm x 3cm (3in x 1in) strips.

ISOMALT SPIRALS

Melt the isomalt in a pot and then carefully add the food colouring, drop by drop, until you achieve the desired colour. Remove from the heat and let the sugar cool down until it becomes thick and malleable. Pinch some off and spiral it around a 6cm (2½in) plastic tube. Ideally each spiral will be about 6–7cm (2½–3in) in length. As each spiral sets, remove carefully from the tube and set aside. Make ten spirals. Store in a sealed container, away from moisture and heat, until ready to serve.

GUAVA PURÉE

Blend the purée and lime juice together and transfer to a squeezy bottle for serving.

TO SERVE

Brush a coconut sponge with a little of the guava purée. Fill each cannelloni tube with the sweet cecily mousse and scrape the ends flat and clean. Arrange an isomalt spiral on the sponge and gently place a cannelloni through it. Place a line of guava purée dots along the centre of the plate and quenelle the coconut sorbet on to the plate. Place a chocolate stick on top and serve.

TIP

When making the isomalt spiral in our professional kitchen, we place some calcium chloride in the base of the box, covered with a sheet of parchment paper. This prevents moisture getting in. However, if using calcium chloride, do not allow it to touch the food in any way – if it does, you must discard the spirals.

IVETA GUDE AND TAREK DAKHLI | PASTRY CHEFS

Sticky pistachio meringue with mandarin orange mousse, elderflower sparkling wine sorbet and mango crisp

This dessert was spinning around in my brain for a good few years before I decided on the final spiral design of the dish. I was looking for something tart to counteract the sweet meringue and lemon wasn't doing it for me. When I experimented with the mandarin orange, it hit the perfect note. For my elderflower sparkler, I pick the blossom at home and then make the 'wine' in the kitchen here. The freshness and heady punch of summer you get when you pop open a bottle is magnificent.

FOR THE MANDARIN ORANGE MOUSSE

125g (4½oz) mandarin purée (we use Boiron or Ravifruit)
125g (4½oz) caster sugar
3g (¼oz) gelatine leaf, pre-soaked in a little water
150ml (5fl oz) Avonmore cream, whipped

FOR THE ELDERFLOWER SORBET

175ml (6fl oz) sparkling elderflower wine (see page 271)
50ml (2fl oz) sugar syrup (see page 271)
20g (¾oz) trimolene or sorbitol
5ml (¼fl oz) fresh lime juice

FOR THE MANGO CRISP

1 mango
80ml (3fl oz) sugar syrup (see page 271)

FOR THE MERINGUE

120g (4oz) egg whites
175g (6oz) caster sugar
50g (2oz) pistachio nuts, crushed

MAKES 6

MANDARIN ORANGE MOUSSE

Boil the purée with the sugar in a pot. Add the softened gelatine leaf and stir to dissolve. Remove from the heat and leave to cool. Refrigerate overnight. To make the mousse, weigh the purée and then weigh out an equal amount of whipped cream. Whisk the purée until smooth, then add the whipped cream and mix to combine. Transfer to a piping bag with a plain nozzle and refrigerate for at least 1 hour before serving.

ELDERFLOWER SORBET

Mix all the ingredients together, churn in an ice cream machine for 20 minutes and freeze or blitz in a Taurus Rowzer or Pacojet.

MANGO CRISP

Preheat the oven to 95°C. Thinly slice the unpeeled mango lengthways on a slicer or mandolin. Dip each slice into the sugar syrup and place on a Silpat, or similar non-stick mat. Put the mango slices into the preheated oven for a minimum of 1 hour. Leave the mango to cool and it will crisp up.

MERINGUE

Preheat the oven to 87°C. Whisk the egg whites with one-third of the sugar. Keep whisking and gradually add the remaining sugar in two more stages until the meringue mix holds a stiff peak. Transfer into a piping bag fitted with an 8mm (¼in) plain nozzle. Mark out a spiral template on a piece of cardboard. Place the template underneath the parchment paper and pipe the meringue evenly following the lines of the spiral template. Repeat this process 6 times. Sprinkle each spiral with the crushed pistachio nuts. Cook in the preheated oven for 2 hours. Do not allow the meringue to colour. Cool and store for serving.

TO SERVE

Lay the meringue spiral in the centre of the plate. Pipe the mandarin mousse between the gaps of the meringue spiral. Place a quenelle or scoop of the elderflower sorbet in the centre and finish with a mango crisp.

Ravioli of pineapple and pina colada sorbet with effervescent elderflower foam

This is a wonderfully floral, flavoursome dessert with its heady combination of elderflower, zippy pineapple and creamy pina colada. It is very clean on the palate and easy on the eye.

FOR THE PINA COLADA SORBET

400ml (14fl oz) coconut milk
85gm (3oz) fresh pineapple juice
85gm (3oz) sugar syrup (see page 271)
25gm (¾oz) trimolene or 100ml (3½fl oz) sorbitol
25ml (¾fl oz) Malibu rum

FOR THE PINEAPPLE

1 whole pineapple, peeled
300ml (10½fl oz) sugar syrup (see page 271)

FOR THE PINEAPPLE CRISP

6 pre-soaked pineapple slices, from above
10gm (½oz) honey
poppy seeds or rapeseeds

FOR THE ELDERFLOWER FOAM

250ml (9fl oz) sparkling elderflower wine (see page 271)
¾ tsp xanthan gum

TO SERVE

Carrick Farm viola petals and micro-cress

MAKES 6

PINA COLADA SORBET

Mix all the ingredients together and churn in an ice cream maker or blitz in a Taurus Rowzer or Pacojet. Pipe the sorbet into 6 dome moulds (7cm x 3cm / 3in x 1in) and freeze.

PINEAPPLE

Slice the pineapple widthways, wafer-thin, and leave to soak in the sugar syrup for at least 1 hour.

PINEAPPLE CRISP

Preheat the oven to 95°C. Place the pre-soaked pineapple slices on a Silpat (or other) non-stick mat and cook in the preheated oven for 60–90 minutes (depending on thickness of the slices) or until completely dry and crispy. Once cooked, remove the pineapple from the oven and immediately mould each slice over an upturned tea cup or mould. Set aside to cool. Place a little honey in the centre of each circle and sprinkle on a few poppy seeds or rapeseeds.

ELDERFLOWER FOAM

Bring the elderflower wine to the boil in a pot. Add the xanthan gum. Transfer to a siphon gun and add two ISI chargers. Shake very well and refrigerate until needed.

TO SERVE

Remove the sorbet from the dome moulds. Place a dome on each plate, slightly off-centre. Cover the dome with a layer of pineapple slices and shape them over the dome to form a smooth cover, with some slices of pineapple flowing down over the mould on to the plate. Place a pineapple crisp on top. Siphon a line of elderflower foam along the length of the plate and decorate with the viola flower petals and the micro-cress.

Passion fruit bavarois with champagne jelly and passion fruit and mango sorbet

The tart, citrus zip of this dessert is brilliant. It's a wonderful palate-cleansing dessert, ideal to serve after a rich main course, or simply to enjoy at any time on a warm summer's day.

FOR THE PASSION FRUIT JELLY

5gm (¼oz) gelatine sheets
250ml (9fl oz) passion fruit coulis (we use Boiron or Ravifruit)
5gm (¼oz) passion fruit pulp
25gm (¾oz) caster sugar

FOR THE BAVAROIS

20gm (¾oz) gelatine leaves
290ml (10fl oz) passion fruit coulis (we use Boiron or Ravifruit)
290ml (10fl oz) Avonmore pouring cream
200gm (7oz) caster sugar
5 egg yolks
435ml (15fl oz) Avonmore cream, whipped

FOR THE PASSION FRUIT AND MANGO SORBET

150ml (5fl oz) passion fruit coulis (we use Boiron or Ravifruit)
50ml (2fl oz) mango coulis (we use Boiron or Ravifruit)
100g (3½oz) sugar syrup (see page 271)

FOR THE CHAMPAGNE JELLY

100ml (3½fl oz) water
juice of ½ lemon
80gm (3oz) caster sugar
375ml (13fl oz) Laurent Perrier Champagne
8 leaves gelatine, pre-soaked in water

FOR THE PINEAPPLE GARNISH

200gm (7oz) finely diced pineapple
60ml (2fl oz) sugar syrup (see page 271)

FOR THE CHOCOLATE STICKS

80gm (3oz) sugar syrup (see page 271)
45g (1½oz) Valrhona cocoa powder
12gm (½oz) glucose syrup

SERVES 10

PASSION FRUIT JELLY

Soak the gelatine in a little cold water until soft. Bring the passion fruit coulis, pulp and sugar to the boil. Once boiling, squeeze any excess water out of the gelatine, add it to the pot and mix until it is completely dissolved. Pour into ten 8cm (3in) foil cups, about 4mm (1/10in) thick, and leave to set in the fridge.

BAVAROIS

Soften the gelatine leaves in a little cold water until soft. Bring the passion fruit coulis to the boil. Squeeze any excess water out of the gelatine, add it to the coulis and stir until the gelatine dissolves. Remove from the heat, then add the pouring cream and mix to combine. Whisk the egg yolks with an electric mixer. Bring the caster sugar to the soft boil stage, then pour the melted sugar slowly into the whisked egg yolks. Whisk once more for about 5 minutes. Add the passion fruit mix from above and finish by folding in the whipped cream. Remove the passion fruit jelly moulds from the fridge and pour the bavarois mixture on top of the jelly – it should be about 6cm (2½in) deep. Refrigerate to set.

PASSION FRUIT AND MANGO SORBET

Mix all the ingredients together and place in a Taurus Rowzer beaker and freeze. Then blitz when required. Alternatively, place in an ice cream machine and churn for 20 minutes and then freeze.

CHAMPAGNE JELLY

Place the water, lemon juice and sugar in a pot and bring to the boil. Pour in the champagne and then squeeze the excess water out of the gelatine leaves and add them to the pot. Remove the pan from the heat and whisk until the gelatine is completely dissolved. Line an ice-cube tray with cling film and fill with the jelly mix. Cover and transfer to the fridge to set.

PINEAPPLE GARNISH

Cover the pineapple with the sugar syrup and leave to infuse in the fridge for 2–3 hours.

CHOCOLATE STICKS

Preheat the oven to 165°C. Combine all the ingredients in a small bowl to form a paste. Lay a sheet of parchment paper on a tray and, using a small disposable piping bag with a tiny cut made at the top, squeeze out a series of thin chocolate lines the full length of the paper (you can cut them as needed later). Bake in the preheated oven for 4 minutes. Remove and set aside to cool.

TO SERVE

Remove the bavarois moulds from the fridge and demould by dipping the mould briefly into warm water. Invert the bavarois and place on the plate, jelly-side up. Place 3 cubes of champagne jelly around the bavarois, with a teaspoon of pineapple garnish in between. Place a quenelle of sorbet on top of the bavarois and top with a chocolate stick.

Warm molten Valrhona Tanariva chocolate dumpling with Baileys ice cream and crisp cocoa layer

Aesthetically this dish looks gorgeous, but there is so much more to it than mere good looks. If you love a traditional chocolate fondant, wait until you taste this dumpling with its hidden, melting ganache centre.

FOR THE BAILEYS ICE CREAM

550ml (20fl oz) Avonmore milk
150gm (5oz) egg yolks
65gm (2¼oz) caster sugar
175ml (6fl oz) Baileys Irish Cream
25gm (¾oz) trimolene

FOR THE CHOCOLATE BATTER

125gm (4½oz) strong flour
25gm (1oz) Valrhona cocoa powder
1 whole free-range egg
125ml (4½fl oz) McGargles IPA (or any pale ale)
½ tsp salt
25gm (1oz) icing sugar
25gm (1oz) Avonmore unsalted butter, melted

FOR THE TANARIVA GANACHE

125gm (4½oz) pear purée (we use Boiron or Ravifruit)
40gm (1½oz) trimolene
300gm (10oz) Valrhona Tanariva milk chocolate (33%), broken up
40gm (1½oz) Avonmore unsalted butter, softened
25gm (1oz) pear liqueur

FOR THE COCOA CRISP

30gm (1oz) plain flour
125gm (4½oz) icing sugar
15gm (½oz) Valrhona cocoa powder
30ml (1fl oz) water
40gm (1½oz) Avonmore unsalted butter, melted
30gm (1oz) desiccated coconut

FOR THE RED ISOMALT RING

100gm (3½oz) isomalt
red food colouring

MAKES 10

BAILEYS ICE CREAM

Bring the milk up to the boil in a pot. In a bowl, mix the egg yolks and caster sugar together, then add one-third of the hot milk and whisk together. Transfer the mixture back into the pot with the remaining milk and cook over a low heat until it begins to thicken. Pour in the Baileys and the trimoline and whisk well. Remove from the heat and leave to cool. Once cool, place in a Taurus Rowzer beaker and freeze. Then blitz when required. Alternatively, place in an ice cream machine and churn for 20 minutes and then freeze.

CHOCOLATE BATTER

Sieve the flour and cocoa powder into a mixing bowl. Add the egg, beer, salt and icing sugar and whisk well until the mix forms a batter. Then add the melted butter and mix to combine. Cover and refrigerate for 1 hour before use.

TANARIVA GANACHE

Place a pot over a medium to low heat and add the pear purée and trimolene and warm through. Add the chocolate and allow it to melt. Add the softened butter and pear liqueur, mix to combine and then remove from the heat. Cover and refrigerate until the mixture has set. Once set, form the ganache into 35gm (1oz) balls. Dip each ball in the chocolate batter and freeze.

COCOA CRISP

Preheat the oven to 170°C. Mix the flour, icing sugar and cocoa powder together in a bowl. Add the water and whisk, then add the melted butter and desiccated coconut. Roll out the mixture between 2 sheets of parchment paper to form a very thin sheet. Place the 2 sheets of paper, with the cocoa layer sandwiched in the middle, between 2 heavy flat baking trays. Cook in the preheated oven for 6–8 minutes, or until crisp. Remove from the oven and, while still warm, cut the layer into ten 10cm (4in) discs and set aside to cool.

RED ISOMALT RING

Melt the isomalt in a pot then add the red colouring, drop by drop, until you reach the desired colour. Let the sugar cool down until it becomes thick and easy to handle. Pinch off some of the mixture and curve a string of the warm sugar mix around a 10cm (4in) plastic tube. Once it has set, remove the ring carefully from the tube and repeat to make 10 rings. Store the rings in a box with a lid, away from moisture and heat.

TO SERVE

Place the cocoa crisp in the centre of a plate. Remove the dumpling from the freezer, place it directly into a deep-fat fryer set to 180°C and cook for 3 minutes until it puffs up. Remove the dumpling, drain and pat dry. Take the isomalt ring and place it and the dumpling on the cocoa crisp (the weight of the dumpling will hold the ring up). Quenelle some Baileys ice cream on the side of the plate and serve immediately. The molten ganache should flow out of the dumpling when it is broken apart with a fork.

TIP

When storing the isomalt rings, we place some calcium chloride in the base of the box and cover it with a sheet of parchment paper. This prevents moisture getting in. If using calcium chloride, it is essential not to allow it to touch the food in any way; if it does, you must discard the rings.

BREDA MAHER | CHEESEMAKER

Breda started making cheese in 1986. 'I loved cooking and was married to a dairy farmer, so making cheese seemed like an obvious thing for me to do,' explains Breda. 'When I started making cheese, most of the local hotels and leading restaurants only served French cheese, yet we had this magnificent supply of top-quality Irish milk. So I set out to make an Irish cheese to rival the famous cheeses of France.' And that is precisely what she did. From her farm in Tipperary, with its fertile peaty soil, clover-rich grass and herd of pedigree Friesian cows, Breda began making Brie- and Camembert-style cheeses that went on to win countless awards. She now employs over twenty people in her state-of-the-art facility on Cooleeney Farm and you'll find her Cooleeney Camembert and goat's cheese on the menu at The K Club.

www.cooleeney.com

Wexford strawberries with vanilla pastry cream, sablé biscuit and Kir Royale jelly

This is a classic recipe – sablé biscuit, pastry cream and sweet Irish strawberries. Posh strawberries and cream. You have the crunch from the biscuit, the velvety thick vanilla custard, the sweetness of the Irish berries and the little acid hit from the balsamic vinegar – all in one perfect mouthful.

FOR THE KIR ROYALE JELLY

180ml (6fl oz) champagne
100ml (3½fl oz) crème de cassis
80ml (3fl oz) water
80gm (3oz) sugar
25gm (1oz) gelatine leaves, soaked in a little water

FOR THE SABLÉ BISCUITS

250gm (9oz) plain flour
100gm (3½oz) Avonmore unsalted butter, cut into cubes
100gm (3½oz) caster sugar
1 free-range egg

FOR THE VANILLA PASTRY CREAM

500ml (17fl oz) Avonmore milk
75gm (2½oz) Avonmore unsalted butter
150gm (5oz) caster sugar
1 bourbon vanilla pod, split in half lengthways
35gm (1¼oz) plain flour
30gm (1oz) cornflour
2 free-range eggs

FOR THE OPALINE CRISP

250gm (9oz) white fondant
125gm (4½oz) glucose
1 tsp Nougasec
10gm (½oz) strawberry compound
2 drops red colouring

FOR THE STRAWBERRY AIR

125ml (4½fl oz) Avonmore milk
5gm (¼oz) strawberry compound
¾ tsp lecithin powder

TO SERVE

24 fresh Wexford strawberries, trimmed and cut in half
40ml (1½fl oz) 12-year-old Villa Manodori balsamic vinegar

SERVES 8

KIR ROYALE JELLY

Boil all the liquid and sugar together in a pot. Remove from the heat, squeeze the excess water out of the gelatine and add it to the pot. Stir to dissolve. Pour the mixture into a mould and refrigerate it overnight. Once it is set, cut it into 2cm (1in) cubes.

SABLÉ BISCUITS

Preheat the oven to 160°C. Mix the flour and butter together in a mixer, or rub the butter into the flour by hand. Add the sugar and mix to combine. Add the egg and knead gently to form a paste. Cover and refrigerate for 2 hours. Dust the counter top with a little flour and roll out the pastry to 3mm (⅒in) thick, then cut out 8 rectangular shapes measuring 10cm x 4cm (4in x 1½in). Place on a Silpat (or similar) non-stick mat or parchment paper and cook in the preheated oven for 8 minutes. Remove the biscuits from the oven, sprinkle them with a little caster sugar and leave to cool.

VANILLA PASTRY CREAM

Place the milk, butter, vanilla pod and 75gm (2½oz) of the caster sugar in a pot and bring to the boil. In a separate bowl, crack the eggs and mix in the remaining sugar, the flour and cornflour and mix to combine. Add one-third of the hot milk mixture to the cold egg mix and whisk to combine, then mix this into the remaining hot milk. Cook the pastry cream, whisking continuously, until the mixture comes to the boil. Pour the pastry cream into a bowl and refrigerate immediately. Once cool, transfer it into a piping bag for service.

OPALINE CRISP

Place the ingredients in a pot and heat to 155°C. Add in the red colouring and mix to combine. Pour the mixture on to a lined flat tray and leave it to harden. Break the hardened mixture into small pieces and blitz in a HotmixPRO or blender until it forms a dust. Line a baking sheet with a Silpat (or similar) non-stick mat. Sprinkle the opaline dust through a fine sieve into a rectangular stencil measuring 10cm x 4cm (4in x 1½in) until the rectangle is full. Repeat 8 times. Remove the

stencil and cook the opaline in an oven set to 160°C until just melted but still holding its shape. Remove from the oven and place the mat on a cold counter top or marble top to crisp up.

STRAWBERRY AIR

Place all the ingredients in a rectangular container. Blend together using a hand-held stick blender until foam appears. Allow the foam to settle until just a layer of air bubbles sits on top.

TO SERVE

Place the sablé biscuit in the centre of the plate. Pipe 2 generous lines of the pastry cream lengthways on top of the biscuit. Place the strawberries along the pastry cream. Place the Kir Royale jelly to one side. Make a small circle of the vanilla cream on the other side and fill the circle with about 5ml (1/4fl oz) of the balsamic vinegar. Using a spoon, place the strawberry air along the top of the strawberries and finish with the opaline crisp.

Toonsbridge ricotta with raspberry leather, Jane Sellers honey and Irish berries

When I visited Toonsbridge Dairy, Jenny-Rose Clarke gave me a small bowl of their fresh ricotta. It was like no ricotta I had tasted before and I was blown away. I went straight out to the jeep, where I had a jar of Jane Sellers honey, and when we tasted the two together I knew I had to create a dessert just for these two star ingredients.

FOR THE RASPBERRY LEATHER

100gm (3½oz) raspberry purée (we use Boiron or Ravifruit)

TO SERVE

150gm (5oz) Toonsbridge ricotta
125gm (4½oz) fresh Irish raspberries
60gm (2oz) fresh Irish blueberries
60 fresh Irish blackberries
200ml (7fl oz) Jane Sellers honey

SERVES 6

RASPBERRY LEATHER

Pour the raspberry purée on to a non-stick Silpat mat (or similar) and transfer to a dehydrator, set to 52°C, for 10 hours. Remove the leather from the mat and cut into strips (15cm x 4cm; 6in x 1½in).

TO SERVE

Pour the honey to form a pool in the centre of the plate. Place 2 tablespoon-sized quenelles of the fresh ricotta in a line on top of the honey, leaving a small gap between each quenelle. Gently lay the raspberry leather over the ricotta quenelles to form a wave of leather. Drop each type of berry on to the honey.

Poached gooseberries in elderflower sparkling wine with tarragon jelly and gooseberry crisps

Gooseberries have a short enough season in Ireland, so it is important to make the most of them while we have them. I love the simplicity of poaching them in the fragrant elderflower sparkling wine to enhance their natural sweetness and then pairing them with the aniseedy tang of the tarragon jelly.

FOR THE ELDERFLOWER SPARKLING WINE SORBET

40ml (1½fl oz) water
40gm (1½oz) caster sugar
280ml (10fl oz) sparkling elderflower wine (see page 271)
10ml (½fl oz) freshly squeezed lemon juice
40ml (1½fl oz) sorbitol

FOR THE TARRAGON JELLY

130gm (4½oz) fresh tarragon leaves, juiced
60gm (2oz) fresh basil leaves, juiced
18gm (¾oz) caster sugar
100ml (3½fl oz) water
40ml (1½fl oz) Crinnaughtaun apple juice
½ tsp agar-agar

FOR THE GOOSEBERRY CRISPS

5 fresh gooseberries
30ml (1fl oz) sugar syrup (see page 271)

FOR THE CHOCOLATE STICKS

See page 275.

FOR THE GOOSEBERRIES

60 ripe gooseberries
300ml (10fl oz) sparkling elderflower wine (see page 271)

SERVES 6

SPARKLING ELDERFLOWER WINE SORBET

Place the water and sugar in a pot and bring up to the boil. Add the rest of the ingredients and then place in a Taurus Rowzer beaker and freeze. Blitz in the Taurus Rowzer when required. Alternatively, place the mixture in an ice cream machine, churn for 20 minutes and then freeze.

TARRAGON JELLY

Pass the tarragon and basil juice through a fine chinois or sieve and muslin cloth and add the strained juices, water and apple juice to a pot with the sugar. Bring to the boil, then add the agar-agar and bring back up to the boil, whisking as you go. Line a 2cm-deep (1in) mould with cling film and pour in the liquid. Allow to cool and then transfer to the fridge to set. Once set, cut the jelly into 2cm (1in) cubes.

GOOSEBERRY CRISPS

Preheat the oven to 95°C. Slice the gooseberries, across the equator, into 2mm (1⁄10in)-thick slices and gently place them in the sugar syrup for 20 minutes. Put a Silpat or similar non-stick mat on a baking tray and lay the pre-soaked gooseberry slices on top. Transfer to the preheated oven for 2 hours until crisp. Remove and allow to cool. Store in an airtight container until needed.

GOOSEBERRIES

Place the gooseberries in a large, wide pan and add just enough sparkling elderflower wine to cover the fruit. Bring up to a simmer and poach gently until the gooseberries are just soft, about 8 minutes. Remove from the heat and keep warm.

TO SERVE

Place the gooseberries in a bowl and sprinkle tarragon jelly cubes around the fruit. Place a quenelle of elderflower sorbet on top, garnish with a chocolate stick and then add gooseberry crisps to serve.

Lime and cream cheese parfait with lavender meringue, lemon curd and lavender-scented honey

The smell of fresh lavender transports me straight to the bottom of my garden in high summer. I love it. But I've always preferred to use lavender in sweet rather than savoury dishes. The floral notes of the lavender meringue here contrast brilliantly with the zesty lime parfait.

FOR THE LIME PARFAIT

60gm (2oz) caster sugar
20ml (¾fl oz) water
75gm (2½oz) free-range egg yolks
400ml (14fl oz) Avonmore cream, whipped
100gm (3½oz) cream cheese
25gm (1oz) Jane Sellers honey
25gm (1oz) roasted hazelnuts, chopped
zest of 1 lime

FOR THE LAVENDER MERINGUE

6 fresh lavender flower-heads
120gm (4oz) free-range egg whites
125gm (4½oz) caster sugar

FOR THE LEMON CURD

240ml (8½fl oz) freshly squeezed lemon juice
250gm (9oz) caster sugar
170gm (6oz) Avonmore unsalted butter
9 free-range eggs

FOR THE LAVENDER HONEY

150ml (5fl oz) Jane Sellers honey
2 fresh lavender flower-heads

MAKES 10

LIME PARFAIT

Boil the sugar and water together until the mixture reaches 116°C. In a bowl, whisk the egg yolks and then slowly add the boiled sugar mixture, whisking on a medium speed until all the sugar has been mixed in. Fold in the whipped cream, cream cheese, honey, hazelnuts and lime zest. Pour the mixture into a mini-rectangle silicone mould tray, to fill 10 small rectangles (75mm x 30mm x 30mm; 3in x 1in x 1in), and freeze.

LAVENDER MERINGUE

Lay the flower-heads on a wire rack and allow to dry for 24 hours, then crush the petals finely. Preheat the oven to 90°C. Whisk the egg whites in a clean, dry bowl and then add the sugar gradually in three stages, while continuing to whisk. Finish by adding the ground lavender flower-heads and whisk until the mixture holds a stiff peak. The mix should be a pale lavender colour. Transfer the meringue mixture to a disposable piping bag, and snip the end of the bag to leave a 5mm-wide (¼in) hole. Place a sheet of parchment paper on a baking tray and pipe rows of meringue along the full length of the sheet, leaving 2cm (1in) between each row. Place in the oven for 1 hour. Cut the meringue sticks into 50 lengths measuring 7.5cm (3in). Crush the remaining meringue sticks finely and set aside for garnish.

LEMON CURD

Add the lemon juice, caster sugar and unsalted butter to a saucepan and bring up to the boil. Whisk in the eggs and continue to cook over a high heat for 2–3 minutes, whisking constantly until the curd starts to thicken. Remove from the heat, pass the mixture through a fine chinois or sieve and refrigerate. When cool, transfer to a HotmixPRO blender (or similar) and blend until smooth. Store in a squeezy bottle.

LAVENDER HONEY

Gently warm the honey in a pot and then remove from the heat. Add the lavender flowers and allow to infuse in the honey for 2 hours. Store in a squeezy bottle.

TO SERVE

Remove the frozen parfait from the moulds and use a sharp knife to cut each one into 2 triangular pieces. Place a circle of the lemon curd in the centre of a plate and place a parfait on top. Pour a circle of the lavender honey around the lemon curd. Neatly arrange the lavender meringue around the parfait. Squeeze a line of the curd on the edge of the plate and sprinkle the crushed lavender meringue over to serve.

Straffan Red rhubarb parfait with tangy opaline, grenadine stewed stalks and cream purée

Straffan Red is a local variety of rhubarb, christened by a gardener here on the estate long before the K Club existed, when the property was still Straffan House. This dish is my take on rhubarb and custard. The cream purée here is interesting – the texture is like a thick custard but the flavour is beguilingly subtle. You can, of course, use any locally grown rhubarb in this dish.

WINE PAIRING

McGargles Stout

I know this may seem an unusual pairing, but I had to do it. McGargles – our local craft brewery – has made a stout for us, The Mulligan, and, believe it or not, the rhubarb dessert and this stout are amazing together. I know – it surprised me too!

FOR THE RHUBARB PURÉE

120gm (4oz) Straffan Red rhubarb stalks, chopped into 1cm pieces
20gm (¾oz) caster sugar
30ml (1fl oz) grenadine syrup

FOR THE RHUBARB PARFAIT

40gm (1½oz) caster sugar
10ml (½floz) water
3 free-range egg yolks
330ml (11fl oz) Avonmore cream, whipped
100gm (3½oz) rhubarb purée, from above

FOR THE OPALINE RING

250gm (9oz) fondant
125gm (4½oz) glucose
1 tsp Nougasec
5gm (¼oz) rhubarb purée, from above

FOR THE CREAM PURÉE

350ml (12fl oz) Avonmore milk
50ml (2fl oz) Avonmore cream
10gm (½oz) caster sugar
½ tsp carrageen moss powder

FOR THE STEWED RHUBARB STALKS

5 Straffan Red rhubarb stalks
200ml (7fl oz) sugar syrup (see page 271)
200ml (7fl oz) grenadine syrup

FOR THE RHUBARB JELLY

100ml (3½fl oz) rhubarb poaching syrup, from above
16gm (½oz) gelatine leaf, pre-soaked in a little water

FOR THE RHUBARB SHAVINGS

100ml (3½fl oz) grenadine
30gm (1oz) caster sugar
2 stalks Straffan Red rhubarb

MAKES 10

RHUBARB PURÉE

Place the rhubarb in a pot with the sugar and grenadine syrup and poach over a medium heat until the rhubarb is nice and soft. Pour the mix into a HotmixPRO blender (or similar) and blitz on high until smooth. Set aside to cool.

RHUBARB PARFAIT

Boil the sugar and water together until the mixture reaches 116°C. In a separate bowl, whisk the egg yolks and slowly add the boiled sugar mix, whisking on a medium speed continuously as you go, until all the sugar mixture has been combined. Fold in the whipped cream and rhubarb purée. Pour the mixture into 10 stainless steel tubes (6cm x 4.5cm; 2½in x 1¾in) and freeze.

OPALINE RING

Preheat the oven to 180°C. Place the fondant, glucose and Nougasec in a pot and cook over a medium heat until the mixture reaches 155°C. Remove from the heat, add the rhubarb purée and mix to combine. Pour the mixture evenly on to a Silpat or similar non-stick mat and allow to cool completely and harden. Once it is hard, break up the opaline mix, place it in a HotmixPRO blender (or similar) and blitz until it forms a powder. Lay a non-stick mat on a baking tray and, using a 14cm x 4cm (5½in x 1½in) template, sieve the opaline powder to fill the template and repeat 10 times to form 10 rectangles. Place in the oven for 2 minutes until the powder has completely melted and softened into a strip, then remove from the oven and fold each strip around a 6cm x 4.5cm (2½in x 1¾in) stainless steel tube to form a ring; the edges should overlap slightly and stick together. Store until needed in an airtight container away from moisture and heat.

CREAM PURÉE

Add the milk and cream to a saucepan and bring up the boil. Reduce to simmer, whisking very occasionally to prevent burning, until the mixture has reduced to 175ml (6fl oz). Remove from the heat. Mix the caster sugar and carrageen powder together and whisk into the cream in the saucepan. Allow the mixture to swell for 3 minutes. Place the pan back on the heat and bring back to the boil, whisking all the time. Remove from the heat, pass the mixture through a fine chinois or sieve and leave to cool. Refrigerate for 5 hours until set. Once it is set, place the mixture in a HotmixPRO blender (or similar), blitz until smooth and then keep refrigerated.

STEWED RHUBARB STALKS

Peel the rhubarb stalks and cut into 5cm (2in) pieces. Mix the sugar syrup and the grenadine syrup in a large, wide pan and bring up to a simmer. Place the rhubarb pieces flat in the syrup and poach gently until soft (about 5 minutes). Remove the rhubarb pieces from the syrup and set aside to keep warm. Leave the syrup to cool to use for the jelly.

RHUBARB JELLY

Heat the rhubarb syrup in a saucepan to 80°C, then remove from the heat. Squeeze out any excess water from the gelatine leaf, add the leaf to the syrup and stir until melted. Pour the syrup into a mould and leave to set in the fridge. Cut the jelly into 1cm (½in) cubes for service.

RHUBARB SHAVINGS

Warm the grenadine and sugar in a pot until the sugar has melted and the mixture is nice and syrupy. Cut the rhubarb sticks into 12cm (4½in) lengths and then shave them lengthways into wafer-thin strips. Soak the rhubarb shavings in the grenadine syrup for 3 minutes. Place in a dehydrator set to 68°C for 8 hours, until crisp.

TO SERVE

To remove the rhubarb parfait from the moulds, run a blowtorch very quickly over the outside of each mould first. Place the parfait into an opaline ring and place the ring in the centre of a serving bowl. Stack 3 pieces of warm stewed rhubarb on top. Add a quenelle of cream purée and place a crisp rhubarb shaving on top. Sprinkle over some rhubarb jelly cubes and pour 20ml (¾fl oz) of rhubarb syrup into the bowl to serve.

MARY McAULIFFE & SHARON VERDELET | MOTHER AND DAUGHTER BREAKFAST CHEF TEAM

AUTUMN / WINTER

Yellow coconut soup with Galway Bay mussels and lemongrass foam

The base recipe for this 'soup' was given to me by an Asian chef who worked with us here at The K Club a few years ago. He spent some time showing me different Asian sauces and cooking techniques and this yellow coconut soup was one that stood out for me. We enrich it with mussel stock, which adds extra oomph to the dish.

WINE PAIRING

Trimbach Gewürztraminer

Literally meaning 'spicy', this wine is the perfect match for anything that has an Asian influence. You could swim in the lychee aromas coming out of the glass here.

FOR THE MUSSELS

1 kg (2lb 3oz) Galway Bay mussels, scrubbed clean
150ml (5¼fl oz) white wine
2 garlic cloves, bashed
2 sprigs of fresh thyme

FOR THE SOUP

75g (2½oz) diced red onion
75g (2½oz) diced white onion
100g (3½oz) garlic, peeled
50g (2oz) lemongrass, bruised and chopped
35gm (1¼oz) chopped galangal
50gm (2oz) candle nut
5gm (¼oz) lemon leaf
10gm (½oz) ginger, chopped
5gm (¼oz) coriander seeds
20ml (¾fl oz) Newgrange Gold rapeseed oil
10gm (½oz) ground turmeric
500ml (17fl oz) chicken stock (see page 270)
mussel cooking liquid, from above
800ml (28fl oz) coconut milk
salt and freshly milled black pepper
25ml (¾fl oz) fresh lime juice

FOR THE LEMONGRASS FOAM

250ml (9fl oz) chicken stock (see page 270)
100gm (3½oz) chopped lemongrass
25ml (1fl oz) fresh lime juice
¾ tsp xanthan gum

TO SERVE

Carrick Farm micro-fennel, to garnish

SERVES 6

MUSSELS

Heat a large pot with a lid on the hob until extremely hot. Add the mussels and pour over the wine. Throw in the garlic and thyme and cover with the lid. Once the mussels open they are cooked; this should only take a few minutes. Discard any mussels that fail to open. Pass through a fine sieve and retain the cooking liquid. Pick the mussels from the shells and remove any remaining beard and set aside.

SOUP

Put the onions, garlic, lemongrass, galangal, lemon leaf, candle nut, ginger and coriander seeds into a HotmixPRO blender (or similar) and blitz for about 30 seconds. Transfer into a pot with the rapeseed oil and gently cook, stirring as you go to prevent the mixture sticking and burning, until all the moisture has evaporated and the mixture is dry. Add the turmeric powder and cook for a further 10 minutes. Pour in the chicken stock, mussel cooking liquid and coconut milk. Gently bring up to the boil, then reduce the heat to a simmer. Cook until it thickens a little and reaches a sauce consistency. Strain the soup through a fine strainer and press the pulp in the sieve with the back of a small ladle to extract all the flavour. Discard the pulp and return the strained liquid to the pot. Finally check the seasoning and finish by adding the fresh lime juice to taste. Cover to keep warm.

LEMONGRASS FOAM

Place all the ingredients in a pot, bring to the boil and leave to simmer for 20 minutes. Let the liquid cool and then pass it through a fine sieve. Bring back to the boil and add the xanthan gum, whisking to combine. Transfer into a siphon gun and add two ISI chargers. Shake well and set aside to serve.

TO SERVE

Place the soup back on the hob to heat through and add the cooked mussels to it. Pour the hot soup into warmed bowls. Run a line of the lemongrass foam either on top of the soup or on the rim of the bowl. Sprinkle with micro-fennel to garnish.

Black Périgord winter truffle risotto with aged acquerello rice, Castlefarm cheese and celeriac foam

This dish is a celebration of black truffle season – the smell of the truffle in the kitchen when we are making this dish is magical; the perfume pervades the kitchen. The acquerello rice is aged for a year, which means it cooks really evenly and you get a much better result. The addition of Jenny Young's local organic hard cheese in place of imported Parmesan gives the dish some Irish roots.

WINE PAIRING

Laurent-Perrier Grand Siècle Champagne

Champagne and truffles make surprisingly good bedfellows; any good vintage would be fine.

FOR THE CELERIAC AND CASTLEFARM CHEESE FOAM

150gm (5oz) celeriac, peeled and sliced
50ml (2fl oz) water
salt and freshly milled black pepper
85gm (3oz) Avonmore milk
30gm (1oz) Castlefarm cheese, grated

FOR THE ACQUERELLO RICE RISOTTO

80ml (3fl oz) virgin olive oil
40gm (1½oz) shallot, very finely chopped
salt and freshly milled black pepper
200gm (7oz) aged acquerello rice, washed
120ml (4fl oz) white port
400ml (14fl oz) fresh chicken stock (see page 270)
60gm (2oz) organic Castlefarm cheese, grated
20ml (¾fl oz) white truffle oil
8ml (¼fl oz) truffle vinegar
20gm (¾oz) black Périgord winter truffle
(or more if you like)
160ml (5½fl oz) crème fraîche

SERVES 4

CELERIAC AND CASTLEFARM CHEESE FOAM

Place the celeriac, water, pinch of salt and pepper in a vacuum-pack bag, seal and place in steamer to cook until soft. Remove from bag and transfer to a blender to blitz until smooth. Place the purée in a pot over a medium heat, add the milk and cheese and whisk until smooth. Place in a siphon gun charged with two ISI chargers and shake vigorously. Set aside until ready to serve.

ACQUERELLO RICE RISOTTO

Pour the olive oil into a warm pan, add the shallots, season and allow to sweat gently over a medium heat for 2–3 minutes so that they cook without colouring. Increase the heat, add in the rice and cook quickly until you hear the husks crack, then deglaze the pan with the port and cook until the port is reduced by 80%. Add half the stock, reduce the heat to medium and cook until all the stock has been absorbed. Add the remaining stock bit by bit until the rice is slightly undercooked, only needing about 3–4 minutes more. To finish, add the cheese, truffle oil and vinegar at this stage. Mix to combine and fold in the crème fraîche, then grate in the fresh truffle and check the seasoning.

TO SERVE

Pour the risotto from the pot into warmed bowls. Slice the truffle directly on to the risotto, using a truffle slicer if you have one. I like to serve 5 slices on top. Siphon the celeriac and Castlefarm cheese foam around the curve of the bowl.

TIP

Always serve risotto flat in the base of a wide bowl, not in circular moulds as you might do with regular rice. I also like to present this dish covered with a lid, so that when it is removed at the table the diner gets the full impact of the truffle aroma.

Charred Kerry prawn tails with tortellini of Jerusalem artichoke and white port sauce

The secret to this dish is roasting the prawns in the shell, as this makes all the difference to the flavour. The earthy Jerusalem artichoke then provides a great base note for the sweet shellfish.

WINE PAIRING

Waterford Estate Sauvignon Blanc 2009

A bit of age on this South African Sauvignon gives a richness to the wine. Lovely.

FOR THE JERUSALEM ARTICHOKE CRISP

1 Jerusalem artichoke (as long as possible)
salt and freshly milled pepper

FOR THE JERUSALEM ARTICHOKE PURÉE

150gm (5oz) peeled Jerusalem artichoke
squeeze of fresh lemon juice
salt and freshly milled white pepper

FOR THE TORTELLINI

250gm (9oz) strong flour
2 whole free-range eggs
3 free-range egg yolks
salt
Newgrange Gold rapeseed oil
extra flour for dusting
Jerusalem artichoke purée, from above
1 egg yolk (for egg wash)
6ml (¼fl oz) good olive oil
salt and freshly milled black pepper

FOR THE PRAWN AND WHITE PORT SAUCE

16 whole Kerry prawns or langoustines (5–7 per kilo grade)
25gm (1oz) Avonmore unsalted butter
2 shallots, finely chopped
1 garlic clove
salt and freshly milled white pepper
50ml (2fl oz) white wine
50ml (2fl oz) white port
100ml (3½fl oz) fish stock (see page 270)
200ml (7fl oz) Avonmore cream

FOR THE PRAWNS

16 whole Kerry prawn tails, from above
salt and freshly milled black pepper
20ml (¾fl oz) Newgrange Gold rapeseed oil
10ml (½fl oz) white port

SERVES 8

JERUSALEM ARTICHOKE CRISP

Peel the artichoke and cut it into halves or quarters (depending on the size). Slice into fine slivers using a mandolin. Cook them in a fryer, set to 170°C, until golden. Remove, drain and season. Set aside for serving.

JERUSALEM ARTICHOKE PURÉE

Place the Jerusalem artichoke in a vacuum-pack bag with the lemon juice and pinch of salt and white pepper. Cook in a steamer for 20 minutes. Transfer the contents of the bag to a blender and blitz for 4 minutes until smooth. Keep warm.

TORTELLINI

Place the flour, egg yolks and whole eggs in a food processor and pulse until the mixture resembles fine breadcrumbs. Add enough oil to bring the crumbs together. Transfer the mix into a bowl and bring together by hand to form a dough. Turn out on to a floured surface and knead quite vigorously for 1 minute. Divide the dough in two, cover with cling film and rest this in the refrigerator for 30 minutes. Pass the dough through a pasta machine, starting at the highest setting and working the pasta through the machine until close enough to zero. Your final sheet of pasta should be so fine that you can see through it. Place the pasta sheet on to parchment paper and use a cutter to cut out eight 10cm (4in) circular rings. Place a teaspoon of Jerusalem artichoke purée in the centre of each pasta disc and dab the edges with a little egg yolk. Fold the pasta in half and tuck the edges in together to form a tortellini shape. Arrange the tortellini on a sheet of parchment paper and set aside.

PRAWN AND WHITE PORT SAUCE

Separate the prawn heads from the tails by pinching the back of the prawn head with your left hand and pulling the tail away with your right. Remove the eyes from the heads with a sharp knife and crush the heads in a bowl; set aside. Place a pot over a medium heat and add the butter to melt. Add the shallots, garlic and a little salt and cook over a low heat, covered with a

lid, until the shallots are soft and translucent. Add the prawn heads to the pot and cook for 10 minutes. Deglaze the pot with the white wine and port and reduce by 80%. Add the fish stock and cream, bring to the boil and then reduce to simmer for 20 minutes until it reaches a nice sauce consistency. Pass through a fine sieve, pressing the mixture all the way through with a ladle to extract the maximum amount of flavour. Season to taste. Keep warm.

PRAWNS

Using a pair of scissors, nip along both sides of the underbelly of the tail, then gently pull away the remaining skin to expose the flesh of each prawn. Season the prawns with salt and milled pepper.

TO SERVE

To cook the tortellini, bring a large pot of salted water to the boil and add in the sheet of parchment paper with the tortellini on it (to prevent the risk of bursting the tortellini as you remove them from the paper). Cook for 3 minutes until al dente. Remove from the heat and drain. Toss the tortellini in olive oil and season with salt and milled pepper to serve. Heat a pan until very hot, add the oil followed by the prawns, shell-side down, and cook until golden (about 2–3 minutes), without turning, to get the charred finish. Deglaze with white port and baste the liquid over the prawns, then serve immediately. Arrange a tortellini of Jerusalem artichoke in the centre of a warm plate and surround with 2 charred prawn tails (as pictured). Aerate the sauce with a stick blender and spoon it over the tortellini and prawns. Finish with the Jerusalem artichoke crisp.

Native shellfish with baby squid, saffron and garlic potato and Bouillabaisse sauce

This is my Irish interpretation of the traditional Marseillais soup. Our native Irish shellfish are so good that you need to do very little to them, but the addition of just enough of the powerfully flavoured sauce really gives it a lift. The smoothness of the saffron and garlic mash then brings all the flavours together.

WINE PAIRING

Terras Gauda Albariño, Galicia

We love this grape variety and this is one of the best examples. It boasts a wealth of flavour to stand up to this robust dish.

FOR THE BOUILLABAISSE SAUCE (MAKES 2 LITRES/3½ PINTS)

olive oil
250gm (9oz) white onion, peeled and diced
125gm (4½oz) fennel bulb, diced
70gm (2½oz) leek, sliced (white part only)
225gm (8oz) celery, diced
35gm (1¼oz) garlic, chopped
125gm (4½oz) tomato purée
500gm (17oz) fresh tomatoes, chopped
375ml (13fl oz) white wine
1.75 litres (3 pints) chicken stock (see page 270)
1.75 litres (3 pints) fish stock (see page 270)
40g (1½oz) fresh thyme
1.5 kg (3lb 5oz) white fish, skin removed
500gm (17oz) conger eel
2kg (4lb 7oz) white fish bones, heads removed
salt and freshly milled white pepper

FOR THE SAFFRON AND GARLIC POTATO

100ml (3½fl oz) Avonmore double cream
2g (½ tsp) saffron filament
1 large potato, peeled and cut into even 1cm (½in) dice
2 garlic cloves, peeled
salt and freshly milled white pepper

FOR THE FISH GARNISH

32 mussels, cleaned
80ml (3fl oz) white wine
1 Ballyheigue lobster, cooked (see page 277 for cooking method)
6 baby squid, tube and tentacles only, cleaned
30ml (1fl oz) Newgrange Gold rapeseed oil
6 large fresh Castletownbere scallops
6 large Kerry prawn tails (5–7 per kilo grade)
20gm (¾oz) Avonmore unsalted butter

SERVES 6

BOUILLABAISSE SAUCE

Sweat off the vegetables in a little olive oil over a medium to low heat, and cook slowly until soft but not coloured. Add the garlic and cook for another 2 minutes. Add the tomato purée and continue to cook until the mixture has thickened slightly. This will cook out the purée. Add fresh tomatoes and white wine and cook until reduced by half. Add both stocks, the fresh thyme, white fish meat, conger eel and bones. Stir well and bring up to the boil, then turn down and leave to simmer for around 30 minutes until the liquid has begun to thicken. Using a stick blender, blitz the sauce well. Strain through a fine strainer and then pass again through a muslin cloth to ensure that no shards of bone get through. Put the sauce back in the pot over a low heat and adjust the seasoning to taste.

SAFFRON AND GARLIC POTATO

In a small pot bring the cream to the boil, then add the saffron stems. Remove from the heat and allow to infuse for 20 minutes, then strain. You should be left with a yellow-coloured cream reduction. Bring a small pot of salted water to the boil and cook the potato with the garlic until soft and cooked through. Strain and mash the potato and garlic. Whisk the mashed potato and garlic, little by little, into the saffron cream until you achieve a creamy mash. You might not need to add all the potato.

FISH GARNISH

Heat a heavy-based pot on the hob until extremely hot. Add the mussels, pour over the wine and cover with a tight-fitting lid. The mussels should open very quickly. Discard any that fail to open. Pass through a fine sieve and retain the liquid. Pick the mussels out of the shells and set aside. Cut the lobster tail into 6 pieces and keep the claws whole. Place the lobster meat and the mussel cooking liquid in a pot and heat gently to warm it through. Add the squid tails and tentacles and cook for 10–15 seconds, or until just tender, and remove. Season the scallops and prawns with salt and pepper and sear in a hot pan with the rapeseed oil until golden brown. Add the unsalted butter and, when it foams up, baste the shellfish quickly with the nutty butter.

TO SERVE

Place a quenelle of the mash in the centre of a warm wide-rimmed bowl. Pour in the bouillabaisse sauce, arrange the fish garnish neatly around the bowl and serve.

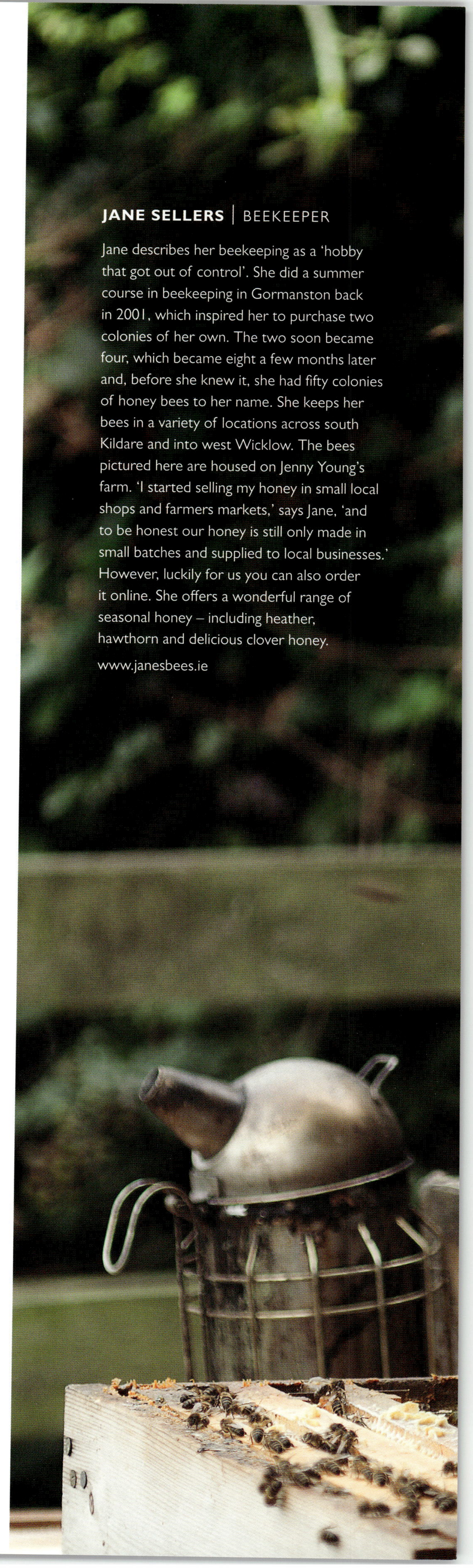

JANE SELLERS | BEEKEEPER

Jane describes her beekeeping as a 'hobby that got out of control'. She did a summer course in beekeeping in Gormanston back in 2001, which inspired her to purchase two colonies of her own. The two soon became four, which became eight a few months later and, before she knew it, she had fifty colonies of honey bees to her name. She keeps her bees in a variety of locations across south Kildare and into west Wicklow. The bees pictured here are housed on Jenny Young's farm. 'I started selling my honey in small local shops and farmers markets,' says Jane, 'and to be honest our honey is still only made in small batches and supplied to local businesses.' However, luckily for us you can also order it online. She offers a wonderful range of seasonal honey – including heather, hawthorn and delicious clover honey.

www.janesbees.ie

Rosace of Castletownbere scallops with black Périgord truffle, chicory and hazelnut and black truffle dressing

The lightly braised chicory in this dish is the secret star. The nutty flavour of the bitter sweet leaves is magic when paired with the creamy scallop and earthy truffle. I love all the contrasts in texture and flavour in this dish.

WINE PAIRING

Jean Leon Vinya Gigi Chardonnay, Penedès

Even though the scallops have such a delicate flavour, the chicory and hazelnuts in this dish need a more robust wine. This Chardonnay from the cool hills of Spain is rich and nutty.

FOR THE BLACK TRUFFLE DRESSING

5gm (¼oz) truffle vinegar
15gm (½oz) white truffle oil
15gm (½oz) best-quality hazelnut oil
20ml (¾fl oz) Newgrange Gold rapeseed oil
35ml (1¼fl oz) sunflower oil
20gm (¾oz) Périgord winter truffle, chopped
25gm (¾oz) hazelnuts, chopped
salt, to taste

FOR THE CHICORY

6 heads white chicory
50ml (2fl oz) water
15gm (½oz) caster sugar
20gm (¾oz) Avonmore unsalted butter
10ml (½fl oz) best-quality hazelnut oil
salt and freshly milled white pepper

FOR THE ROSACE

6 large Castletownbere scallops
40gm (1½oz) black Périgord winter truffle
10ml (½fl oz) Newgrange Gold rapeseed oil
salt and freshly milled white pepper

SERVES 4

BLACK TRUFFLE DRESSING

Put all the ingredients into a bowl and mix to combine. Adjust the seasoning with a little salt.

CHICORY

Strip the chicory leaves and remove any yellow parts, leaving just the white. Set aside 12 of the largest leaves and then slice the rest lengthways into 3mm-thick (⅒in) strips. Place the water, caster sugar and unsalted butter in a saucepan and bring to the boil. Add the chicory and cook quickly until the leaves are just soft, then add the hazelnut oil. Adjust the seasoning and leave to cool. Lightly grease four 8cm (3in) stainless steel rings and line the inside of each ring with the uncut chicory leaves. Fill the centre with the softened chicory strips and transfer to a steamer to heat through for 8 minutes.

ROSACE

Preheat the oven to 140°C. Cut the scallops into 3mm (⅒in)-thick slices. Slice the truffle into wafer-thin slices. Grease a sheet of parchment paper and four 8cm (3in) stainless steel rings with rapeseed oil. Lay alternative slices of scallop and black truffle inside the rings to form a rosace or circle. Season with salt and milled white pepper and cook for 1 minute in the oven.

TO SERVE

Place the chicory on a warm plate and remove the ring. Gently remove the ring from the scallops and lay the rosace of scallop and truffle on top of the chicory. Run a circle of black truffle and hazelnut dressing around the rosace to serve.

Seared Dordogne foie gras with green lentils and Madeira sauce, Straffan Red rhubarb compote and truffle custard

The combination of foie gras, truffles and lentils is not a new one, but it's a great one. We make the rhubarb compote in spring and then store it for this dish. I love the slightly acidic hit it provides to cut through the richness of the foie gras.

WINE PAIRING

Château de Rayne-Vigneau Sauternes

There is no better match. This is a classic: sweet but crisp, earthy with putty flavours from the botrytis. Heaven with foie gras.

FOR THE STRAFFAN RED RHUBARB COMPOTE

4kg (9lb) Straffan Red rhubarb, chopped
400ml (14fl oz) grenadine
200gm (7oz) caster sugar
8 leaves of baby spinach, to serve

FOR THE RHUBARB SHAVING

50ml (2fl oz) grenadine
15gm (½oz) caster sugar
1 stick of rhubarb

FOR THE MADEIRA SAUCE

30gm (1oz) Avonmore unsalted butter
15gm (½oz) diced carrot
15gm (½oz) diced celery
15gm (½oz) diced shallot
15gm (½oz) diced leek
sprig of fresh thyme
150ml (5fl oz) Madeira
300ml (10fl oz) ruby port
1.5 litre (2½ pints) veal jus (see page 270)

FOR THE GREEN LENTILS

100gm (3½oz) green puy lentils, soaked overnight
200ml (7fl oz) white chicken stock (see page 270)
25gm (1oz) smoked bacon rind
30gm (1oz) unsalted Avonmore butter
1 carrot, peeled and diced
1 stick of celery, peeled and diced
½ leek, diced
1 white onion, finely chopped
sprig of fresh thyme

FOR THE TRUFFLE CUSTARD

40gm (1½oz) free-range egg yolk
pinch of salt
pinch of caster sugar
125ml (4½fl oz) Avonmore cream
½ leaf gelatine, soaked in water
10ml (½fl oz) white truffle oil

FOR THE FOIE GRAS

1 x 600gm (1lb 5oz) Dordogne foie gras lobe
200gm (7oz) rock salt

SERVES 8

STRAFFAN RED RHUBARB COMPOTE

Place the rhubarb and grenadine in a pot and cook over a medium heat until it has stewed right down and is just dry. Add the sugar and cook for another 10 minutes. Taste and check for bitterness; if it needs more sugar, add it little by little, but leave it a little bitter.

RHUBARB SHAVING

Warm the grenadine and sugar in a pot to make a syrup. Cut the rhubarb sticks into 12cm (4½in) lengths and slice wafer-thin slices lengthways. Soak in the grenadine syrup for 3 minutes. Remove and place in the dehydrator, set to 68°C, for 8 hours until crisp.

MADEIRA SAUCE

Melt the butter in a pot and add the diced vegetables and sprig of thyme. Cook over a low heat until the vegetables are soft but still hold their shape (this gentle cooking method extracts the natural sugars). Add the Madeira and ruby port, increase the heat to high and cook until the liquid is reduced by 75%. Add the veal jus and cook over a medium heat for a further 30 minutes. Remove from the heat and pass through a fine sieve and muslin cloth, letting it drain slowly to remove any impurities (do not push it through). Season with salt to taste. (This sauce can be made 1–2 days in advance and stored in the refrigerator.)

GREEN LENTILS

Drain the pre-soaked lentils and rinse thoroughly, then cook in the chicken stock with the bacon rind for about 20 minutes until the lentils are almost cooked through but still have a little bite. Remove from the heat and drain. Place the butter in a pan over a low heat and add the diced vegetables and fresh thyme. Cook until the vegetables are soft and cooked through but not coloured. Add the vegetables to the lentils and set aside to cool.

TRUFFLE CUSTARD

Place the egg yolks in a bowl with the pinch of salt and sugar. Heat the cream gently in a pot and, when warm, whisk into the egg yolk mix and then return to the pot to cook for 1 minute over a low heat. Squeeze any excess water from the gelatine and add it to the custard; mix until dissolved. Finally add the white truffle oil, mix to combine and then remove from the heat and leave to cool. Transfer into a squeezy bottle.

FOIE GRAS

Cover the lobe of foie gras completely in the rock salt and leave to stand for 1 hour at room temperature. Rinse, pat dry and vacuum pack. Place in the fridge until fully firmed up, then place in a waterbath, set to 56°C, for 10 minutes. Plunge the bag immediately into heavily iced water to cool down. Once it is firm again, repeat the process and place back in the waterbath, set to 60°C, for 14 minutes. Once again plunge the bag immediately into heavily iced water to cool down. When it is firm, remove from the vacuum-pack bag, cover tightly in cling film and allow it to set in the fridge.

TO SERVE

Remove the foie gras from the fridge. Using a hot knife, cut it into 2cm (1in) slices per portion. Leave to stand for 10 minutes to come up to room temperature (this is important). Place the pot of lentils back on the heat and cover with just enough Madeira sauce to barely bind the lentils together. Quenelle the rhubarb compote and place on a baby spinach leaf on a warm plate. Place the rhubarb shaving on top. Draw a 10cm (4in) circle of truffle custard on the plate and fill with the lentil mix. Season the fois gras, then seal it in a hot non-stick pan until golden brown on each side and place on top of the lentils.

BLACK WINTER TRUFFLE

Marbled terrine of Dordogne foie gras with five spice opaline tube and celeriac foam, and quince purée

Celeriac and foie gras provide a classic flavour match here, while the Madeira glaze between the layers of this terrine add an extra richness to the dish. The acidity from the quince then works to cut through that richness and provide a tart counterpoint.

WINE PAIRING

Thomas Barton Sauternes

This is an incredibly good drinking Sauternes – sweet without being cloying and a lovely texture and flavour. Pair any Sauternes with foie gras and you won't go wrong.

FOR THE MADEIRA GLAZE

30gm (1oz) Avonmore unsalted butter
15gm (½oz) diced carrot
15gm (½oz) diced celery
15gm (½oz) diced shallot
15gm (½oz) diced leek
sprig of fresh garden thyme
150ml (5fl oz) Madeira
300ml (10fl oz) ruby port
1.5 litre (2½ pints) veal jus (see page 271)
salt

FOR THE MARBLED TERRINE

2 lobes Dordogne foie gras, soaked overnight in milk
24gm (1oz) salt
12gm (½oz) milled black pepper
12gm (½oz) caster sugar
12gm (½oz) five spice powder
120ml (4fl oz) Madeira
120ml (4fl oz) Armagnac
120ml (4fl oz) red port

FOR THE CELERIAC FOAM

350gm (12oz) celeriac
400ml (14fl oz) Avonmore cream
salt and freshly milled white pepper

FOR THE FIVE SPICE STICKS

55gm (2oz) sugar syrup (see page 271)
10gm (½oz) glucose syrup
27gm (1oz) five spice powder

FOR THE OPALINE TUBES

100gm (3½oz) fondant
50gm (2oz) glucose syrup
2gm (½ tsp) Nougasec
2gm (½ tsp) five spice powder

FOR THE QUINCE PUREÉ

75gm (2½oz) caster sugar
½ fresh vanilla pod
juice of 1 lemon
juice of 1 orange
1 Granny Smith apple, peeled and cored
3 quince, peeled and cored

MAKES 16 PORTIONS

MADEIRA GLAZE

Melt the butter in a pot over a low heat and add the vegetables and thyme. Cook over a low heat until the vegetables are soft but not coloured – to extract the natural sugars. Add the Madeira and ruby port, increase the heat to high and allow the liquid to reduce by 75%. Add the veal jus, reduce the heat to medium and cook for 30 minutes more. Pass through a fine sieve and muslin cloth and then place the sauce in a pot and reduce over a low heat until it forms a very thick syrup. Season with salt to taste.

MARBLED TERRINE

Remove the foie gras lobes from the milk and pat dry. Using a hot knife, slice the lobes widthways into 1.5cm (½in)-thick slices. Mix all the dry ingredients together in a bowl. Place the slices flat on a tray and sprinkle the dry mix over them. Finally, sprinkle the alcohol over the lobes, cover with cling film and refrigerate overnight. Remove the slices from the marinade and pat dry. Sear each slice very quickly in a hot pan until golden brown on each side and cool quickly. Keep the excess fat, pass through a fine sieve and reserve to serve.

BUILDING THE TERRINE

Line a terrine mould (25cm x 9cm x 7cm; 10in x 3½in x 3in) with cling film. Warm the Madeira glaze until it just melts. Line the base of the mould with slices of foie gras, packing them tightly side by side, leaving no gaps, so that the bottom of the mould is completely covered. Brush them with a thick layer of Madeira glaze. Repeat the process until the mould is full. It is very important to leave no gaps between the slices of foie gras. Fold the cling film over the top of the terrine and place a light weight on top (we use a litre carton of milk). Place the terrine in the fridge and allow it to set.

CELERIAC FOAM

Peel the celeriac and chop it into small pieces. Place in a pot and cover with the cream, then season to taste with salt and pepper. Cook slowly over a gentle heat, taking care not to boil the cream. When the celeriac is soft, place the mix into a HotmixPRO blender, or similar, and blend until very smooth. The consistency should be that of a thick soup. Pour into a siphon bottle charged with two ISI gas chargers, shake vigorously and refrigerate for service.

FIVE SPICE STICKS

Preheat the oven to 155°C. Warm the sugar and glucose syrups together in a pot. Add the five spice powder and whisk to form a paste. Place the mixture into a disposable piping bag and nick a 2mm (1/10in) hole in the tip. Lay a Silpat or similar non-stick mat on a flat baking tray and pipe the paste in a straight line the full length of the tray. Place in the preheated oven and cook for 8 minutes, or until hard. Remove and, once cool, break into 12cm (4½in) lengths for service.

OPALINE TUBES

Preheat the oven to 160°C. Place the ingredients in a saucepan and bring to the boil. Pour on to a flat tray and leave to harden. Break into smaller pieces and then blend them in a HotmixPRO, or similar, until blended to dust. Cut out a rectangular stencil measuring 7cm x 4cm (3in x 1½in) and place the template on a Silpat or similar non-stick mat on a baking tray. Put the opaline dust into a fine sieve and sprinkle over the stencil until the shape has been filled. Repeat this 16 times, to make 16 opaline rectangles. Remove the stencil and cook the opaline in the preheated oven until just melted but still holding its shape. Remove from the oven and roll over a 2.5cm (1in)-diameter cylinder to form tube shapes. Store the tubes in an airtight container.

QUINCE PUREÉ

Place the caster sugar, vanilla pod, lemon and orange juice in a saucepan. Finely slice the apple and the quince and very quickly add them to the sugar mix before they have a chance to discolour. Cook over a low heat until the fruit is soft. Pour into a HotmixPRO blender, or similar, and blend until very smooth. Cool and store in a bottle.

TO SERVE

Using a very hot knife, cut the terrine into 1cm (½in)-thick slices. Place a slice in the centre of a plate. Fill each opaline tube with the celeriac foam and place one beside the foie gras. Push a five spice stick through the centre of the foam. Add dots of quince purée in a line and garnish with some of the foie gras fat around the plate. Serve with a warm baby brioche on the side.

TIP

As you roll the opaline tubes, if the opaline begins to firm up simply transfer it back to the oven for 30 seconds to warm through again. When storing the opaline tubes in our professional kitchen, we place some calcium chloride in the base of a box, covered with a sheet of parchment paper, to prevent moisture getting in. However, it is essential not to allow calcium chloride to touch the food in any way. If it does, you must discard the tubes.

HELEN GEE | JAM MAKER

Helen Gee launched G's Gourmet Jams from her kitchen in Abbeyleix in County Laois in 1998. Although the business has expanded considerably over the years, Helen continues to make her jams the good old-fashioned way – stirred and poured by hand in big open pots on the stove. Helen has won countless awards for her jams, which are tangy and sharp, bursting with natural fruit flavour, unlike other sugar-laden commercial brands. Helen's four children are all involved in the business in various ways. Her son Cyril, a tillage farmer, currently grows raspberries, rhubarb and other fruit for Helen to transform into delicious jams, curds, chutneys and relishes.

www.gsgourmetjams.ie

Truffled Dordogne foie gras ganache with Périgord melanosporum and yellow plum purée

This dish is just pure, unadulterated luxury. Foie gras rolled in truffle – what could be more lavish? It's a close-your-eyes kind of a dish. Melanosporum is the formal name for black truffle. We source ours from the village of Saint Alvare in the Périgord region.

WINE PAIRING

Château d'Yquem 1988

I know this is bordering on the ridiculous, as it's uber expensive, but of all the wines we've tasted at The K Club – and we've got to taste the good stuff – this is the one that will take the legs out from under you. And this recipe deserves something special.

FOR THE FOIE GRAS GANACHE

100gm (3½oz) Dordogne foie gras, soaked overnight in milk
2gm (½ tsp) salt
1gm (¼ tsp) milled black pepper
1gm (¼ tsp) caster sugar
1gm (¼ tsp) five spice powder
12ml (½fl oz) Madeira
12ml (½fl oz) Armagnac
12ml (½fl oz) red port
35ml (1¼fl oz) ice cold water
30gm (1oz) grated black Périgord winter truffles

FOR THE MIRABELLE PLUM PURÉE

100gm (3½oz) preserved mirabelle plums (see page 274)

FOR THE BRIOCHE CHAPELURE

10gm (½oz) unsalted Avonmore butter
50gm (2oz) brioche loaf, crumbed (see page 275)
salt and freshly milled white pepper

MAKES 4

FOIE GRAS GANACHE

Remove the foie gras from the milk and pat dry. Using a hot knife, slice the lobes widthways into 1.5cm (½in)-thick slices. Mix together all the dry ingredients (except the truffle) in a bowl. Place the slices flat on a tray and sprinkle the dry mix over them. Drizzle over the alcohol, cover with cling film and refrigerate overnight. Remove the foie gras from the marinade and pat dry. Place the foie gras in a HotmixPRO blender (or similar), set the temperature to 63°C and let it melt. Then set the blender to high, add the ice cold water and blitz to combine. Pass the mix through a fine sieve and leave to set in the fridge. Once set, roll the ganache into balls (about 25gm/1oz each). Roll the balls in the grated truffle and return to the fridge until required.

MIRABELLE PLUM PURÉE

Remove the stones from the preserved plums and blitz the fruit in a HotmixPRO blender (or similar) until smooth. Pass through a fine sieve and set aside until required.

BRIOCHE CHAPELURE

Melt the butter in a saucepan and add the brioche crumbs. Cook until golden brown and crispy. Drain on kitchen paper and season with a little salt and freshly milled white pepper to taste.

TO SERVE

Spoon a little mirabelle plum purée in the centre of the plate. Place a ball of truffled ganache on top and sprinkle a line of the brioche chapelure at the side of the plate to serve.

Terrine of Irish mutton stew with thyme and flat-leaf parsley emulsion

This is my contemporary take on the traditional Irish stew. Undoubtedly the hard work here is in the preparation. Once you have made the terrine, it is just a slice and serve job, making it a fantastic dish to make for a special dinner party.

WINE PAIRING

Anthony Barton Saint-Émilion

This is a medium-bodied French classic from the family that built The K Club. Soft and round, this wine bats well above its weight.

FOR THE MUTTON STEW

1 shoulder of mutton, on the bone
1 pig's trotter
8 banana shallots, peeled, with trimmed root left on
3 leeks, washed
3 carrots, peeled
10 celery sticks
10 leaves of Savoy cabbage
10 baby potatoes, peeled
200gm (7oz) potatoes, peeled and chopped into cubes
5 litres (9 pints) mutton stock (see page 271)
bouquet garni (to include fresh thyme, sage and rosemary)
5gm (¼oz) chopped flat-leaf parsley

FOR THE THYME AND FLAT-LEAF PARSLEY EMULSION

100ml cooking liquid, from above
5ml (¼fl oz) cider vinegar
20ml (¾fl oz) Newgrange Gold rapeseed oil
¼ tsp chopped garden thyme
¼ tsp chopped flat-leaf parsley

FOR THE BABY VEGETABLES

300ml (10fl oz) cooking liquid, from above
20 baby carrots
10 baby parsnips
10 baby leeks

TO SERVE

micro-celery, to garnish
fresh thyme, to garnish

SERVES 10

MUTTON STEW

Put the shoulder of mutton, pig's trotter, all the vegetables and bouquet garni into a large pot and pour over the mutton stock. Simmer gently on a low heat and remove the vegetables from the pot as they are cooked, including the baby potatoes, setting them aside for later. When the mutton and trotter are soft and fully cooked through – the meat should be falling off the bone – remove them from the liquid, leaving the cubed potato in the pot.

Reduce the liquid by 50–60% until it becomes sticky. Set aside 100ml (3½fl oz) of the reduced cooking liquid and keep for the emulsion. Transfer the rest to a blender and blitz for a few minutes. Place 20ml (¾fl oz) of the liquid on a plate and refrigerate to cool, then test if it has set. If it has not set, you need to reduce it further.

Flake the shoulder of mutton from the bone. Place the meat on a sheet of cling film and roll tightly into long, thin rolls about 30cm x 2cm (12in x 1in). Set aside in the fridge.

Line the terrine mould with cling film and then cover with the blanched Savoy cabbage leaves. Warm the jellied cooking stock a little and add the chopped parsley.

To construct the terrine, unwrap the rolls of mutton and fill the terrine mould by dipping the mutton rolls and the mixture of vegetables into the warmed jellied cooking stock and filling the terrine up to the top – varying the layers as you go to give a mosaic effect. Season each layer with a little salt and freshly milled black pepper as you go. Fold over the cabbage leaves and allow to set overnight, covered, in the fridge.

THYME AND FLAT-LEAF PARSLEY EMULSION

Blend the cooking liquid, vinegar and rapeseed oil in a blender. Once emulsified, remove from the blender and add the thyme and flat-leaf parsley.

BABY VEGETABLES

Bring the cooking liquid to the boil and add the baby vegetables. Remove each one as they are cooked. They should be soft and cooked through but still holding their shape. Set aside to keep warm.

TO SERVE

Cut the terrine into 2cm (1in)-thick slices per portion. Place a slice on a warm plate, then draw a thick line of emulsion below it and arrange the baby vegetables on top. Sprinkle with the fresh herbs and serve.

Widgeon with spiced parsnip purée, preserved baby artichokes and eggnog foam

The spiced parsnip purée brings the punch of seasonal flavours to this deep winter dish – with the sweet, heady spices in the eggnog foam introducing a touch of Christmas home comfort. Paired with the earthy richness of the game bird, it all comes together beautifully.

WINE PAIRING

Santa Digna Rosé

Any rosé with a bit of sweetness would work here. The eggnog sauce demands it, but the slight red berry character of this rosé will suit the widgeon.

FOR THE WIDGEON

4 widgeon
20ml (¾fl oz) Newgrange Gold rapeseed oil, plus extra for sealing
4 sprigs of fresh thyme
salt and freshly milled black pepper

FOR THE STOCK

4 widgeon carcasses, from above
1.5 litres (2½ pints) brown chicken stock (see page 270)

FOR THE BRAISED LEGS

8 widgeon legs, from above
salt and freshly milled black pepper
20ml (¾fl oz) vegetable oil
widgeon stock, from above
30gm (1oz) chopped onion
30gm (1oz) chopped leek
20gm (¾oz) chopped celery
30gm (1oz) chopped carrot
1 garlic clove
4 juniper berries
10 crushed black peppercorns
1 small sprig of fresh sage and thyme
1 small bay leaf

FOR THE SPICED PARSNIP PUREÉ

40gm (1½oz) Avonmore unsalted butter
400gm (14oz) parsnips, peeled and cut into 1cm (½in) dice
salt and freshly milled white pepper
2gm (½ tsp) freshly grated nutmeg
3gm (¾ tsp) cinnamon stick
280ml (10fl oz) Avonmore cream

FOR THE EGGNOG FOAM

200ml (7fl oz) Avonmore full-fat milk
1 clove
35gm (1¼oz) free-range egg yolks
75gm (2½oz) caster sugar
200ml (7fl oz) Avonmore cream
2gm (½ tsp) ground cinnamon
1gm (¼ tsp) grated nutmeg
30ml (1fl oz) Jameson whiskey

FOR THE PRESERVED BABY ARTICHOKES

10 preserved baby artichokes (see page 274)
25ml (1fl oz) clarified butter (see page 272)

TO SERVE

24 sprigs of micro-chervil

SERVES 8

WIDGEON

Carefully remove the legs and breasts from the carcass of each bird. Put the breasts into a vacuum-pack bag with the rapeseed oil, thyme and seasoning. Keep the legs aside for braising (see below). Seal the bag and place a fine needle probe in the centre of one breast. Transfer to a waterbath, set to 60°C, until the needle probe hits 54°C. Remove the breasts from the bag and season with salt and milled black pepper. Add a dash of oil to a hot pan and pan-fry the breasts, skin-side down, until golden brown.

STOCK

Preheat the oven to 160°C. Chop the widgeon carcasses into small pieces. Place on a baking tray and transfer to the oven for 20 minutes, or until golden brown. Drain off the excess fat and place the bones in a pot with the brown chicken stock. Bring up to the boil and reduce to a gentle simmer for 4 hours. Skim off the fat as it rises to the top, to keep the stock clear. Check for a good strong flavour before passing through a fine sieve. If the flavour has not developed enough, leave it to simmer for as long as needed until the flavour is there.

BRAISED LEGS

Preheat the oven to 120°C. Season the legs with salt and milled black pepper. Pour the oil into a hot pan and place the legs in, skin-side down, until golden brown. Turn them over and quickly seal the other side, then remove the legs from the pan and set aside. Add the mirepoix (chopped vegetables and herbs) to the pan and cook until golden. Deglaze with a little stock. Return the legs to the pan and then pour over just enough stock to cover the legs. Cover with a disc of parchment paper. Transfer to the preheated oven and cook until the legs are nice and tender (about 90 minutes). Remove the legs from the stock and keep warm. Pass the stock through a fine sieve and muslin cloth and keep for serving. The sauce should be nice and syrupy, but, if not, simply put it back over the heat and reduce it until you achieve the desired consistency.

SPICED PARSNIP PURÉE

Melt the unsalted butter in a saucepan and add the diced parsnip with a little salt and milled white pepper to taste. Cover and cook over a low heat to sweat the parsnip without colouring it. Cook until the parsnip begins to soften, then add the nutmeg, cinnamon and cream. Continue to cook over a low heat until the parsnip is very soft. Transfer to a HotmixPRO blender (or similar) and blitz on high until very smooth.

EGGNOG FOAM

Add the milk and clove to a saucepan and place over a high heat to bring to the boil, then remove from the heat. In a bowl, mix the egg yolks and sugar together and then pour over the milk and whisk quickly and thoroughly to combine. Place the mixture back in the saucepan and cook over a low heat until the custard thickens a little. Remove from the heat and allow to cool. Once the custard is cooled, add the cream, nutmeg, cinnamon and whiskey and mix to combine. Cover and leave to infuse in the fridge for 4 hours. Pour the mixture into a siphon bottle charged with two ISI gas chargers, shake vigorously and set aside for service.

PRESERVED BABY ARTICHOKES

Remove the artichokes from the jar, drain and pat dry. Cut the artichokes in half. Add the clarified butter to a hot pan and brown the artichokes until golden.

TO SERVE

Spoon two pools of spiced parsnip purée on to a warmed plate and drag a spoon lengthways through one of them. Place the braised leg on one pool of purée and the sliced breast on the other. Position the baby artichoke next and spoon some sauce around. Finally dot the eggnog foam on the plate and garnish with micro-chervil.

Wild game sausage with glazed pear, smoked Hardyman's belly bacon, curly kale and thyme-scented jus

This is an intensely flavoured sausage made with pheasant, rabbit, mallard and venison. It's a game-lover's dream. The sweet, glazed pear then balances out the intense game flavours. The smokiness of the bacon and the fresh thyme go brilliantly together.

WINE PAIRING

Cambria Pinot Noir, Santa Maria Valley, California

Pinot is making a real resurgence, and this dish demands the earthy quality of a great Pinot Noir.

FOR THE WHITE WINE MARINADE

180ml (6fl oz) white wine
1 carrot, peeled and chopped
1 celery stick
1 white onion, peeled and chopped
1 sprig of fresh thyme

FOR THE WILD GAME SAUSAGE

80gm (2¾oz) pheasant legs, minced
80gm (2¾oz) mallard, minced
80gm (2¾oz) venison neck, minced
80gm (2¾oz) rabbit shoulder, minced
10gm (½oz) unsalted Avonmore butter
40gm (1½oz) chopped shallot
25gm (1oz) chopped fresh sage
80gm (2¾oz) golden raisins, soaked overnight
80gm (2¾oz) barley, soaked overnight
salt and freshly milled black pepper
100gm (3½oz) natural hog skins

FOR THE SMOKED BELLY BACON

100gm (3½oz) smoked Hardyman's belly bacon
1 sprig of fresh thyme
½ garlic clove
10ml (½fl oz) Newgrange Gold rapeseed oil

FOR THE THYME-SCENTED JUS

pheasant carcass, chopped
venison bones, chopped
mallard carcass, chopped
rabbit carcass, chopped
80gm (2¾oz) carrot, chopped
60gm (2oz) onion, chopped
40gm (1½oz) celery, chopped
1 garlic clove
3 sprigs of fresh thyme
3 litres of chicken stock (see page 270)

FOR THE PEARS

5 preserved Victorian Garden pears (see page 274)
50gm (2oz) icing sugar

FOR THE CURLY KALE

1 head of curly kale
1 carrot, peeled and cut into batons
30gm (1oz) Avonmore unsalted butter
50ml (2fl oz) chicken stock (see page 270)

SERVES 10

WILD GAME SAUSAGE

Put all the marinade ingredients in a large pot and bring up to the boil. Boil for 10 minutes and then leave to cool completely. Mix all the meat together and place in the marinade for 5 hours.

Sweat the chopped shallot and sage in the butter and, when cool, add it to the pot containing the sausage meat. Add the pre-soaked raisins and barley, and season with salt and milled black pepper. At this stage it is best to do a taste test: take some of the sausage meat mixture and cook it in the steamer; taste it to check the seasoning and flavour, and adjust as required.

Once you are happy with the seasoning, fit a disposable piping bag with a plain 1.5cm (½in) nozzle and fill the bag with the sausage meat mixture. Tie one end of the hog skin and draw the skin up along the nozzle. Press the mixture into the hog skin and twist into 10cm (4in) sausage lengths (about 60gm/2oz each in weight). Tie the other end and repeat the process 10 times. Place the sausages in a vacuum-pack bag and insert a probe into the centre of one of the sausages. Cook in a waterbath set to 74°C until the probe temperature reaches 72°C.

SMOKED BELLY BACON

Place the belly and the thyme in a vacuum-pack bag and seal. Cook in a waterbath set to 76°C for 3 hours, then remove the bag from the waterbath and transfer it to a bowl of iced water to cool.

THYME-SCENTED JUS

Preheat the oven to 170°C. Place the chopped bones on a tray and roast in the oven, stirring occasionally, for about 20 minutes or until golden brown. Add the vegetables and 2 sprigs of fresh thyme and cook for an additional 15 minutes. Remove from the oven and scrape everything into a pot. Deglaze the oven tray with the chicken stock and pour the juices into the pot with the bones. Place on the hob and bring to the boil, then reduce the heat and simmer for about 3 hours over a low heat. Pass the liquid through a sieve, discard the bones and reduce the liquid to a sauce consistency. Before serving, add the final sprig of fresh thyme for flavour.

PEARS

Cut each pear in half and slice each half lengthwise into 6 slices to create a fan effect, keeping the top of the pear attached to the stem (as pictured). Dust each pear with icing sugar and caramelise with a blowtorch or under a salamander or hot grill.

CURLY KALE

To prepare the curly kale, pick the leaves off the tough stem and discard the stem. Put the butter and the stock in a pot, bring to the boil, then add the carrots and cook until just tender. Add the curly kale and toss it around for a few seconds until wilted. Drain and set aside.

TO SERVE

Once cooked, remove the sausages from the vacuum-pack bag and season with salt and pepper. Add 25gm (1oz) of unsalted butter to a hot pan and, once the butter is foaming, fry the sausages until golden brown on all sides. Set aside to keep warm. Slice the belly into 5mm (¼in)-thick slices and fry in the same pan until golden brown. Place the fan of pear to the side of the plate. Add the curly kale and the carrot to the centre of the plate and top with the belly bacon. Finish with a wild game sausage on top, then use a spoon to pool the thyme-scented jus around it.

Squab pigeon breast with Jerusalem artichoke purée, slow-cooked leg and peanut butter ice cream, pine nut oil

The first time my pastry chef made this peanut butter ice cream I knew I had to create a pigeon dish to serve it with. The nutty, almost woody flavour of the ice cream just said 'pigeon' to me for some reason. You'll just have to try it to see what I mean!

WINE PAIRING

Bourgogne Lombeline Pinot Noir

An earthy Pinot, the rich pigeon, the twist of the peanut ice cream – this is a dish and a match they'll be talking about for years.

FOR THE PIGEON

4 squab pigeons
20ml (¾fl oz) rapeseed oil
2 sprigs of fresh thyme
salt and freshly milled black pepper
20ml (¾fl oz) clarified butter

FOR THE JERUSALEM ARTICHOKE PURÉE

80gm (3oz) Jerusalem artichoke, peeled
squeeze of fresh lemon juice
salt and milled white pepper
30ml (1fl oz) Avonmore cream

FOR THE BUTTERNUT SQUASH CRISP

1 butternut squash

FOR THE PEANUT BUTTER ICE CREAM

500ml (17½fl oz) Avonmore milk
100gm (3½oz) free-range egg yolks
75gm (2½oz) caster sugar
200gm (7oz) peanut butter
180gm (6oz) procrema

FOR THE THYME CHAPELURE

10gm (½oz) Avonmore unsalted butter
2gm (½ tsp) dried thyme
20gm (¾oz) panko breadcrumbs

FOR THE PARSNIP CRISP

1 small parsnip, peeled
salt

MAKES 8

THE PIGEON

Remove the legs and breasts carefully from the carcass. Set the pigeon legs aside for braising (see below). Place the breasts into a vacuum-pack bag with the oil, thyme and a little seasoning. Seal and place the fine needle probe in the centre of one breast. Cook in a waterbath set to 60°C until the needle proble reaches 54°C. Remove the breasts from the bag, season with salt and milled black pepper and seal skin-side down in a hot pan with 10ml (½fl oz) of clarified butter until golden brown.

For the legs

Remove the thigh bone from the legs, and cut the end of the leg bone. Season the legs with a little salt and milled black pepper. Lay the legs skin-side down on a board, fold over the thigh and push the leg bone through the skin. Then place each leg on a sheet of cling film and roll up tightly, letting the leg bone pierce the cling film on each roll. Tie each end with string. Cook in a waterbath set to 72°C for 3 hours. Remove and season again with salt and milled black pepper and seal in a hot frying pan with the remaining clarified butter until golden brown.

JERUSALEM ARTICHOKE PURÉE

Place the artichoke in a vacuum-pack bag with a squeeze of lemon juice and a pinch of salt and white pepper. Cook in a steamer for about 20 minutes. Transfer to a HotmixPRO blender or similar and blend with the cream for 4 minutes until smooth.

BUTTERNUT SQUASH CRISP

Cut the butternut squash on a slicer into 2mm (1/10in)-thick strips. Cut the centre out using a 3cm (1in) cutter and place in the dehydrator set to 54°C for 6 hours until dry and crisp. Store in an airtight container until required.

PEANUT BUTTER ICE CREAM

Boil the milk in a saucepan. Mix the egg yolks and caster sugar together in a bowl, add one-third of the milk and whisk together. Then place the mixture into the pot with the remaining hot milk. Add the peanut butter and cook over a low heat until it begins to thicken, but do not boil. Pass through a fine chinois or sieve and allow to cool. Add the procrema and once the mixture is cold, place in a Taurus Rowzer beaker and freeze. Then blitz when required. Alternatively, place in an ice cream machine and churn for 20 minutes and then freeze.

THYME CHAPELURE

Melt the butter in a pan, add the thyme and allow it to infuse for a few minutes. Add the panko breadcrumbs and cook until golden brown. Drain on kitchen paper and allow to cool.

PARSNIP CRISP

Slice the parsnip on a slicer into 2mm (1/10in)-thick lengths. Heat the oil in a deep fryer to 360°C and fry the parsnip crisps until just golden. Remove and place on a paper towel to drain. Season with a little salt and allow to cool.

TO SERVE

Run a line of the thyme chapelure along one side of a warm plate. Place a small scoop of the peanut butter ice cream on top of the chapelure and top the ice cream with the butternut squash crisp. Spoon some Jerusalem artichoke purée on to the plate and place the leg on top. Place the breast of the pigeon on next and drizzle over a little pine nut oil. Finish with the parsnip crisp.

EDWARD JOHNSTON | SHEEP FARMER

Edward Johnston leads something of a double life – as a successful solicitor in Dublin and a sheep farmer in County Mayo. A native of Achill Island, Edward grew up raising Blackface mountain lamb on his family farm. Together with his neighbour and friend John Corrigan, the pair today supply exceptional quality Achill Island Blackface lamb under the name Caor Acla. 'Our Caor Acla lamb is farmed and reared using the traditional methods handed down by our ancestors,' Edward explains. 'It is the only sustainable way to produce lamb of this quality in such a harsh environment.' The resulting lamb is an exceptional gourmet meat. The animals feed on the local grasses and herbs native to the bogland and grasslands by the coast, and this distinctive terroir lends the meat its own unique taste.

www.caoracla.ie

THE K CLUB GARDENERS

Ravioli of celeriac and Périgord truffle, seasonal baby vegetables and carrot and Sauternes butter sauce

I think vegetarian dishes are all too often an afterthought on a menu. I wanted to create a really exciting vegetarian dish to offer complex layers of flavour. The result is a time-consuming dish to prepare but a fantastic one to serve up.

WINE PAIRING

Trimbach Frédéric Emile Riesling 2001

An older Riesling develops beautiful kerosene flavours, a love it or hate it wine. We love it. It's great with truffles.

FOR THE CARROT BUTTER SAUCE

250gm (9oz) Avonmore unsalted butter
1 kg (2lb 3oz) peeled carrots, minced
125gm (4½oz) white onion, diced
½ glass Sauternes
750ml (26fl oz) vegetable stock (see page 271)
500ml (17fl oz) freshly squeezed orange juice, strained
salt and freshly milled white pepper

FOR THE PASTA

250gm (9oz) strong flour
3 free-range egg yolks
2 whole free-range eggs
salt
Newgrange Gold rapeseed oil
extra flour for dusting

FOR THE RAVIOLI FILLING

200gm (7oz) celeriac, peeled and diced
200ml (7fl oz) Avonmore cream
salt and freshly milled pepper

FOR RAVIOLI ASSEMBLY

flour, to dust
beaten egg yolk
4 thin slices of Périgord truffle

FOR THE BASIL OIL

50gm (2oz) basil leaves, stalks removed
100ml (3½fl oz) Newgrange Gold rapeseed oil

TO SERVE

baby beetroots, roasted and peeled
baby carrots, scrubbed and parboiled
baby turnips, scrubbed and parboiled
50gm (2oz) trompette mushrooms, washed, dried and sautéed in unsalted butter
baby artichokes, peeled and sautéed in clarified butter
4 thin slices of Périgord truffle

SERVES 4

CARROT BUTTER SAUCE

Melt the butter in a pot, add the minced carrot and onion and sweat them over a medium heat until cooked through but not coloured. Pour in the Sauternes and cook out until reduced by 50%. Add the orange juice and chicken stock and reduce by 50%. Pass the mix through a fine sieve and store the liquid, covered, in the fridge overnight to set. After the mixture has set, separate the butter that will have solidified on top from the stock and dice it into small squares. Reduce the stock by 50% and then whisk in the diced butter until the sauce thickens and the butter is emulsified into it. Taste and adjust the seasoning as required. Strain and set aside.

PASTA

Place the flour, egg yolks and whole eggs in a food processor and pulse until the mixture resembles fine breadcrumbs. Season with a little salt. Add just enough oil to bring the crumbs together, transfer to a bowl and bring together by hand. Turn out on to a floured surface and knead for 1 minute. Split the dough in two, cover each piece with cling film and rest these in the fridge for 30 minutes.

RAVIOLI FILLING

Place the diced celeriac in a pot, cover with the cream, season and bring slowly up to the boil. Once the celeriac is soft and the cream has reduced, remove the pot from the heat, strain and purée the celeriac in a food processor. Check the seasoning and adjust if required. Suspend the celeriac purée in a muslin cloth to allow all the excess moisture to come out – you want a dry purée.

RAVIOLI ASSEMBLY

Remove the pasta dough from the fridge and dust it lightly with flour. Using a pasta machine, roll out the pasta dough as thinly as possible, starting at the highest number on the dial and moving down a notch each time until you reach 1. Using a 10cm (4in) cutter, cut out 2 discs from the sheet of pasta – this will make 1 ravioli. Take a large spoon of the celeriac mixture and place it in the centre of one of the pasta discs; place a slice of the Périgord truffle on top. Brush the edges of the other pasta disc with the beaten egg yolk and press the two pieces together, forming a flying-saucer shape – making sure to squeeze out any air trapped between the two discs as you go. Repeat this process four times. Arrange the four ravioli on a sheet of parchment paper and set aside.

BASIL OIL

Blanch the basil leaves in boiling water for 20 seconds, then plunge them immediately into ice-cold water. Strain and dry the leaves. Place them in a blender and slowly add the rapeseed oil as you blitz to combine.

TO SERVE

To cook the ravioli, bring a large pot of salted water to the boil and add in the sheet of parchment paper with the ravioli on it (to prevent the risk of bursting the ravioli as you remove them from the paper). Cook for 4 minutes until al dente. Remove from the heat and drain. Toss in olive oil and season with salt and milled pepper to serve. Place one ravioli in the centre of a warm wide-rimmed bowl and gently spoon the carrot butter sauce around it. Place a garnish of baby vegetables around the ravioli and on top of the sauce and drizzle with basil oil. Finally, place a slice of Périgord truffle on top.

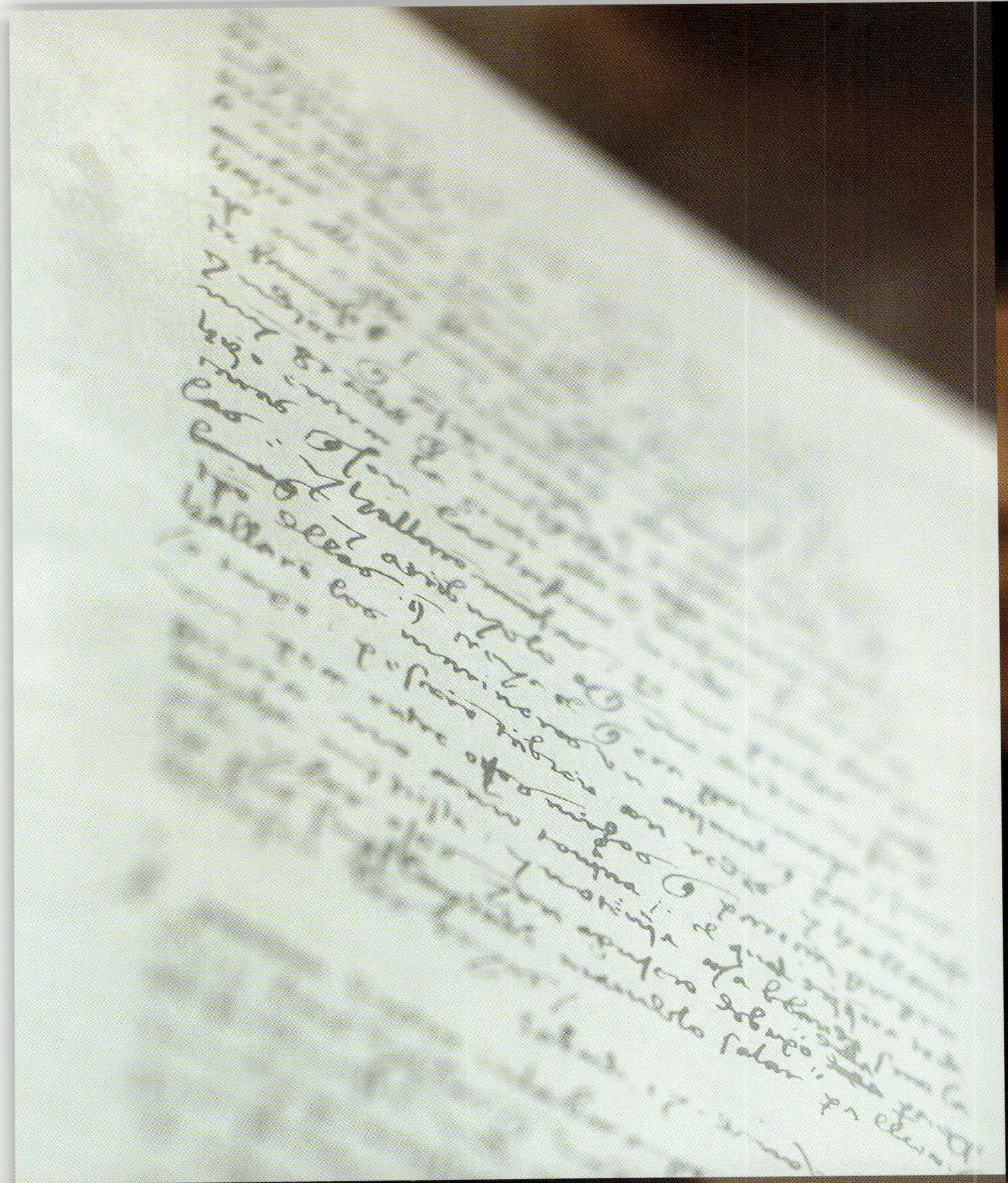

Ballyheigue Kerry Head lobster with traditional thermidor sauce

This is one of Dr Smurfit's favourites. Even though it is possibly over a century old, it is still a great dish. In my version I make a slightly lighter thermidor sauce, with the addition of whipped cream to allow the subtle flavour of the lobster to shine through.

WINE PAIRING

Domaine Mosnier Chablis Premier Cru

This Chablis is slightly richer, due to its Premier Cru status, but it is still flinty and crisp – perfect for cutting through the richness of the lobster sauce.

FOR THE THERMIDOR SAUCE

200ml (7fl oz) Avonmore milk
40gm (1½oz) white onion, chopped
½ bay leaf
6 whole black peppercorns
30gm (1oz) Avonmore unsalted butter
20gm (¾oz) plain flour
25gm (1oz) grated Coolattin chedder
15gm (½oz) blue cheese
50ml (2fl oz) whipped Avonmore cream
hollandaise sauce, from below
15gm (½oz) Dijon mustard
2 dashes Worcestershire sauce
10gm (½oz) finely grated Parmesan cheese

FOR THE LOBSTER

2 live Ballyheigue Kerry Head lobsters (400–500gm each) (14–18oz)
salt and freshly milled black pepper

FOR THE HOLLANDAISE SAUCE

30ml (1fl oz) white wine vinegar
1 shallot, finely sliced
1 sprig of fresh thyme
5 black peppercorns
3 free-range egg yolks
80ml (3fl oz) warm clarified butter (see page 272)
salt and freshly milled white pepper

SERVES 2

THERMIDOR SAUCE

Begin by making a mornay sauce. Bring the milk, onion, bayleaf and peppercorns to the boil. Reduce the heat to its lowest setting and allow to infuse for 15 minutes. In a separate pan melt the unsalted butter over a low heat and stir in the flour to form a smooth paste. Cook this roux, without colouring, for a minute or two until it takes on a sandy texture. Remove the roux from the heat and then add the strained milk to the pan. Place the pan over a gentle heat and whisk constantly until the sauce thickens and there are no lumps. Add in the cheddar and blue cheese and mix to combine.

LOBSTER

For detailed instructions on how to prepare and cook the lobster tails and claws, please turn to page 277. Then cut the tail meat into 6 even slices and chop the claw and knuckle meat into 3cm (1in) pieces. Season with the salt and milled white pepper and set aside to keep warm.

HOLLANDAISE SAUCE

Place the vinegar, shallot, thyme and peppercorns in a pot and allow to boil until the liquid is reduced by 70%. Pass through a fine sieve and retain the liquid. Place the egg yolks and reduced liquid in a glass bowl and whisk over a pot of hot water until the sauce reaches ribbon stage or holds its form. Then slowly whisk in the warm clarified butter until it is fully emulsified.

TO SERVE

To finish the thermidor sauce, fold the whipped cream, hollandaise sauce, Dijon mustard, Parmesan cheese and Worcestershire sauce into the base mornay sauce. To test the sauce and make sure it will glaze, place a spoonful on a plate and place under the salamander or grill; it should turn an even golden brown. Place the lobster meat back in the shell on the warm serving plate and cover generously with the thermidor sauce. Glaze under the salamander or grill until golden brown and serve immediately.

T-bone of wild Atlantic turbot, gnocchi of Carrick Farm's micro-watercress, raw Clarinbridge oyster sauce and beluga caviar

When you taste this dish, close your eyes and you could be standing on the pier, the sense of the sea is so strong. The raw oyster sauce captures the briny freshness of the ocean perfectly. I also love the contrast of the cold sauce paired with the hot fish and gnocchi; it really works. We use beluga caviar in this dish, but you can use sevruga or any sturgeon caviar.

WINE PAIRING

Domaine Laroche Chablis Grand Cru

You cannot get much better than Chablis and oysters, except maybe Guinness and oysters, but this rich Grand Cru and the magnificent turbot make a noble partnership.

FOR THE TURBOT

2–3 kg (4½lb–6½lb) whole Atlantic turbot
40ml (1½fl oz) clarified butter (see page 272)
50gm (2oz) Avonmore unsalted butter
salt and freshly milled white pepper

FOR THE RAW OYSTER SAUCE

8 Clarinbridge oysters
5 drops Villa Manodori balsamic vinegar
5 drops freshly squeezed lemon juice
285ml (10fl oz) Avonmore cream
pinch cayenne pepper
50gm (2oz) beluga caviar

FOR THE CUCUMBER SOLFRINO

1 cucumber, peeled

FOR THE WATERCRESS GNOCCHI

500gm (1lb) Maris Piper potatoes, peeled and diced
250gm (8oz) micro-watercress, finely chopped
150gm (5oz) strong flour
salt and freshly milled black pepper
40ml (1½fl oz) clarified butter (see page 272)

SERVES 8

TO PREPARE THE TURBOT

Remove the head and tail from the fish. Cut along the outside of the fillet on both sides, using a knife to cut between the fillet and the skirt. Using a heavy-duty metal scissors, cut along this line to remove the skirt. Then cut along the natural dividing line that runs lengthways between each fillet. Turn over onto the opposite side and repeat the process. Using a cleaver or a saw, cut through the bone again on each side of the meat, without tearing or cutting into the flesh, to leave you with 2 individual pieces of turbot on the bone. Turn the fish so that it is running the width of the board and, using a knife, cut the turbot into 3cm-wide (1in-wide) pieces. Then use a saw or cleaver to cut through the bone to leave you with T-bone shapes. Be aware that, as you remove the portions, the tail gets thinner, so you will have to make the cuts wider to get the same amount of meat on each T-bone. Trim any dark skin from the T-bone but leave the white skin on the opposite side.

RAW OYSTER SAUCE

Open the oysters and place the flesh and all the oyster juice into a HotmixPRO blender (or similar). Add the lemon juice, balsamic vinegar and cream and blitz. Pass through a fine sieve or chinois and season with a little cayenne pepper; there is no need to season with salt, as the oyster is naturally salty. Add the caviar and chill the sauce in the fridge.

CUCUMBER SOLFRINO

Using a small solfrino cutter remove small balls of cucumber flesh from the whole cucumber.

WATERCRESS GNOCCHI

Steam the potatoes until tender, then pass them through a fine sieve. Stir in the strong flour, a little at a time, until the mixture forms a firm dough (you may not need to use all the flour). Mix in the chopped micro-watercress and season with salt and freshly milled black pepper. Roll the mixture into long lengths, about 1cm (½in) in diameter. Cut the rolls into 2cm-long (1in-long) gnocchi pieces and pinch the end of each gnocchi slightly. Add the gnocchi to a pot of boiling salted water. The gnocchi are cooked when they float to the surface. Drain, pat dry and allow to cool a little. Place the clarified butter in a non-stick pan and fry the gnocchi until golden brown on each side. Set aside on kitchen paper and keep warm.

TURBOT

Season the T-bones with salt and freshly milled white pepper. Add the clarified butter to a hot pan and place the T-bone flesh-side down in the pan until golden brown on each side. Add the unsalted butter to the pan and let it form a nut brown foam, then lower the heat and baste the fish with a spoon until just cooked (about 4 minutes).

TO SERVE

Spoon the chilled raw oyster sauce on to a warmed plate. Neatly arrange the hot watercress gnocchi on top. Sprinkle some cucumber solfrino balls around the gnocchi. Place a T-bone of turbot on top of the gnocchi and garnish with micro-watercress.

MICHAEL HEALY AND PAT DOYLE |

WILD IRISH GAME

Wild Irish Game is one of the longest established and most highly respected wild game suppliers in Ireland. The business was founded by Michael Healy and his late wife Jane in 1997 in Glenmalure, County Wicklow. Over the years Michael has become something of a chef's secret weapon, thanks to the quality of the game he supplies – including wild venison, mallard, wigeon, teal and much more. In 2014 the Healys joined forces with the Doyle family in order to expand the business, but the company remains 100 per cent family- and Irish-owned and is dedicated to the same level of professional integrity as the day the company was founded.

www.wildirishgame.ie

Thornhill duck breast with Peking glaze, slow-cooked leg and crispy crackling, golden raisin chutney and pine nut oil

This Asian-inspired take on Thornhill duck is hugely popular. We also serve this gorgeous Cavan-reared duck in the traditional way, on the trolley. However, one of the highlights of this version is the crispy crackling, which is removed from the duck and cooked separately to make a decadent, non-greasy crisp.

WINE PAIRING

Yalumba Patchwork Shiraz, Barossa Valley

This is a monster of a wine, full of spice and rich black fruit. It goes perfectly with this flavoursome dish.

FOR THE DUCK

1 whole Thornhill duck
1 sprig of fresh thyme
1 garlic clove
20ml (¾fl oz) Newgrange Gold rapeseed oil
salt and freshly milled black pepper
40gm (1½oz) Avonmore unsalted butter
1 tsp sesame seeds, toasted, to garnish

FOR THE GOLDEN RAISIN CHUTNEY

60gm (2oz) muscovado sugar
50ml (2fl oz) champagne vinegar
300gm (10oz) golden raisins, soaked in water overnight
25gm (1oz) Avonmore unsalted butter
50gm (2oz) chopped onion
salt and freshly milled white pepper

FOR THE PINE NUT OIL

20gm (¾oz) pine nuts
40ml (1½fl oz) Newgrange Gold rapeseed oil
salt and freshly milled white pepper

FOR THE PEKING GLAZE

50ml (2fl oz) oyster sauce
5ml (¼fl oz) dark soy sauce
10gm (½oz) granulated sugar
5ml (¼fl oz) sesame oil
20ml (¾fl oz) thin soy sauce
1gm (¼ tsp) freshly milled black pepper
100ml (3½fl oz) water
100ml (3½fl oz) honey

FOR THE TURNIP FONDANT

1 turnip
10ml (½fl oz) Newgrange Gold rapeseed oil
1 sprig of fresh thyme
1 garlic clove, bashed
salt and freshly milled white pepper
20gm (¾oz) Avonmore unsalted butter

SERVES 4

DUCK LEGS

Remove both breasts and legs from the carcass. Debone the legs and roll each into a cylinder shape, wrapping each one very tightly in cling film. Place them in a vacuum-pack bag with the garlic, thyme, rapeseed oil, salt and pepper and seal. Transfer to a waterbath, set to 70°C, and slow cook for 12 hours. Once cooked, remove and place the duck (still in the sealed bag) immediately into iced water to cool.

DUCK BREAST

Using a very sharp knife remove the skin from the breast in one piece without cutting into the flesh. Place the breasts in a vacuum-pack bag and season with a little salt and freshly milled black pepper. Seal and insert a needle probe into the centre of the breast. Transfer to a waterbath, set to 60°C, and cook until the probe reaches a temperature of 52°C.

DUCK SKIN CRACKLING

Preheat the oven to 180°C. Cut the skin in half lengthwise. Season with a little salt and freshly milled pepper and place between two sheets of parchment paper. Place the sheets on to a baking tray and place another tray on top. Cook in the preheated oven for 30 minutes. Remove the top tray and cook for another 10 minutes, or until the skin is golden and crispy. Brush with Peking glaze and sprinkle with toasted sesame seeds.

GOLDEN RAISIN CHUTNEY

Place the sugar in a pot and heat until it is light caramel in colour. Add the vinegar to make a gastrique sauce. Once the sugar is dissolved, remove the pot from the heat and set aside to cool. Squeeze any excess water out of the raisins. Place the unsalted butter in a separate pot and melt over a medium heat. Add the onions, season and cook slowly until soft but not coloured. Pour in the gastrique sauce, add the raisins and cook over a medium heat until the liquid has all but evaporated. Transfer to a jar and allow to cool until needed.

PINE NUT OIL

Preheat the oven to 145°C. Roast the pine nuts in the preheated oven until golden. Place the pine nuts and rapeseed oil in a blender and blend on high until smooth. Season to taste. Pass through a fine sieve and store in a bottle.

PEKING GLAZE

Mix all the Peking glaze ingredients together in a pot and boil until the liquid has reduced to form a thick syrup. Set aside.

FOR THE TURNIP FONDANT

Slice the turnip widthways into 3cm (1in)-thick rounds. Place in a vacuum-pack bag with the rapeseed oil, thyme and garlic. Season with a little salt and pepper and seal the bag. Cook in a steamer for 45 minutes, or until the turnip is soft. Remove from the bag and pat dry. Using a 5cm (2in) cutter, cut the turnip into as many fondants as it will make.

TO SERVE

Put the duck legs in the sealed bag back into the waterbath, set to 65°C, for 15 minutes to warm through. Remove from the bag and seal in a hot pan until the skin is golden brown on all sides and then cut each leg in half. To finish the turnip fondants, add the butter to a hot pan and when it foams up add the turnip fondants and baste until they turn golden brown in the nutty butter. Remove the duck breasts from the bag and seal the meat very quickly in a hot pan until nicely browned. Paint with Peking glaze and place under a hot grill for 1 minute and then cut in half before serving. Paint the Peking glaze lengthwise down a warm plate and place the crackling on top. Place a quenelle of raisin chutney on the skin. Next arrange the duck breast and leg pieces on the strip of glaze. Place the turnip fondants with a small sliver of the breast resting on top. Drizzle the pine nut oil each side of the duck and serve.

Cutlet of wild Wicklow Hills venison, Jane Sellers local apiary honeycomb, pickled Straffan Red rhubarb, ceps and chocolate oil

Wild venison has a different flavour to its farmed cousin; it's stronger and earthier and so needs to be paired well on the plate. Jane Sellers' honey lends just the right smooth, sweet note. If you haven't yet tasted honey and ceps together – wait until you taste this.

WINE PAIRING

Pio Cesare Barolo

Barolo is the king of wine in Italy. Barolos are sublime and the richness of the wine matches the earthiness of the venison here perfectly.

FOR THE PICKLED STRAFFAN RED RHUBARB

4 stalks Straffan Red rhubarb
100ml (3½fl oz) red wine
100ml (3½fl oz) grape juice
100ml (3½fl oz) grenadine syrup
30ml (1fl oz) cider vinegar

FOR THE CHOCOLATE OIL

50gm (2oz) Valrhona chocolate (70%)
10gm (½oz) Valrhona cocoa powder
10gm (½oz) Valrhona cocoa nibs
20ml (¾fl oz) olive oil
40ml (1½fl oz) sunflower oil

FOR THE MARINADE

1.5 litres (3¼ pints) red wine
40gm (1½oz) chopped onion
30gm (1oz) chopped carrot
30gm (1oz) chopped leek
2 garlic cloves, peeled
1 sprig of fresh rosemary
1 sprig of fresh thyme
5gm (¼oz) crushed black peppercorns

FOR THE VENISON

40gm (1½oz) Avonmore unsalted butter
20ml (¾fl oz) vegetable oil
2 racks of wild Wicklow Hills venison, French-trimmed

FOR THE FRESH CEPS

250gm (9oz) fresh ceps
50ml (2fl oz) Newgrange Gold rapeseed oil
30ml (1fl oz) Madeira
salt and freshly milled black pepper, to taste

FOR THE HONEYCOMB

100gm (3½oz) Jane Sellers honeycomb, cut into 6 even slices
6 baby spinach leaves, to garnish

SERVES 6

PICKLED STRAFFAN RED RHUBARB

Peel and slice the rhubarb into 4cm-long strips (1½in) and place in a bowl or large jar. Add the liquids to a pot and bring to the boil and then reduce the heat to simmer until the liquid is reduced by half. Pour the liquid over the rhubarb and cover with cling film, or a lid, and leave to cool. Store in the fridge overnight before using.

CHOCOLATE OIL

Place all the ingredients in a glass bowl over a pot of gently simmering water to allow them to melt slowly. Stir occasionally. Keep warm.

VENISON

Place all the marinade ingredients in a large pot and bring to the boil. Reduce the heat and simmer for 40 minutes, then remove from the heat to cool completely. Place the whole venison racks in a tray and cover the meat completely with the marinade. Cover with cling film and leave to marinate in the fridge for 8 hours. Remove the venison from the marinade, pat dry and transfer the racks into a vacuum-pack bag, season with a little salt and milled black pepper and seal. Place in a waterbath set to 60°C. Insert a needle probe into the centre of the meat and cook until the probe temperature reaches 56°C. Remove the venison from the bag and season well with salt and milled pepper.

CEPS

Trim the ceps and scrape off any debris from the stalks. Wash very gently with cold water and pat dry. Slice the ceps into strips lengthwise, about 3mm (1/10in) thick. Place the oil in a hot pan and fry the ceps very quickly. Deglaze the pan with Madeira. Season with salt and pepper to taste.

TO SERVE

Add the vegetable oil to a hot pan and seal the venison until it is golden brown on all sides. Whisk the chocolate oil well. Cut the venison racks into even-sized cutlets. Arrange the pickled rhubarb around the warm plate, with a piece of honeycomb placed on a spinach leaf. Neatly arrange the ceps on top of the venison. Drizzle the chocolate oil over.

JOHN DUNNE | BUTCHER

David Hicks set up Hicks Foods in 1983 with an aim to supply quality meats to order for a discerning range of clients in the catering industry. The company has since developed a sterling reputation for supplying the highest-quality meat sourced and selected from the Dawn Meats Group. The cutting, boning, rolling and portioning of the meat is prepared to the individual specification of the chefs they work with. 'We pride ourselves on maturing our beef in the traditional way in our purpose-built dry ageing room,' says Hicks butcher John Dunne. 'We were chuffed that our beef was used by Finbarr to create his Beef Tuath dish for the Ryder Cup teams.'

www.hicksfoods.ie

An Beef Tuath – Beef fillet, potato and garlic foam, roasted shallot and wild mushroom crown, and Bunratty mead sauce

When we hosted the Ryder Cup in 2006, Bord Bia asked me to come up with a dish that celebrated Irish beef for a special dinner to welcome both teams. This is the dish I created. The name came from the Department of Irish and Celtic Languages in Trinity College; they chose 'Beef Tuath' (meaning 'Beef of the Kingdom') to reflect the fact that the four main components of the dish represent the four provinces of Ireland.

WINE PAIRING

Marqués de Cáceres Gaudium

This is a stunning monster of a Spanish red. Why not French, you may ask, but the great thing about this wine is it exhibits French influence paired with Spanish style.

FOR THE BEEF

8 x 95gm (3½oz) pieces Irish beef fillet
salt and freshly milled black pepper

FOR THE POTATO FOAM

250gm (9oz) Maris Piper potatoes, peeled
55gm (2oz) crème fraîche
35gm (1¼oz) garlic confit (see page 55)
25ml (1fl oz) Avonmore milk
100ml (3½fl oz) vegetable stock (page 271)
salt and freshly milled black pepper, to taste

FOR THE GLAZED ORGANIC CARROTS

2 large organic carrots, peeled
250ml (9fl oz) chicken stock (see page 270)
50ml (2fl oz) Jane Sellers honey
50gm (2oz) unsalted butter
salt and freshly milled white pepper, to taste

FOR THE SHALLOT AND WILD MUSHROOM CROWN

28 shallots, peeled
40ml (1½fl oz) vegetable oil
1 sprig thyme
40gm (1½oz) butter
160gm (5½oz) cooked mixed wild mushrooms (morels, girolles, ceps or black trompettes)

FOR THE MEAD SAUCE
(makes approximately 100ml/3½fl oz)

10ml (½fl oz) vegetable oil
25gm (1oz) diced beef trim
40gm (1½oz) Jane Sellers honey
65ml (2½fl oz) Bunratty mead
15ml (½fl oz) cider vinegar
100ml (3½fl oz) veal jus (page 271)
65ml (2½fl oz) brown chicken stock (page 270)
salt and freshly milled black pepper

SERVES 4

THE BEEF

Season the beef with salt and freshly milled black pepper and then vacuum pack all eight pieces in one bag. Insert the fine needle probe directly into the middle of one fillet and place in a waterbath, set to 60°C. When the temperature probe in the meat hits 52°C, the meat is cooked medium-rare.

POTATO FOAM

Place the potatoes in 300ml (10fl oz) of water, season and cook until soft. Strain and keep 100ml (3½fl oz) of the cooking stock. Pass the potatoes through a fine sieve or moulie and keep warm. Place the mashed potato in a pot and add in the crème fraîche, garlic confit and the milk, then whisk together thoroughly until smooth. Gradually add the reserved potato cooking stock and mix to form a thick soup consistency. Bring the mix up to the boil and then transfer it into an ISI siphon bottle. Add one charger of ISI gas and leave to rest for one hour, shaking from time to time to work in the gas. Dispense when required.

GLAZED ORGANIC CARROTS

Peel down the carrots to 5cm (2in) in diameter. Cut each carrot into 4cm (1½in) lengths. Using a 3cm (1in) cutter, remove the centre of the carrot pieces to leave you with four 4cm x 5cm (1½in x 2in) cylindrical carrot shapes. Place the stock, honey and butter in a small pot and bring to the boil. Season with salt and milled white pepper to taste and reduce the heat to a simmer. Cook gently until the sauce is reduced by half to form a light glaze. Add in the carrot shapes and cook until soft, basting with the stock as you go.

SHALLOT AND WILD MUSHROOM CROWN

Seal the shallots in a hot pan with the oil until golden brown. Add in the butter and thyme and cook until soft. Drain and allow to cool. Grease four cylinder moulds (6cm deep x 5cm wide; 2½in deep x 2in wide) with a little butter. Line each mould with 7 cooked shallots, pointed end upwards, then fill the centre of each ring with the wild mushrooms, pressing the mix firmly in place. Transfer to the fridge to set for 1 hour. Place on a tray and transfer to a steam oven set to 90°C for 10–12 minutes. Remove and place directly on to kitchen paper to allow any excess liquid to drain off.

MEAD SAUCE

Preheat the oven to 150°C. Add the oil to a very hot pot and seal off the beef trim until it is nicely browned on all sides. Add the honey and caramelise the beef in the honey. Deglaze with the cider vinegar and mead. Lower the heat and allow the liquid to reduce by 80% and then add in the veal jus and brown chicken stock. Increase the heat until the liquid is just coming to the boil and then cover with a lid and transfer to the preheated oven. Allow to cook slowly until the liquid achieves a nice sauce consistency; this should take about 30 minutes. Pass the sauce through a fine sieve and muslin cloth. Repeat this process if necessary until you have a completely smooth sauce. Taste, and season if necessary.

TO SERVE

Remove the beef from the bag, season once more with salt and freshly milled black pepper. Heat a pan with clarified butter and quickly seal the beef on each side. Warm four plates. Place two beef medallions on each plate. Next, transfer the shallot crown to the plate and demould. Place one glazed carrot on the plate and fill the centre with the potato foam from the ISI bottle. Pour over the mead sauce and serve immediately.

TIP

The mead sauce is better if made a couple of days before you need it.

Slow-cooked Irish ox cheek and tongue, pickled girolles, Nolan's black pudding and Bunratty mead sauce

This dish is pure winter. I love braising, as it allows me to work with otherwise underused cuts of meat – and the effect is magic. I have also raided our preserves larder for the pickled girolles in this dish, but you can make them on the day if you need to. James Nolan is a butcher from Kilcullen. I grew up eating his black pudding and it has been great to see him win a number of awards in recent years.

WINE PAIRING

Barton & Guestier Château Magnol

This wine is predominantly Cabernet Sauvignon and has a richness and silkiness that complements the rich ox cheek. Try any good Bordeaux with this dish.

FOR THE PICKLED GIROLLES

200gm (7oz) fresh girolles
45ml (1½fl oz) champagne vinegar
25gm (1oz) sugar
250ml (9fl oz) water
½ star anise
¼ cinnamon stick
2 juniper berries
1 small bay leaf
1 small sprig of fresh thyme
1 small sprig of rosemary
2gm (½ tsp) yellow mustard seeds
2 whole cloves

FOR THE OX CHEEK

1 kg (2lb 3oz) Irish ox cheek
salt and freshly milled black pepper
30ml (1fl oz) vegetable oil
50gm (2oz) onion, chopped
1 celery stick, chopped
80gm (3oz) leek, chopped
80gm (3oz) carrot, chopped and peeled
1 sprig of fresh rosemary or thyme
4 garlic cloves, smashed with side of knife
3 litres (5 pints) brown veal stock (see page 270)
10 slices black Périgord truffle

FOR THE MEAD SAUCE

ox cheek trimmings, from above
salt and freshly milled black pepper
20ml (¾fl oz) vegetable oil
60gm (2oz) Jane Sellers honey
80ml (3fl oz) Bunratty mead
ox cheek cooking liquid, from above

FOR THE PICKLED OX TONGUE

1 pickled ox tongue
100gm (3½oz) carrots, roughly chopped
100gm (3½oz) onions, roughly chopped
50gm (2oz) celery, roughly chopped
½ garlic bulb, smashed with side of knife
1 bayleaf
100gm (3½oz) leeks, roughly chopped
10gm (½oz) crushed black peppercorns
5gm (¼oz) crushed coriander seeds
3 large sprigs of fresh thyme
5 litres (9 pints) chicken stock (see page 270)

FOR THE SPINACH PURÉE

500gm (17oz) baby spinach
100ml (3½fl oz) Avonmore cream
2 garlic cloves, peeled
pinch freshly grated nutmeg
salt and freshly milled black pepper
10ml (½fl oz) white truffle oil

FOR THE MOUSSELINE POTATOES

200gm (7oz) Maris Piper potatoes, peeled and chopped
180ml (6fl oz) Avonmore cream
40gm (1½oz) Avonmore unsalted butter
salt and freshly milled white pepper

FOR THE BLACK PUDDING

1 ring of Nolan's black pudding
20gm (¾oz) Avonmore unsalted butter
40 whole red grapes, peeled
100ml (3½fl oz) Bunratty mead

SERVES 10

PICKLED GIROLLES

Peel the stalks of the girolles lightly with a knife, wash very quickly in salted water, place on a cloth and dry well. Place all the other ingredients in a pot and bring the liquid up to the boil, then turn down to the lowest possible heat and leave to simmer for 15–20 minutes. Allow to cool completely. Place the girolles in a sterilised Kilner jar, or similar, and pour the pickling liquor over them. Close the lid and place the jar in a steamer for 15 minutes to seal. Preserve until required for use.

OX CHEEK

Preheat the oven to 160°C. Trim the ox cheeks to remove the extra meat around the daube. Retain the trimmings for the mead sauce below. Cut the daubes into 12 pieces (about 80gm/3oz each) and season with salt and milled black pepper. Seal in a hot pan with the vegetable oil until golden brown all over. Remove from the pan and pat dry. In the same pan, brown the chopped vegetable mirepoix and herbs. Add the veal stock and bring to the boil, then reduce to a simmer and cook until the liquid has reduced by a third. Add the seared ox cheeks to the pan, cover and transfer to the preheated oven for 3 hours, or until the meat is beautifully soft and tender. Once cooked, remove the ox cheek from the sauce and set aside to keep warm. Retain the cooking liquid to make the mead sauce.

MEAD SAUCE

Cut the ox cheek trimmings into 2cm (1in) chunks and season with salt and pepper. Add the oil to a hot pan and seal the trimmings until golden brown. Add the honey, stir to coat the meat and let it caramelise. Add the mead and cook until the liquid has reduced by half. Pour in the ox cheek cooking liquid and continue to cook until the sauce reaches a nice thick consistency that will coat the back of a spoon. Season to taste. Pass the sauce through a fine sieve and muslin cloth.

PICKLED OX TONGUE

Place all the ingredients in a large saucepan. Bring the liquid up to the boil and then reduce to a simmer. Allow to simmer away gently for 3½–4 hours, or until the tongue is completely tender. Remove the tongue from the stock and, while it is still hot, peel off the hard skin, then allow to cool. Slice the tongue into 2mm-thick (1/10in-thick) slices.

SPINACH PURÉE

Blanch the spinach by placing it in boiling, salted water for about 60 seconds and then cooling immediately in ice-cold water. Remove the spinach from the water and squeeze out all excess liquid. Place the cream, garlic and spinach in a saucepan over a medium heat and cook until the cream has thickened. Season with a generous pinch of grated nutmeg, and salt and pepper to taste. Put the mixture into a HotmixPRO blender (or similar) and blend until you achieve a very smooth finish. Finally, add the truffle oil. Once cool, scoop the mixture into a disposable piping bag and nick a 1cm (½in) hole in the nozzle of the bag.

TO ASSEMBLE THE TONGUE CANNELLONI

Lay out the sliced tongue and pipe a line of spinach along one edge. Wrap the tongue around the spinach and roll up to form a cylinder shape. Place the tongue on a tray, cover with cling film and steam for 8 minutes until hot.

MOUSSELINE POTATOES

Place the potatoes in a steamer and cook until soft, then pass through a fine sieve and keep warm. Place the cream in a large heavy-bottomed pan over a medium heat and allow it to reduce by 30%, then add the butter. Once the butter has melted into the cream, add the potato bit by bit and whisk vigorously to form a nice, runny purée. Season with salt and pepper to taste.

BLACK PUDDING

Preheat the oven to 160°C. Remove the outer skin from the black pudding and cut into 2cm (¾in)-thick slices. Grease an oven tray with the unsalted butter and place the pudding slices on top. Transfer to an oven preheated to 160°C and roast for 10 minutes, turning over after 5 minutes. Place a pan over a medium heat on the stove and add the grapes and mead. Cook until the grapes are soft. Remove from the heat and allow the grapes to cool.

TO SERVE

Put the ox cheeks and the mead sauce into a large pan over a medium heat and allow them to warm through, basting the meat continually with the sauce to glaze. To plate up, pour the mousseline into the centre of a warm serving dish. Place the ox cheek on top and then pour the mead sauce around it. Lay a slice of black truffle on top. Arrange the tongue cannelloni and black pudding, placing some grapes on top of the pudding. Draw a line of honey on the plate and sprinkle some pickled girolles over to serve.

Cutlet of aged Irish beef with bone marrow and Castlefarm cheese croûtons, and traditional Bordelaise sauce

This is a dish to be enjoyed in the heart of winter. For a time there we were not allowed to serve bone marrow, but now it's back and it's a joy to cook with, adding such a punch of flavour to any beef dish. The Bordelaise sauce is my tribute to classic, old-style sauce-making. It's far from easy to make but well worth the effort.

WINE PAIRING

La Réserve de Léoville-Barton 2008

Second wines from famous estates can offer great value in terms of quality winemaking. This one is connected to the estate, but any rich Saint-Julien Bordeaux would be perfect.

FOR THE BORDELAISE SAUCE

100gm (3½oz) shallots, finely chopped
1 sprig of thyme
1 garlic clove, peeled
200ml (7fl oz) red wine
150ml (5fl oz) veal jus (see page 271)
salt and freshly milled black pepper

FOR THE FONDANT POTATO

100ml (3½fl oz) brown veal stock (see page 270)
2 large potatoes
10ml (½fl oz) vegetable oil
1 small sprig of fresh thyme
1 small garlic clove, smashed

FOR THE BEEF

450gm (1lb) aged Irish cutlet of beef
1 sprig of fresh thyme
1 small sprig of fresh rosemary
1 garlic clove
20ml (¾fl oz) Newgrange Gold rapeseed oil
salt and freshly milled black pepper
20ml (¾fl oz) vegetable oil
50gm (2oz) Avonmore unsalted butter

FOR THE BELLY BACON LARDONS

50gm (2oz) Newbridge belly bacon
4 spring onions
20gm (¾oz) Avonmore unsalted butter

FOR THE BONE MARROW CROÛTONS

1 whole bone marrow
10gm (½oz) crème fraîche
1 sprig of fresh flat-leaf parsley, chopped
salt and freshly milled black pepper
2 slices white soda bread
5ml (¼fl oz) Newgrange Gold rapeseed oil
10gm (½oz) Castlefarm cheese, grated

SERVES 2–3

BORDELAISE SAUCE

Mix the shallots, thyme, garlic and wine together in a bowl; cover and leave to infuse for 24 hours. Then transfer to a pot and bring to the boil, reduce the heat and simmer until the liquid has been reduced by 70%. Slowly add the veal jus to the liquid and continue to cook over a low heat until the sauce is reduced to a lovely dark sauce consistency. Season with salt and milled black pepper to taste. Set aside to keep warm.

FONDANT POTATO

Preheat the oven to 160°C. Add the brown veal stock to a pot and boil until reduced by half. Top and tail each potato and cut them lengthwise into 6 even wedges. Take each piece and peel and turn it until you have shaped each one into even oval shapes. Place the oil in a hot frying pan and seal the potatoes until golden brown on each side. Drain off any excess oil from the pan and then add the thyme, garlic and reduced stock and transfer to the preheated oven for about 10 minutes until the potato is soft and cooked through but still holding its shape. The stock should be very syrupy and coat the potatoes nicely. Season with salt and pepper to taste. Set aside to keep warm.

THE BEEF

Place the cutlet with the herbs, garlic and rapeseed oil in a vacuum-pack bag and season and seal. Transfer to a waterbath set to 62°C. Place a needle probe directly into the centre of the beef and cook until the probe reaches 60°C. Remove the beef from the bag and season again with salt and pepper.

BELLY BACON LARDONS

Cut the bacon into 2cm x 3cm (¾in x 1¼in) lardons. Melt the butter in pan over a medium heat, add the lardons and fry off until turning golden brown, then add the spring onion for the last minute to brown a little. Drain off excess fat and set aside to keep warm.

BONE MARROW CROÛTONS

Preheat the oven to 160°C. Place the bone marrow in a bowl and roughly crush it with a fork. Add the crème fraîche and parsley and season with a little salt and milled black pepper. Brush the soda bread with the rapeseed oil and toast it in the preheated oven until golden brown and crisp. Remove and allow to cool.

TO SERVE

To finish the beef, heat the vegetable oil in a very hot pan and seal the cutlet on each side until golden brown. Add the unsalted butter and let it foam, then baste the beef with the nutty butter for 2 minutes. Using a spoon, top each croûton with the marrow mix and a sprinkle of cheese. Place under a hot grill to cook until golden brown. Arrange the potatoes, spring onions and belly bacon lardons neatly in the centre of a warm serving bowl. Place the cutlet on top and then the bone marrow croûtons. Bring to the table and carve the cutlet in even slices, place on a warm plate with some of the garnish and pour over the warm Bordelaise sauce from a sauce boat.

Mallard duck breast with braised leg, potato blini, wild Carbury blackberries and Dingle Gin gimlet sorbet

The best part of this dish for me is the braised leg. With all the modern techniques we have introduced in the kitchen, we still braise the old-fashioned way and I love the depth of flavour you get as a result. Carbury is the name of the parish in County Kildare where I live. Every season, I pick kilos of blackberries to bring into the kitchen. For me, wild blackberries and duck are a match made in heaven. The Dingle Gin used here is my nod to the new – it comes from a recently established craft distillery based in Kerry.

WINE PAIRING

O'Dwyer Cabernet Sauvignon, Clare Valley, Australia

This benchmark Aussie Cabernet Sauvignon is full of rich blackberry fruit and a good dollop of eucalyptus. It is perfect with the richness of the mallard. And it's an Irish-owned vineyard to boot.

FOR THE DINGLE GIN GIMLET SORBET

200ml (7fl oz) Dingle Original Gin
100ml (3½fl oz) fresh lime juice
30ml (1fl oz) sorbitol

FOR THE PICKLED CUCUMBER SLICE

1 cucumber
10ml (½fl oz) rice wine vinegar
2gm (½ tsp) sel de Guérande
2gm (½ tsp) chopped fresh dill

FOR THE MALLARD

4 wild mallard
50 wild blackberries
20ml (¾fl oz) rapeseed oil
4 sprigs of fresh thyme
salt and freshly milled black pepper

FOR THE STOCK

4 mallard carcasses
2 litres (3½) brown chicken stock (see page 270)

FOR THE LEGS

8 mallard legs, from above
20ml (¾fl oz) vegetable oil
salt and freshly milled black pepper
30gm (1oz) chopped onion
30gm (1oz) chopped leek
20gm (¾oz) chopped celery
30gm (1oz) chopped carrot
1 garlic clove
4 juniper berries
10 crushed black peppercorns
1 small sprig each of fresh sage and thyme
1 small bay leaf
mallard stock, from above

FOR THE POTATO BLINIS

2 free-range eggs, separated
18gm (½oz) yeast
130ml (4fl oz) Avonmore milk, gently warmed
55gm (2oz) baked potato
55gm (2oz) strong flour
salt and freshly milled white pepper
20ml (¾fl oz) clarified butter

SERVES 8

DINGLE GIN GIMLET SORBET

Place the gin in a pot and warm. Flame off the alcohol, then add the lime juice and sorbitol. Place in Taurus Rowzer beaker and freeze. Then blitz when required. Alternatively, place in an ice cream machine and churn for 20 minutes and then freeze.

PICKLED CUCUMBER SLICE

Peel the cucumber and slice it lengthways – about 2mm (1⁄10in) thick. Place the slices on a small tray and mix with the rice vinegar, dill and salt. Leave to marinate for 30 minutes. Remove the cucumber and wash off the marinade. Keep refrigerated for service.

THE MALLARD

Remove the legs and breasts carefully from the carcasses. Place the breasts in a vacuum-pack bag with the rapeseed oil, thyme and seasoning. Seal and place a fine needle probe in the centre of one breast. Cook in the waterbath, set to 60°C, until the needle probe reaches 54°C. Remove the meat from the bag, season with salt and milled black pepper and set aside.

THE STOCK

Preheat the oven to 160°C. Chop the carcasses into small pieces. Place on a tray and brown in the preheated oven for about 20 minutes, or until golden brown. Drain off any excess fat and place the carcasses in a large pot with the brown chicken stock. Bring to the boil and leave to simmer for 4 hours on a low heat. Skim off the fat as it rises, to keep the stock clear. Check for a good strong flavour before passing through a fine sieve.

THE LEGS & THE SAUCE

Preheat the oven to 140°C. Season the legs with salt and milled black pepper. Pour the vegetable oil into a hot pan and cook the legs, skin-side down, until golden brown. Turn them over and quickly seal the other side, then remove from the pan and set aside. Add the mirepoix (vegetable and herb mix) to the pan and cook until golden. Deglaze the pan with a little mallard stock. Place the legs in the pot and cover with stock. Cover with a disc of parchment paper and cook in the preheated oven until the legs are nice and tender. Remove the legs from the stock and keep warm. Pass the sauce through a fine sieve and muslin cloth and set aside for service.

POTATO BLINIS

Add the yeast to the egg yolks and dissolve. Add the warm milk and warm potato, then sieve in the strong flour and whisk well. Whisk the egg whites in a clean, dry bowl until they form soft peaks, then fold them into the batter. Season to taste. Heat the clarified butter in a non-stick pan. Place 7cm (3in) rings in the hot pan, spoon the batter into them and cook until golden brown on each side. Once cooked, set aside to keep warm.

TO SERVE

In a hot pan, seal the mallard, skin-side down, until golden brown. Place the cucumber diagonally across the warm plate and quenelle the sorbet on top. Spoon the sauce to one side of the cucumber. Slice the breast in two and place a half either side of the cucumber. Position the potato blini with the braised leg on top. Arrange the blackberries around the plate. Finish with a sprinkle of fresh thyme leaves.

JOHNNY LYNCH | BUFFALO DAIRY FARMER

'It might surprise you to learn,' begins Johnny Lynch, 'that, although buffalo are a familiar sight in India and Italy, they actually can't stand the heat. They much prefer a cooler climate and they love rain.' So, needless to say, Johnny's 172-strong herd of buffalo based in Macroom, County Cork, are a very happy bunch. They calve all year round, supplying Johnny with a constant flow of milk, which he uses to make 1200 kilos of cheese a week – with the vital input of skilled local cheesemaker Sean Ferry. 'We produce Irish buffalo mozzarella, halloumi, ricotta and feta. Cheesemaking begins each morning at 4.30am and the cheese is made by 1pm and ready for delivery to our chefs. So it's about as fresh as you can get.' You'll find Macroom Buffalo Mozzarella on the menu at The K Club.

www.macroombuffalocheese.com

Glazed wild pheasant breast with homemade sausage, lemon and thyme paint and pear and cranberry sorbet

Every part of the pheasant is used in this classic winter dish; nothing is wasted. The white carrot purée adds further comfort to the earthy flavour of the game. Then the citrus-infused paint gives everything a lift, while the sweet pear works beautifully with the tartness of the cranberry.

WINE PAIRING

Louis Jadot Pommard
Premier Cru 1999

Game and Pinot are great bedfellows. The slight farmyard quality of a good Pinot goes really well with game and works with the tart cranberry here perfectly.

FOR THE PEAR AND CRANBERRY SORBET

100gm (3½oz) pear purée (we use Boiron or Ravifruit)
70gm (2½oz) cranberry purée (we use Boiron or Ravifruit)
40gm (1½oz) sugar syrup (see page 271)
40ml (1½floz) water
25ml (1fl oz) sorbitol

FOR THE PEAR TUILE

1 pear
50ml (2fl oz) sugar syrup (see page 271)

FOR THE LEMON AND THYME PAINT

100gm (3½oz) caster sugar
50ml (2fl oz) fresh squeezed lemon juice
40ml (1½fl oz) water
zest of ½ lemon
1 pinch dried thyme

FOR THE PHEASANT

2 whole wild pheasants
salt and freshly milled black pepper
10ml (½fl oz) Newgrange Gold rapeseed oil
1 sprig of fresh thyme

FOR THE PHEASANT SAUSAGE

100ml (3½fl oz) white wine
15gm (½oz) finely chopped onion
20gm (¾oz) finely chopped carrot
15gm (½oz) finely chopped celery
15gm (½oz) finely chopped leek
½ garlic clove
1 small sprig of fresh thyme
7–8 needles of fresh rosemary, pulled from the stalk
200gm (7oz) leg meat
20gm (¾oz) barley
20gm (¾oz) golden raisins, pre-soaked overnight
5gm (¼oz) finely chopped fresh sage
30g (1oz) natural hog casings, from a good butcher
salt and freshly milled black pepper
20ml (¾fl oz) clarified butter (see page 272)

FOR THE WHITE CARROT PURÉE

15gm (½oz) Avonmore unsalted butter
10gm (½oz) chopped shallots
100gm (3½oz) white carrots, peeled and diced
50ml (2fl oz) white chicken stock (see page 270)
50ml (2fl oz) Avonmore cream
salt and freshly milled white pepper

FOR THE BRUSSELS SPROUT LEAVES

10gm (½oz) Avonmore unsalted butter
20 Brussels sprout leaves
salt and freshly milled white pepper

SERVES 4

PEAR AND CRANBERRY SORBET

Mix all the ingredients together and place in a Taurus Rowzer beaker and freeze. Then blitz when required. Alternatively, place in an ice cream machine and churn for 20 minutes and then freeze.

PEAR TUILE

Preheat the oven to 90°C. Slice the pear lengthways into 2mm-thick (1/10in) slices. Dip the slices in the sugar syrup. Lay a non-stick Silpat mat (or similar) on a baking tray and arrange the pear slices on the mat. Transfer to the oven for about 90 minutes, or until the slices have crisped up. Remove and store in an airtight container until required.

LEMON AND THYME PAINT

Mix all the ingredients together in a saucepan, place over the heat and bring up to the boil. Allow to cook and reduce until it forms a nice syrup. Cool and refrigerate for service.

THE PHEASANT

Carefully remove the breast and legs from the carcass. De-bone the legs, remove the skin and set the meat aside to make the sausage later. Season the breasts with salt and milled black pepper, rub with the rapeseed oil and put them into a vacuum-pack bag with the fresh thyme and seal. Place a fine needle probe into one of the breasts and cook in a waterbath, set to 70°C, until the probe reaches 67°C. Remove the breasts from the bag and pat dry.

PHEASANT SAUSAGE

Place the white wine, carrot, onion, leek, celery, garlic, thyme and rosemary in a pot over a high heat and bring up to the boil, then remove from the heat and allow to cool. Place the leg meat in a bowl, pour this liquid over and mix well. Leave to marinate for 2 hours. Remove and drain the meat and push through a fine mincer. Mix the minced meat with the barley, golden raisins and sage. Transfer the mixture to a piping bag fitted with a 2cm (3/4in) plain nozzle. Tie one end of the hog casing and attach the other end to the piping bag nozzle, then push the mixture through. Twist the long sausage into 4 even-sized sausage shapes. Cut and tie the ends of each of the 4 sausages. Place the sausages in a vacuum-pack bag and stick the needle probe into the centre of one sausage. Cook in a waterbath, set to 74°C, until the probe reaches 72°C. Remove the sausages from the bag, pat dry and season with salt and freshly milled black pepper.

WHITE CARROT PURÉE

Melt the unsalted butter in a saucepan over a low to medium heat. Add the chopped shallots and cook until softened but not coloured. Add the diced white carrot, chicken stock and cream and cook until the carrot is soft. Put the mixture into a HotmixPRO blender (or similar) and blend on high until smooth. Set aside to keep warm.

BRUSSELS SPROUT LEAVES

Melt the unsalted butter in a pan over a medium heat, add the Brussels sprout leaves and cook briefly until just wilted. Season and then set aside to keep warm.

TO SERVE

To finish the pheasant breasts, place a frying pan over a high heat, add a dash of oil and seal the breasts in the pan, skin-side down, until golden brown. Finish the pheasant sausages by adding the clarified butter to the pan and quickly frying the sausages until golden brown. Paint a generous line of lemon and thyme paint down the centre of a warmed plate. Baste a pheasant breast with some of the paint and then cut the breast in half lengthways and place on the plate. Add a spoon of white carrot purée to the plate and then drag the spoon through the purée. Place a sausage on top. Place a pear crisp next to the breast meat. Add a quenelle of pear and cranberry sorbet and finish with a sprinkling of wilted Brussels sprout leaves.

SAM COURTNEY | K CLUB BUTCHER

Wild native hare, braised salsify, liver and heart farce, potato mousseline and micro-sorrel

I found this recipe one of the hardest to commit to paper, due to the detail needed to explain the preparation of the hare. When you prepare the hare in this way, you get a true appreciation for what a beautifully formed animal it is. My parents would have been reared on hare and rabbit and I would have eaten it quite often as a child, but simply boiled and roasted. This version is my tribute to a wonderful rural Irish ingredient.

WINE PAIRING

Jean-Louis Chavy Puligny-Montrachet Premier Cru Burgundy

You've got to bring out the big guns for this dish. Puligny, which is rich yet elegant, can enhance this hare and leave you with food memories for years.

FOR THE HARE

2 wild hare, skinned
salt and freshly milled black pepper
2 sprigs of fresh thyme
40ml (1½fl oz) Newgrange Gold rapeseed oil

FOR THE STOCK

2 hare carcasses, from above, and all trimmings
2 litres (3½ pints) brown chicken stock (see page 270)

FOR THE LEGS

4 wild hare legs, from above
salt and freshly milled black pepper
20ml (¾fl oz) vegetable oil
hare stock, from above
30gm (1oz) chopped onion
30gm (1oz) chopped leek
20gm (¾oz) chopped celery
30gm (1oz) chopped carrot
1 garlic clove, bashed
4 juniper berries
10 crushed black peppercorns
1 small sprig of fresh sage and thyme
1 small bay leaf
fine lemon zest, to garnish

FOR THE LIVER AND HEART FARCE

wild hare hearts, livers and kidneys, from above
salt and freshly milled black pepper
20ml (¾fl oz) clarified butter (see page 272)
25ml (1fl oz) Madeira
25gm (1oz) Avonmore unsalted butter
25gm (1oz) finely chopped shallot
¼ clove garlic, finely chopped
3 leaves of fresh sage, chopped
1gm (¼ tsp) mace, pounded

FOR THE MOUSSELINE POTATOES

200gm (7oz) Maris Piper potatoes, peeled and chopped
180ml (6fl oz) Avonmore cream
40gm (1½oz) Avonmore unsalted butter
salt and freshly milled white pepper

FOR THE BRAISED SALSIFY

25ml (1fl oz) clarified butter (see page 272)
8 sticks of salsify, peeled and cut in half
200ml (7fl oz) chicken stock (see page 270)
½ garlic clove
1 sprig of fresh thyme
30gm (1oz) Avonmore unsalted butter
salt and freshly milled white pepper

TO SERVE

2 fresh micro-sorrel leaves

SERVES 4

TO PREPARE THE HARE

Before you start to prepare the hare, it is very important to note that all the trimmed meat and bones are set aside and retained for the stock. To begin, remove the insides from each hare. Retain the heart, liver and kidneys and set aside to make the farce. Remove the front legs, double rack, whole saddle and back legs. Chop the front legs and the remaining carcass into small chunks. Take the double rack and chop the ribcage bones on each side, leaving the bones about 6cm (2½in) in length. Then chop each side of the centre bone to leave 2 individual racks. Cut along the edge of the eye of the meat and the bone of each rack, and with your hand push down the ribcage meat to leave the bones exposed. Clean and trim off excess rib meat to leave a trimmed rack. Place the 4 racks flat in a vacuum-pack bag and season with a little milled black pepper and salt, a small sprig of fresh thyme, plus 10ml (½fl oz) of the rapeseed oil and seal. Place a fine needle probe in the centre of one of the racks and transfer to a waterbath set to 58°C. Cook until the needle probe reaches 52°C, then remove the racks from the bag and season with salt and

milled black pepper. Seal each rack very quickly in a hot pan with 10ml (½fl oz) rapeseed oil – you want to sear the outside but not colour the lovely pink meat inside.
Next remove any excess trim from the double saddles and place the saddles in a vacuum-pack bag. Season with a little milled black pepper and salt, a small sprig of fresh thyme and 10ml (½fl oz) of the rapeseed oil and seal. Place a fine needle probe in the centre of one of the saddles and transfer to a waterbath set to 58°C. Cook until the needle probe reaches 52°C. Remove the saddles from the bag, season with a little milled black pepper and salt and seal very quickly in a hot pan with the remaining 10ml (½fl oz) rapeseed oil until golden brown on each side.

HARE STOCK

Preheat an oven to 160°C. Chop the hare carcasses into small pieces. Place on a baking tray and transfer to the preheated oven for about 20 minutes, or until golden brown. Drain off the excess fat and place the bones in a pot with the brown chicken stock. Bring to the boil, then reduce to a low simmer for 4 hours. Skim off the fat as it rises to the top, to keep the stock clear. Check for a good strong flavour before passing through a fine sieve.

THE LEGS

Preheat an oven to 140°C. Cut the legs into 3cm (1in)-thick slices, cutting through the bone with a cleaver or heavy chopping knife as you would for osso buco. Retain the excess trimmings for the stock. Season the legs with salt and milled black pepper. Pour the oil into a hot ovenproof pan and place the legs in the pan, skin-side down, and cook until golden brown. Turn the legs over and quickly seal the other side, then remove them from the pan and set aside. Add the mirepoix (chopped vegetables and herbs) to the pan and cook until golden. Deglaze with a little stock. Return the legs to the pan and pour over just enough stock to cover them. Cover with a disc of parchment paper and transfer the pan to the oven and cook until the legs are nice and tender (about 90 minutes). Then remove the legs from the stock and keep them warm. Pass the stock through a fine sieve and muslin cloth and keep for service. The sauce should be a nice smooth consistency. If not, simply put it back over the heat and reduce until you achieve the desired consistency.

LIVER AND HEART FARCE

Season the hearts, livers and kidneys with salt and milled black pepper. Add the clarified butter to a very hot pan and flash-fry the offal for about 30 seconds on each side. Deglaze with the Madeira. Be careful not to overcook the offal; you want to keep everything pink. Once cooked, roughly chop up the mixture to form a coarse farce. Melt the unsalted butter in a pot over a low heat, add the finely chopped shallots and garlic with a little pinch of salt and cover with a lid. Sweat the shallots for a few minutes without letting them colour, then add the fresh sage and mace and cook for 4 minutes. Add this mixture to the meat farce and season if needed with salt and milled black pepper.

MOUSSELINE POTATOES

Place the potatoes in a steamer and cook until soft, then pass through a fine sieve and keep warm. Place the cream in a large heavy-bottomed pot over a medium heat and allow it to reduce by 30%, then add the butter. Once the butter has melted into the cream, add the potato, bit by bit, and whisk vigorously to form a nice, runny purée. Season with salt and pepper to taste.

BRAISED SALSIFY

Preheat an oven to 140°C. Place the clarified butter in a hot ovenproof pan and seal the salsify until it is golden brown. Add the chicken stock, garlic, fresh thyme and unsalted butter and bring to the boil. Then half cover the pan and transfer it to the oven to braise for 30 minutes, or until the salsify is nice and tender. Remove the salsify from the stock and set aside to keep warm.

TO SERVE

Remove the loin from the saddle of hare and cut each loin lengthways. Place the salsify on a warmed plate. Spoon on some mousseline potato and place the braised hare leg on the bed of mousseline and top with a sprinkle of lemon zest. Add a quenelle of the warm offal farce. Cut the racks into 3 pieces and place each one neatly on the plate. Place the loin on top of the salsify and pour over the braising sauce. Garnish with wild micro-sorrel.

Fennel and pear tart with piccalilli, fennel foam and pear tuile

This vegetarian dish is beautiful to look at and even better to taste. The homemade piccalilli for me is the star – with its fresh, tangy flavour, it adds great zip to the dish. I love the buttery pastry against the earthy pear and fennel. When you pair a fruit and vegetable together, the natural sugars in the fruit really work to enhance the flavour of the vegetable.

WINE PAIRING

Baron de Ley Rioja Reserva

I'm a Spanish girl at heart and I love this wine. It's soft, earthy and spicy and perfect with the aniseed flavours of the fennel in this fabulous veggie dish.

FOR THE POACHED VICTORIAN GARDEN PEARS

500ml (17fl oz) water
50gm (2oz) caster sugar
4 whole Victorian Garden pears, peeled and cored

FOR THE PICCALILLI

brine, made by dissolving 85gm (3oz) salt in 250ml (9fl oz) water
110gm (4oz) baby onions, peeled and halved
110gm (4oz) small cauliflower florets
3gm (¾ tsp) ground ginger
3gm (¾ tsp) ground turmeric
3gm (¾ tsp) mustard seeds
5gm (¼oz) Pommery mustard
190ml (7fl oz) cider vinegar
45gm (1½oz) demerara sugar
½ garlic clove, chopped
110gm (4oz) red pepper, deseeded
110gm (4oz) gherkins, chopped
3–5gm (¼oz) arrowroot, dissolved in a little water

FOR THE FENNEL JUICE FOAM

300ml (10fl oz) fennel bulb, juiced
3gm (¼oz) xanthan gum

FOR THE BRAISED FENNEL BULB

1 fennel bulb
150ml (5fl oz) fish stock
½ tsp fennel seeds
1 sprig of fresh thyme
½ bay leaf

FOR THE FENNEL BULB PURÉE

1 fennel bulb, finely chopped
400ml (14fl oz) Avonmore cream
50gm (2oz) fresh dill
salt and milled white pepper

FOR THE PEAR TUILE DISCS

200ml (7fl oz) sugar syrup (see page 271)
1 pear

FOR THE TARTS

300gm (10oz) puff pastry
poached pears, from above
braised fennel bulb, from above
egg wash

TO SERVE

6 baby turnips, peeled and halved and cooked al dente, to garnish
2 baby leeks, blanched, to garnish
12 edible nasturtium flowers, to garnish

MAKES 6

POACHED VICTORIAN GARDEN PEARS

Place the water and the caster sugar in a pot over a low heat and gently warm to dissolve the sugar. Add the pears, so that they are covered with the syrup. Let the liquid lightly simmer to poach the pears until just soft. Remove from the heat and allow to cool. Cut each pear in three lengthways, then cut each wedge into 6 slices.

PICCALILLI

Place the onions and cauliflower in the salt water brine and leave for 1 hour. Remove from the water and pat dry. Place the ground ginger, ground turmeric and mustard seeds in a pot and heat gently to release their flavour. Remove from the heat and add the Pommery mustard, garlic, cider vinegar and demerara sugar to the dry mix. Add the cauliflower, baby onions, red peppers and gherkins to the pickle and cook until very slightly softened. Thicken the mixture with the dissolved arrowroot and allow to cool.

FENNEL JUICE FOAM

Boil the fennel juice in a pot. Add the xanthan gum and pass through a fine sieve. Pour into a siphon bottle, charge with two ISI gas chargers, shake vigorously and set aside in the fridge for service.

BRAISED FENNEL BULB

Cut the fennel bulb into 6 pieces. Place in a vacuum-pack bag with the remaining ingredients. Seal and cook in a steamer for 30 minutes.

FENNEL BULB PURÉE

Place the fennel in a pot and cover with the cream. Season with a little salt and milled white pepper. Bring to the boil and then reduce to simmer until the fennel bulb is soft. Blitz the mixture with the fresh dill in a HotmixPRO blender or similar until smooth. Season to taste.

PEAR TUILE DISCS

Preheat the oven to 95°C. Finely slice the pear on a slicer or mandolin. Cut out 4cm (1½in) discs of pear from the slices and place them in the sugar syrup. Line a baking tray with a Silpat or similar non-stick mat and lay the pear discs out flat. Cook in the preheated oven for 45 minutes. Remove the discs from the tray and allow to cool. Store in an airtight container.

TO ASSEMBLE THE TARTS

Roll out the puff pastry to form a 3mm (⅒in)-thick sheet. Refrigerate for 30 minutes to allow the pastry to rest. Cut out twelve 10cm (4in) discs using a plain pastry cutter. Take 6 of the discs and, using an 8cm (3in) cutter, remove the centre of each of them (retaining the outer rim). Egg-wash the edge of the six 10cm (4in) bases and lay the outer 10cm (4in) rims on top. Inside the rim, place the poached pear slices on one half and the braised fennel on the other. Finish by egg-washing the rim. Place the 6 tarts on a Silpat or similar non-stick mat and refrigerate for a minimum of 20 minutes to rest before cooking. Preheat the oven to 170°C. Place the tarts in the oven for 18 minutes.

TO SERVE

Lay a row of piccalilli neatly on one side of the plate and add the turnip and baby leeks to garnish. Place the pear tuile discs on top and finish with nasturtium flowers. Make a neat circle of the hot fennel purée on the plate and place the tart on top. Place 3 dots of the fennel juice foam on the piccalilli and serve.

PAUDIE SPILLANE | FISH SUPPLIER

Paudie Spillane worked with the Killarney Mountain Rescue Team for fourteen years, so, when it comes to rising to a challenge, you can be sure he won't shy away. 'When Finbarr calls me up and says he needs some wild Atlantic turbot or the best crab I can get my hands on, I get a great kick out of making sure we impress him every time,' says Paudie, with his trademark dynamic energy. Spillane's Seafood was founded by Paudie's parents, Michael and Finola, in 1973 and the family have built the business up to be one of Ireland's best, supplying fresh and fresh-frozen fish to restaurants and hotels across Ireland. They also run their own fish smokery on site and export their artisan smoked salmon all over the world.

www.spillaneseafoods.com

Little igloo of chestnut and eggnog custard

This dish has made the front cover of magazines. People love it. A pastry chef, Ann Bradley, who was with us back in the early days created the first version of this dish with the igloo shape and over the years we have played around with new fillings. It comes on and off the menu, but it's so popular we can't keep it off for long. We made it for 200 people once, which I can only say we won't be doing again!

FOR THE WHITE SPONGE

125ml (4½fl oz) beaten egg mix
65gm (2¼oz) caster sugar
65gm (2¼oz) plain flour

FOR THE CHESTNUT PARFAIT

3 free-range egg yolks
40gm (1½ oz) caster sugar
65gm (2¼oz) chestnut purée
250gm (9oz) Avonmore cream, whipped

FOR THE KIRSCH JELLY

62ml (2¼fl oz) kirsch
15ml (½fl oz) water
12gm (½oz) caster sugar
5gm (¼oz) gelatine (1 leaf), soaked in water
5ml (¼fl oz) lemon juice

FOR THE EGGNOG CUSTARD

1 free-range egg
2 free-range egg yolks
1 tbsp sugar syrup (see page 271)
90ml (3fl oz) milk
30ml (1fl oz) brandy
30ml (1fl oz) dark rum

FOR THE SUGAR SPIRAL

50gm (2oz) isomalt
droplet yellow food colouring

FOR THE MERINGUE

50gm (2oz) free-range egg white
65gm (2¼oz) caster sugar

12 griottine cherries, to garnish

SERVES 4

WHITE SPONGE

Preheat the oven to 170°C. Whisk the eggs and sugar until the mixture reaches ribbon stage (nice thick foam). Fold in the sieved flour slowly, bit by bit, then pour out on to a parchment-lined, flat baking tray and bake in the preheated oven for 7 minutes. Leave to cool and cut out four 8cm-diameter (3in) discs.

CHESTNUT PARFAIT

Whisk the egg yolks to sabayon or ribbon stage. Bring the sugar to the soft boil stage and pour it over the egg yolks. Whisk until cold. Add the chestnut purée and mix well to combine. Fold in the whipped cream. Pour the mixture into four 8cm (3in)-diameter dome-shaped flexiform moulds. Top with an 8cm (3in) disc of white sponge. Cover and store in the freezer overnight.

KIRSCH JELLY

Put all the ingredients into a pot and bring up to the boil. Remove from the heat. Squeeze any excess water from the gelatine and then add to the pot and whisk until dissolved. Line an ice-cube tray with cling film and fill with the jelly mix. Cover and transfer to the fridge to set.

EGGNOG CUSTARD

Whisk the egg and egg yolks together with the sugar syrup. In a separate pot, bring the milk, rum and brandy to the boil. Add the warm milk mixture to the egg mixture and whisk. Cook over a gentle heat to form a nice thick sauce. Leave to cool and keep refrigerated until ready to serve.

SUGAR SPIRAL

Melt the isomalt in a pot over a low heat. When it is completely melted, you can add the droplet of yellow food colouring. Leave to cool a little and then pour out on to a tray and work it with your hands while it is still warm until it becomes elastic. Wrap it around a 1cm (½in) tube (we use a steel) in a spiral fashion. Once set, remove carefully and set aside to serve.

MERINGUE

Whisk the egg whites a little to break them up. Add the sugar in three stages, whisking as you go. Whisk until the mixture forms stiff peaks. Remove the parfait moulds from the freezer and demould. Pipe the meringue mix immediately on to the set parfait and smooth it with a palette knife to form a dome shape. Fill a small piping bag with the meringue mixture and add the 'igloo' design to the dome.

TO SERVE

Transfer the igloo to a serving plate and brown the meringue gently with a blowtorch, moving rapidly. Dot the custard to the side of the igloo and drag through with a spoon. Place 3 griottine cherries and 3 cubes of kirsch jelly on the plate. Place the sugar spiral in the top of the igloo dome and serve.

KEVIN McGRATTAN | SOUS CHEF

Warm Baileys and chocolate chip soufflé

I am a big fan of runny soufflés. The way to eat this dessert is to scoop out your first mouthful, then pop the ice cream into the hollow and simply luxuriate in the combination of the hot, rich soufflé and the cold ice cream. Desserts don't get much better than this.

FOR THE PASTRY CREAM

8 free-range egg yolks
55gm (2oz) caster sugar
25gm (1oz) flour
20gm (¾oz) cornflour
15gm (½oz) cocoa powder
500ml (17fl oz) Avonmore milk

FOR THE MERINGUE

500gm (17oz) egg white
250gm (9oz) caster sugar

FOR THE SOUFFLÉ

cocoa powder, for dusting moulds
caster sugar, for dusting moulds
500gm (17oz) pastry cream, from above
100ml (3½fl oz) Baileys Irish Cream
75gm (2½oz) chocolate chips
400gm (14oz) meringue, from above

TO SERVE

vanilla ice cream (see page 276)
chocolate sauce (see page 214)

SERVES 5

PASTRY CREAM

Whisk the egg yolks and sugar together. Sieve the flour, cornflour and cocoa powder and whisk into the egg mix. In a small pot bring the milk to the boil and pour it into the egg mixture. Transfer everything back into the pot and cook over a medium heat, mixing constantly, until the cream thickens. Remove from the heat and allow to cool.

MERINGUE

Place the egg whites and sugar into a mixing bowl and whisk until the mixture will hold a stiff peak.

SOUFFLÉ

Preheat the oven to 200°C. Grease five 10cm (4in) soufflé moulds with butter. Dust with a mix of cocoa powder and caster sugar. Beat the pastry cream, Baileys and chocolate chips together. Add 100gm (3½oz) of the meringue mix and beat well. Gently fold in the remaining meringue mix. Fill the moulds to the rim and level off with a knife, then run your clean thumb around the rim of the mould. Place in the preheated oven and bake for 18 minutes.

TO SERVE

Serve the soufflé immediately, with a quenelle of vanilla ice cream and some chocolate sauce on the side.

Warm Victorian Garden pear with chocolate frangipane, granita and pear air

I love to serve these warm pears in autumn – the frangipane in the middle when you cut into the pear is a lovely surprise and gives the dish an extra layer. The contrast of the warm pear and the cold granita really gets your taste buds going and adds an extra layer of decadence to the dish.

FOR THE PEAR GRANITA

100gm (3½oz) pear purée (we use Boiron or Ravifruit)
30gm (1oz) sugar syrup (see page 271)
40ml (1½fl oz) water
20ml (¾fl oz) Pear William liqueur

FOR THE CHOCOLATE FRANGIPANE

60gm (2oz) caster sugar
55gm (2oz) ground almonds
6gm (¼oz) Valrhona cocoa powder
6gm (¼oz) plain flour
60gm (2oz) Avonmore unsalted butter
1 egg

FOR THE POACHED PEARS

6 Victorian Garden pears
2 litres (3½ pints) sugar syrup (see page 271)

FOR THE PEAR CONE

85gm (3oz) caster sugar
65gm (2¼oz) pear purée (we use Boiron or Ravifruit)
37gm (1¼oz) strong flour
25ml (1fl oz) olive oil
12gm (½oz) Avonmore unsalted butter, softened

FOR THE PEAR AIR

75gm (2½oz) pear purée (we use Boiron or Ravifruit)
125ml (4½fl oz) water
2–3gm (½ tsp) lecithin

FOR THE CHOCOLATE SAUCE

60gm (2oz) Avonmore cream
70ml (2½fl oz) water
30gm (1oz) Valrhona cocoa powder
90gm (3oz) sugar
3gm (½ leaf) gelatine leaf, soaked in water

MAKES 6

PEAR GRANITA

Mix all the ingredients together in a bowl. Transfer the mixture to a flat tray lined with parchment paper and spread it out. Place the tray in the freezer and scrape with a fork frequently while freezing to encourage the mixture to form crystals. Store the granita in the freezer until needed.

CHOCOLATE FRANGIPANE

Mix all the dry ingredients in a bowl and then rub in the butter. Add the egg and mix well to combine (or you can use a mixer for this). Cover and refrigerate.

POACHED PEARS

Preheat the oven to 160°C. Peel the pears and, using a corer, carefully remove the core of the pear but leave the stem attached. Place the peeled pears in a deep pot, pour over the sugar syrup and poach the pears over a medium heat until they are part-cooked. Remove from the heat and leave to cool. Once cool, remove the pears from the syrup and trim the base of each pear to make it flat, so that they will stand up. Fill the centre of the pears with the chocolate frangipane mix. Place the pears on a flat tray lined with a Silpat (or similar) non-stick mat and bake in the preheated oven for about 10 minutes. Check to make sure that the frangipane is cooked inside the pear by lifting the pear – the mixture should not leak out once the frangipane is cooked.

PEAR CONE

Mix all the ingredients in a bowl and whisk into a paste. Line a flat baking sheet with a sheet of parchment paper or a Silpat mat (or similar) and place a plastic 6cm (2½in) ring on the paper. Fill the ring with a thin, even layer of the paste and repeat six times on the same sheet of parchment paper or Silpat mat. Cook in an oven preheated to 160°C until golden. While still warm, form the pear crisps into a cone shape and then set aside to cool. Once they are cool, store them in a container with a lid until needed.

PEAR AIR

Place all the ingredients in a rectangular container (this shape helps a good foam to form) and blend together using a hand-held stick blender until foam appears. Allow the foam to settle until the top is covered in air bubbles.

CHOCOLATE SAUCE

Bring the cream and water to the boil in a pot.
In a separate bowl, mix the cocoa powder and sugar together and then add the dry mix to the hot liquid, stirring well. Bring it back to the boil and then pass it through a fine sieve. Squeeze the excess water out of the gelatine and add it to the warm liquid. Whisk to dissolve the gelatine. Place the sauce in a squeezy bottle for service.

TO SERVE

Pour a puddle of chocolate sauce into the base of a warm wide-brimmed bowl. Place the warm poached pear on top. Fill the pear cone with pear granita and stick it into the side of the soft pear. Spoon on the foam and serve.

TIP

The pears can be poached and preserved in the syrup in sterilised, sealed jars and stored for up to 6 months.

JACK ROGERS | RAPESEED OIL

The Rogers family produce Newgrange Gold rapeseed oil from their farm in the heart of the Boyne Valley, County Meath, within sight of the famous heritage sites of Newgrange and Knowth. This is where they grow, press and bottle the oil with complete traceability. A few years ago we decided to swap all imported olive oil in The K Club kitchens with locally produced Irish rapeseed oil and we chose Newgrange. The oil is high in essential fatty acids – omega 3, 6 and 9 – and low in saturated fat and boasts a wonderful fruity flavour.

www.newgrangegold.ie

Baked Cooleeney cheese with Jane Sellers local apiary honey pearls and toasted hazelnuts

Breda Maher's cheese is sweet and tangy and full of flavour. When you warm it, it becomes lovely and gooey, and the crunchiness from the toasted hazelnuts mixed with the honey complement it beautifully.

WINE PAIRING

Clos Sainte Hune Alsace Riesling

We love aged Riesling with this dish. It just works. The slight petrol notes of the wine, the oily character, but also the searing acidity, cut through the creamy baked cheese wonderfully.

FOR THE HONEY PEARLS

100gm (3½oz) Jane Sellers honey
80ml (2¾fl oz) champagne
4gm (¼oz) agar-agar
1 litre (1¾ pints) vegetable oil, chilled to 2°C

FOR THE CHEESE

1 x 200g (7oz) round Cooleeney cheese
120g (4¼oz) hazelnuts
80ml (2¾fl oz) Jane Sellers honey

SERVES 2–4

HONEY PEARLS

Place the honey and champagne in a pot and bring to the boil. Whisk in the agar-agar and allow to cool to 50°C, then pour into a disposable piping bag. Make a small cut at the tip of the bag to allow a very small amount to leak out. Pipe the full bag into the container of chilled oil; the little pearls will set as they sink in the oil. Pass the liquid through a sieve to extract the pearls. Rinse the pearls in cold water to remove any excess oil.

THE CHEESE

Preheat the oven to 120°C. Place the cheese on a baking sheet and cook in the preheated oven until soft – about 15 minutes. Lightly smash the hazelnuts and toast them in a hot, dry pan until golden brown. Add the honey and stir around to mix.

TO SERVE

Place the hazelnuts in the bottom of a presentation glass dish. If needed, you can run the blowtorch over the top of the cheese to brown it. Carefully place the cheese on top of the hazelnuts. Finish by spooning the pearls on top and drizzle over runny honey to serve.

Bay leaf panna cotta, caramelised apple and sweet spiced bread croûtons

The idea of a bay leaf panna cotta might surprise you, but it works wonderfully well. Bay leaf has a naturally refreshing flavour and, paired with the caramelised apple and lightly spiced croûtons, it creates a dish that oozes autumn.

FOR THE BAY LEAF PANNA COTTA

500ml (17fl oz) Avonmore cream
10 fresh bay leaves
40gm (1½oz) caster sugar
3½ gelatine leaves, pre-soaked in water

FOR THE BAY LEAF TUILE

50gm (2oz) plain flour
50gm (2oz) icing sugar
50gm (2oz) Avonmore unsalted butter
50gm (2oz) free-range egg whites
1 dried bay leaf, crushed

FOR THE CARAMELISED COX'S APPLE

150gm (5oz) caster sugar
50gm (2oz) Avonmore unsalted butter
2 pinches ground nutmeg
5 whole cloves
1 cinnamon stick, smashed
8 Cox's Orange Pippin apples, peeled, cored and diced into 1cm (½in) cubes

FOR THE SWEET SPICED BREAD CROÛTONS

spiced bread loaf (see page 276)
50gm (2oz) icing sugar

SERVES 10

BAY LEAF PANNA COTTA

Place the cream and the bay leaves in a saucepan and bring to the boil. Remove from the heat and allow to infuse for 20 minutes. Add the caster sugar and bring the cream back to the boil and then pass the mixture through a fine chinois or sieve. Squeeze any excess water from the softened gelatine leaves and whisk into the mixture until the gelatine is completely dissolved. Pour immediately into a cone mould (4cm/1½in wide x 8cm/3in high) and allow to set in the fridge. (To make the cone moulds, we use squares cut from heavy-duty black plastic bags. We fold these to the required shape and size, then stand them up in hollowed-out egg cartons.) Once set, remove the panna cotta from the moulds for service.

BAY LEAF TUILE

Preheat the oven to 160°C. Blitz all the ingredients together to form a paste. Using a flat piece of hard plastic, cut out a triangular template with a 4cm (1½in) base and 12cm (4½in) sides. Place a Silpat or similar non-stick mat on a baking tray and use the plastic template to spread the tuile mix evenly to fill the template 12 times. Transfer the baking tray to the oven and cook for 5 minutes until golden brown. Remove the mat from the baking tray and cool immediately on a marble top or wire rack to avoid over-colouring. Store the 12 tuiles (you only need 10 but it's always good to have some spare) in an airtight container for service.

CARAMELISED COX'S APPLE

Place the sugar in a pot over a medium heat and cook until it reaches a light-brown colour. Add the unsalted butter and the spices and mix together well, then add the apple and simmer for 2 minutes over a medium heat. Drain the apple from the liquid and set aside to keep warm. Pass the cooking liquid through a fine chinois or sieve. Bring it up to the boil and reduce until it reaches sauce consistency. Set aside.

SWEET SPICED BREAD CROÛTONS

Preheat an oven to 160°C. Slice the bread into 5mm (¼in)-thick slices, then cut the slices into 30mm x 5mm croûtons (1¼in x ¼in). Toss the croûtons in the icing sugar to coat them and then shake off any excess sugar. Line a baking tray with a Silpat or similar non-stick cooking mat.

Place the croûtons on the mat and cook in the oven for 5 minutes until golden brown. Remove and leave to cool.

TO SERVE

Place a panna cotta cone in the centre of a plate and pour on the apple caramel sauce. Neatly arrange the warm Cox's apple around the plate and place the spiced bread croûtons on top. Finally, tilt a triangle tuile on the side of the panna cotta and serve.

Glazed lemon tart with baked black fig ice cream and fig paper

Citrus fruit and figs work really well together. The deep, dark sweetness of the figs contrasts beautifully with the zesty top note of citrus. I love that this dish embraces the crossover in seasons, when the zippy spark of summer is mellowing towards autumn.

FOR THE LEMON TART FILLING

250ml (9fl oz) Avonmore cream
200ml (7fl oz) freshly squeezed lemon juice
400gm (14oz) caster sugar
9 free-range eggs
icing sugar, to dust

FOR THE SWEET PASTRY BASE

320gm (11oz) Avonmore unsalted butter
200gm (7oz) icing sugar
1 free-range egg
500gm (17oz) plain flour

FOR THE BLACK FIG PAPER

10 dried figs
20 ripe black figs
20ml (¾fl oz) red port

FOR THE BAKED BLACK FIG PURÉE

100gm (3½oz) Avonmore unsalted butter
150gm (5oz) demerara sugar
24 black figs
50ml (2fl oz) red port

BAKED BLACK FIG ICE CREAM

250gm (9oz) free-range egg yolks
1 litre Avonmore milk
150gm (5oz) caster sugar
210gm (7½oz) baked fig purée, from above
50gm (2oz) mascarpone cheese
150ml (5fl oz) Avonmore cream
150gm (5oz) procrema

FOR THE CHOCOLATE STICK

see page 94

TO SERVE

sprigs of sweet cicely

SERVES 8

LEMON TART FILLING

Place the cream, lemon juice and caster sugar in a saucepan and bring up to the boil, then remove from the heat. Whisk the eggs in a bowl and pour the warm cream and lemon mixture into the eggs, whisking to combine. Set aside to cool.

SWEET PASTRY BASE

Whisk the unsalted butter and the icing sugar together. Add the egg and sieve in the plain flour. Mix to form a soft dough. Cover the bowl with cling film and refrigerate for 1 hour. Place the dough on a floured marble surface or bench and roll out until 3mm (1⁄10in) thick. Place a rectanglular tart-tin frame (38cm x 11cm x 3cm; 15in x 4in x 1in) on a Silpat or similar non-stick mat and grease with a little unsalted butter. Line the tin with pastry, leaving a little of the pastry hanging over the edge, and transfer it to rest in the fridge for 30 minutes; this will prevent shrinkage during cooking. Preheat the oven to 170°C. Line the pastry with cling film and cover the base with rice or baking beans, right up to the top. Fold in the edge of the cling film and place the non-stick mat and tart tin on a baking sheet. Transfer to the oven and bake for 25 minutes. Remove the cling film and rice (or beans) and allow to cool. Trim any excess pastry from the edge of the tart tin and pour in the lemon filling, right up to the top. Reduce the oven to 100°C and bake the tart until the filling is just firm, about 20 minutes. Leave to cool, still in the tart frame, on a wire rack.
Cut the tart into 10 equal-sized slices and trim off the overhanging pastry edging. Cut a triangle shape and a round out of each slice. Sieve icing sugar on top of each piece and caramelise it with a blowtorch until golden brown. Set aside.

BLACK FIG PAPER

Preheat the oven to 160°C. Place the dried figs in an ovenproof dish and transfer to the oven to heat through for a few minutes; this will help soften them up. Cut them in half and use a knife to scrape out the flesh. Mix the warm dried fig flesh with the red port. Take the fresh figs and peel them right down to the red flesh. Mash them to a pulp and add to the dried fig and red port mixture. Cut the sealed edges off a large vacuum-pack bag to leave you with 2 plastic sheets. Place one sheet on a marble surface or counter top and spread the pulped fig mixture on top of the sheet to form a square or rectangle. Place the second sheet of plastic on top and, using a small saucepan, flatten the fig mixture to a thickness of approximately 2mm (1⁄10in). Place the sheet on a tray and freeze for a couple of hours to set. Remove the top layer of plastic and cut the compressed fig into 12cm x 6cm (4½in x 2½in) strips. Peel off the bottom layer of plastic and store the fig strips in the freezer until required.

BAKED BLACK FIG PURÉE

Preheat the oven to 150°C. Melt the butter and sugar in an ovenproof pan and add the whole black figs and the port. Transfer to the oven to bake for 25 minutes until soft. Remove from the oven and retain 100ml (3½fl oz) of the cooking liquid for later. Place the figs and remaining liquid in a HotmixPRO (or similar) blender. Purée and leave to cool.

BAKED BLACK FIG ICE CREAM

Whisk the egg yolks and sugar together in a bowl. Boil the milk in a saucepan and pour 200ml (7fl oz) of the hot milk into the cold egg mixture and whisk. Return this egg mixture to the rest of the hot milk in the pot, whisk and continue to cook on a low heat for 2 minutes. Pass through a fine chinois or sieve and leave to cool. Add the baked fig purée, cream, mascarpone and procrema and mix to combine. Allow to cool. Pour the mixture into a Taurus Rowzer beaker and freeze and then blitz in the Taurus Rowzer when needed. Alternatively, you could churn the mixture in an ice cream machine for 20 minutes and freeze.

TO SERVE

Remove the black fig paper from the freezer, place one strip in the centre of the plate and allow to thaw for about 5 minutes. Place a glazed lemon tart triangle and circle neatly on the fig paper and add a quenelle of black fig ice cream. Place a chocolate stick on top of the ice cream and spoon over some baked fig syrup to serve.

MICHAEL KAVANAGH | EGGS

Michael Kavanagh is the third generation, and the third Michael Kavanagh, to run MK Country Fresh Eggs. This Dublin family has been supplying eggs and egg products to the Irish catering trade for twenty years. The free-range eggs they supply to The K Club are reared on their farm in Monaghan.

www.cfe.ie

Valrhona Macae chocolate ganache tart with tonka bean mousse, chocolate paint and buttermilk sorbet

You have to love chocolate to fully appreciate this dessert. The spicy darkness of the Macae, at 62%, packs a serious punch, but it's not bitter; rather, it exudes layers of complex dark chocolate flavour. The tonka bean mousse then adds a creamy smoothness to the dish and the buttermilk sorbet is there to clean the palate between mouthfuls of intense chocolate.

FOR THE CHOCOLATE TUILE

125ml (4fl oz) freshly squeezed orange juice
250gm (9oz) icing sugar
50gm (2oz) plain flour
25gm (1oz) cocoa powder
150gm (5oz) unsalted butter

FOR THE BUTTERMILK SORBET

250gm (9oz) Kilbeg natural yoghurt
75ml (2½fl oz) Avonmore buttermilk
75ml (2½fl oz) Avonmore milk
65ml (2¼fl oz) sugar syrup (see page 271)
25ml (1fl oz) Avonmore cream
25ml (1fl oz) liquid glucose
5gm (¼oz) ascorbic acid
60gm (2oz) sorbitol

FOR THE CHOCOLATE PASTRY

320gm (11oz) Avonmore unsalted butter, at room temperature
200gm (7oz) icing sugar
1 free-range egg
300gm (10½oz) plain flour
200gm (7oz) cocoa powder

FOR THE MACAE CHOCOLATE GANACHE

400gm (14oz) Valrhona Macae 62% dark chocolate buttons
500ml (17fl oz) Avonmore cream
400gm (14oz) liquid glucose

FOR THE TONKA BEAN MOUSSE

100ml (3½fl oz) Avonmore cream
1 tonka bean, crushed
24gm (1oz) caster sugar
1gm gelatine leaf (¼ leaf), pre-soaked in a little water
15gm (½oz) Valrhona Macae 62% dark chocolate buttons

FOR THE CACAO BROWN LIQUEUR PEARLS

150ml (5fl oz) Bols Cacao Brown liqueur
8gm (¼oz) caster sugar
2gm (½ tsp) agar-agar
5 litres (9pints) vegetable oil, chilled to 2°C

FOR THE CHOCOLATE PAINT

50gm (2oz) Valrhona Macae 62% dark chocolate buttons
15gm (½oz) cocoa powder
10gm (½oz) icing sugar
50ml (2fl oz) sunflower oil
20gm (¾oz) Valrhona Grue de Cacao, to garnish

SERVES 10

CHOCOLATE TUILE

Warm the orange juice and icing sugar in a pot until the sugar dissolves. Sieve the plain flour and cocoa powder together in a bowl and then add the orange juice mixture. Melt the unsalted butter and whisk it into the mixture to form a paste. Refrigerate overnight.

Preheat the oven to 160°C. Spread some of the mixture on to a Silpat (or similar) non-stick mat, place on a baking tray and bake in the oven for 10 minutes. Cut into 12cm x 1cm (4½in x ½in) strips while the paste is still hot and before it hardens. Store the strips in an airtight container for service.

BUTTERMILK SORBET

Mix all the ingredients together in a bowl. Pour the mixture into a Rowzer beaker and freeze. Blitz in the Taurus Rowzer when needed. Alternatively, churn the mixture in an ice cream machine for 20 minutes and then freeze.

CHOCOLATE PASTRY

Mix the unsalted butter and icing sugar together in a bowl. Add the egg and mix well. Sieve in the plain flour and cocoa powder and bring together to form a thick dough. Cover the bowl with cling film and refrigerate for 1 hour. Roll out the dough on a floured marble top or counter until 3mm (1⁄10in) thick. Grease a rectangular tin frame (38cm x 11cm x 3cm; 15in x 4in x 1in) with a little unsalted butter and place it on a greased Silpat (or similar) non-stick mat. Line the tin frame with the pastry, leaving a little of the pastry hanging over the edge, then transfer to the fridge to rest for 30 minutes (to prevent shrinkage during cooking). Preheat the oven to 170°C. Line the rested pastry with cling film and fill with rice or baking beans, right up to the top. Fold in the edge of the cling film and place the non-stick mat with the frame on it on a baking sheet. Bake in the oven for 25 minutes, then remove the cling film and rice (or beans) and return the tin to the oven for another 5 minutes. Leave to cool on a wire rack. Trim off any excess pastry from the edge of the tart.

MACAE CHOCOLATE GANACHE

Place the Macae chocolate buttons in a bowl. Boil the cream in a saucepan and pour on to the chocolate buttons. Add the liquid glucose and mix well together. Pour the mixture into the lined chocolate pastry tart tin and allow to set. Cut the tart into 10 equal slices.

TONKA BEAN MOUSSE

Place the cream and the tonka bean in a saucepan and bring to the boil, then remove from the heat and set aside to infuse for 20 minutes. Add the sugar to the cream mixture and place the pan back on the heat and bring up to the boil. Pass the cream mixture through a fine chinois or sieve. Squeeze any excess water from the gelatine and stir it into the cream mixture until it dissolves. Pour this mixture over the Abinao chocolate buttons in a bowl and whisk until the chocolate melts. Leave to cool and refrigerate until set. Whisk the mousse in a mixer until smooth, then transfer to a disposable piping bag and refrigerate until ready to use.

CACAO BROWN LIQUEUR PEARLS

Boil the liqueur in a saucepan, whisk in the sugar and agar-agar and bring the liquid back to the boil. Remove from the heat and allow to cool to 54°C. Transfer to a disposable piping bag and snip a tiny cut at the tip of the bag to allow a small amount to drip out. Place the bag over the oil and allow drops to fall into the oil until the bag is empty. The little pearls will set as they sink in the oil. Pass the oil through a sieve to extract the pearls and then wash them with cold water to remove any excess oil.

CHOCOLATE PAINT

Put the chocolate buttons, cocoa powder, icing sugar and sunflower oil in a heatproof bowl and place over a pot of simmering water to melt. Whisk until the chocolate is melted and the mixture is well combined. Remove from the heat and store at room temperature. Keep the Grue de Cacao for sprinkling on top.

TO SERVE

Using a paint brush, paint a line of the chocolate paint along the plate. Sprinkle a light line of the Grue de Cacao along the length of the paint. Place a slice of the ganache tart across the painted line and pipe three 2cm-high (1in-high) tonka bean mousse rosettes on top. Neatly arrange the chocolate tuile strips between the tonka bean mousse rosettes. Place a teaspoon of the Cocoa Brown pearls on the side of the plate and finish with a quenelle of the buttermilk sorbet.

Chocolate ravioli of autumn fruits, nuts and Jane Sellers honey, black treacle ice cream

This is a long-standing recipe here at The K Club. It is lovely and Christmasy and is a triumph on the taste buds. The chocolate ravioli and its hint of orange and layers of rich autumn fruits bring together all the wonderful flavours that we associate with this time of year.

FOR THE CHOCOLATE PASTA

750gm (1lb 10oz) strong flour
250gm (9oz) cocoa powder
20gm (¾oz) salt
1 free-range egg
500ml (17fl oz) free-range egg yolks
125ml (4½fl oz) water

FOR THE FRUIT AND NUT FILLING

50gm (2oz) pine nuts, chopped
50gm (2oz) walnuts, chopped
50gm (2oz) nibbed almonds
130gm (4½oz) Jane Sellers honey
100gm (3½oz) dates
100gm (3½oz) dried prunes
100gm (3½oz) golden raisins
zest of ½ orange

TO ASSEMBLE THE RAVIOLI

chocolate pasta, from above
fruit and nut filling, from above
egg wash, to seal
20ml (¾fl oz) best-quality hazelnut oil, to serve

FOR THE CACAO BROWN LIQUEUR JELLY

190ml (7fl oz) Bols Cacao Brown liqueur
20gm (¾oz) caster sugar
25ml (¾fl oz) water
10gm (½oz) gelatine leaf, pre-soaked in water

FOR THE PEAR PURÉE

2 fresh ripe pears, peeled and cored
100ml (3½fl oz) sugar syrup (see page 271)
20ml (¾fl oz) Poire William liqueur

FOR THE BLACK TREACLE ICE CREAM

250ml (9fl oz) Avonmore milk
500ml (17fl oz) Avonmore cream
3 free-range egg yolks
125gm (4½oz) black treacle

FOR THE SUGAR STICK

50gm (2oz) isomalt
droplet yellow food colouring

TO SERVE

60gm (2oz) toasted hazelnuts, crushed
zest of 1 orange

SERVES 6

CHOCOLATE PASTA

Mix all the dry ingredients together. Add the eggs and water and bring together to form a dough. Knead this really well on a floured surface until you have a stiff dough. Wrap the dough in parchment paper and refrigerate for 1 hour. Using a pasta rolling machine, roll the dough into fine sheets about 1mm (1/20in) thick.

FRUIT AND NUT FILLING

Preheat the oven to 160°C. Roast the nuts in the oven for 2 minutes. Warm the honey in a pot, add the nuts, dried fruit and orange zest and mix well to combine. Set aside to cool.

THE RAVIOLI

Cut the chocolate pasta sheets into discs using an 8cm (3in) stainless steel cutter. You will want 24 discs. Place a small (40gm/1½oz) ball of the fruit and nut filling on to 12 of the pasta discs and egg-wash the edges. Lay a second disc on top of the filling and squeeze the edges together to form a flying-saucer-shaped ravioli. Cook the ravioli in 5 litres (9 pints) of boiling water for 4 minutes; the pasta should be al dente. Remove the ravioli from the water and toss them in a bowl with the hazelnut oil to prevent them from sticking to each other.

CACAO BROWN LIQUEUR JELLY

Place the liqueur, caster sugar and water in a pot and bring to the boil. Remove from the heat, allow to cool a little and add the squeezed gelatine leaf to the mixture. Whisk until the gelatine is completely dissolved. Pour into a 1cm-deep (½in) mould lined with cling film and leave to set in the fridge. Once set, remove from the mould and cut the jelly into 2cm-wide (1in) triangles.

PEAR PURÉE

Finely slice the pear and place it in a saucepan with the sugar syrup and Poire William liqueur. Bring to the boil, cover with a parchment lid and reduce to a simmer until the pear is very soft. Transfer to a HotmixPRO blender (or similar) and blend on high until smooth. Set aside to keep warm.

BLACK TREACLE ICE CREAM

Put the milk, cream and treacle into a saucepan and bring up to a simmer. In a bowl, whisk the egg yolks. Pour 150ml (5fl oz) of the warm milk and cream mixture into the cold egg yolks and mix to combine. Return this mixture to the pot of warm milk and cream and cook over a low heat for 2 minutes until slightly thickened. Allow to cool. Transfer to a Taurus Rowzer beaker and freeze. Blitz in the Taurus Rowzer when required. Alternatively, you could churn the mixture in an ice cream machine for 20 minutes and freeze.

SUGAR STICK

Melt the isomalt in a pot over a low heat. When it is completely melted, you can add the droplet of yellow food colouring. Leave to cool a little and then pour out on to a tray and work it with your hands while it is still warm until it becomes elastic. Pull it into thin straight lines and lay them down on a Silpat (or similar non-stick) mat. Once set, remove carefully and break into even-sized 10cm (4in) pieces.

TO SERVE

Place three triangles of jelly to the side of each plate. Pierce through with a sugar stick. Place a tablespoon of crushed hazelnuts on the other side of the plate. Arrange a circle of pear purée in the middle of the plate and balance two chocolate ravioli on top. Grate over some fresh orange zest. Finally, place a quenelle of treacle ice cream on top of the crushed hazelnuts and serve.

Petits fours

Basil truffles

Makes 70 pieces

350gm (12oz) Valrhona Ivoire chocolate 35%
550gm (1lb 3oz) Valrhona Abinao chocolate 85%
100gm (3½oz) fresh basil leaves, roughly chopped
500ml (17½fl oz) Avonmore cream
cocoa powder

METHOD

Place the Ivoire chocolate and 150gm (5oz) of the Abinao chocolate in a bowl. Place the cream in a pot and add the fresh basil. Bring the cream up to the boil briefly, then remove from the heat and allow the basil to infuse for 30 minutes. Return to the heat and bring back to the boil, then pour the cream over the chocolate and whisk until it melts and is smooth. Leave to cool and refrigerate overnight. Melt the remaining Abinao chocolate in a bowl over hot water. Roll the chocolate and basil cream ganache into 15gm (½oz) balls. Place a small amount of the melted chocolate in your hand and lightly coat the ball, then roll in the cocoa powder to coat. Store in an airtight container in the fridge.

Raspberry sorbet and white chocolate stick

Makes 70–80 pieces

1kg (2lb 3oz) raspberry purée
450ml (16fl oz) sugar syrup (see page 271)
50ml (2fl oz) fresh lemon juice
150ml (5fl oz) sorbitol
300gm (10oz) Valrhona Ivoire chocolate 35%

METHOD

Mix together all the ingredients except the Ivoire chocolate. Place in a Rowzer beaker and freeze, then blitz in the Rowzer when required. Alternatively, place the mixture in an ice cream machine, churn for 20 minutes and then freeze. Place the sorbet in a disposable piping bag and cut a 1cm (½in) hole in the tip. Lay a Silpat (or similar) non-stick mat on a flat tray and very quickly pipe 2 lines of sorbet, touching side by side, the full length of the mat, then pipe another line on top of these and place in a blast freezer or freezer. Cut the solid sorbet into 2cm (1in) pieces and place a lolly stick in each one. Return to the freezer to set. Melt the Ivoire chocolate in a bowl and dip each lolly into it to coat. Place on a mesh rack and allow to drip, then place on a parchment-lined tray and store in the freezer until needed.

Vanilla rice pudding arancini

Makes 40–50 pieces

FOR THE RICE PUDDING

325ml (11fl oz) Avonmore milk
325ml (11fl oz) Avonmore cream
100gm (3½oz) pearl rice
1 bourbon vanilla pod, cut in half lengthways
75gm (2½oz) caster sugar

FOR THE COATING

800ml (28fl oz) coconut milk
100gm (3½oz) tempura flour
panko breadcrumbs

METHOD

To make the rice pudding, place all the ingredients in a pot and cook over a medium heat until the rice is cooked. You need to stir occasionally to prevent the rice sticking to the bottom of the pot, but do not over-stir the rice. Once cooked, allow to cool and refrigerate overnight.

To make the coating, mix the coconut milk and tempura floor together. Roll the rice pudding into 3cm (1in) balls and dip into the coconut batter. Shake off any excess batter and roll the balls in the panko breadcrumbs. Heat the oil in a deep fryer to 360°C and fry until golden brown.

Blackcurrant jelly

Makes 60–70 pieces

25gm (1oz) pectin
150gm (5oz) caster sugar
1kg (2lb 3oz) blackcurrant purée
1050gm (2lb 5oz) granulated sugar
220gm (8oz) glucose syrup

METHOD

Mix together the pectin and the caster sugar. Place the blackcurrant purée in a pot and heat to 120°C. Whisk in the pectin and sugar and bring back to the boil. Add the granulated sugar and heat to 223°C. Place a 2cm-deep (1in-deep) stainless steel mould on a baking tray lined with a Silpat or similar non-stick mat and pour the mixture directly into the mould. It will set very quickly. Once set, cut into triangle shapes and coat in caster sugar. Store in an airtight container.

Orange opaline lollies

Makes 60 pieces

250gm (9oz) fondant
125gm (4½oz) glucose syrup
4gm (¼oz) nougasec
4ml (¼fl oz) orange essence

METHOD

Place the fondant, glucose and nougasec in a pot and heat to 155°C. Add the orange essence and pour directly on to a Silpat (or similar) non-stick mat to set. Once set and cold, break into small pieces and blend in a blender until it forms a very fine powder. Preheat the oven to 160°C. Line a baking tray with a Silpat (or similar) non-stick mat. Place a 5cm (2in) disc stencil on the mat. Place the opaline powder into a fine sieve and sprinkle the powder over the stencil until full. Repeat as many times as you can to fill the length of the mat, leaving a 10cm (4in) gap between each row of discs. Remove the stencil and cook the opaline discs in the oven until just melted but still holding their shape. At this stage, lay a lolly stick in the centre of each disc. Lift the mat off the warm tray and place on a cold counter top or marble slab to cool and become crisp.

Tonka bean chocolates

Makes 60 pieces

300gm (10½oz) Valrhona Abinao chocolate 85%
500ml (17fl oz) Avonmore cream
6 tonka beans, grated
1 bourbon vanilla pod, cut lengthways
800gm (1lb 12oz) Valrhona Abinao chocolate 85%, for dipping

METHOD

Place the Abinao chocolate in a bowl. Place the cream in a saucepan with the grated tonka beans and vanilla pod and bring to the boil. Remove from the heat and allow to sit and infuse for 30 minutes. Bring the cream back to the boil and pour over the chocolate. Whisk until the chocolate melts and is smooth. Pour into a 2cm (1in)-deep rectangular stainless steel mould and leave to cool, then refrigerate overnight. Remove and cut the ganache into 4cm by 2cm (1½in x 1in) rectangles.

Place the second amount of Abinao chocolate in a bowl and melt over hot water. Once it reaches 45°C, remove from the heat and stir constantly until it drops back to 27°C. Place the bowl back over the pot of hot water and bring the temperature back up to 30°C. Place each ganache rectangle on a fork and dip into the melted chocolate until evenly coated. Place on a mesh rack and allow to drip. Finish quickly by decorating with three fine lines of chocolate and allow to cool. Store in an airtight container.

THE WINE CELLAR

The K Club Wine Story

A grand house in a slice of Irish countryside associated with equestrian dynasties and a lush golf green might not be where you'd expect to find a rich wine legacy, but the briefest stroll through the handsome house at the heart of The K Club Resort offers many clues as to its historic and contemporary significance in Ireland's sometimes surprising relationship with wine.

As storytellers go, sommelier Lisa O'Doherty is a natural – and it helps that she has her pick of truly great stories – but you don't even have to catch one of her complementary cellar tours for the house to begin to unravel its secrets. The walls of the high-ceilinged corridors themselves have a tale to tell.

Here in one corner is a magnificent display of iconic wine bottles of various sizes, their contents long-consumed but not forgotten, and still sporting labels designed by the likes of the esteemed modern Irish artist Francis Bacon. There is the faded sepia portrait of the handsome Sir Anthony Barton, who was born in this very house and inherited two of Bordeaux's most prestigious Cru Classé châteaux. And next to him is a photograph capturing the original scale of Straffan House as built by his forefather Hugh Barton, himself the grandson of one of Ireland's intriguing 'Wine Geese' diaspora.

From Straffan House's origins as a 17th-century bolt-hole to the resort's Ryder Cup lists, which required the sourcing of obscure Californian wines – and by way of one of Ireland's most prestigious collections of iconic Bordeaux and Burgundy, and a suite of Venetian wine glasses especially commissioned for a dinner for the world's ten richest men – the story of wine in this corner of Kildare is an eventful one that has been unfolding for several centuries.

The house, its history and the Barton connection

Modelled on a château at Louveciennes near Versailles, the original Straffan House was built in 1830 by an Irish-born Bordeaux-based wine producer named Hugh Barton. However, as anyone who has taken Lisa's tour already knows, the real story of the remarkable Barton legacy begins a century or even two before that.

The tour begins in the old entrance hall of the original house – now the east wing of the hotel – where a large painting of 1601's infamous Battle of Kinsale pays homage to what was the last stand of the old Gaelic aristocracy. The victory of Queen Elizabeth I's troops at Kinsale proved a watershed in Ireland's destiny and, when many of the defeated Gaelic nobility fled to Catholic Spain for refuge, they left a vacuum that would be filled by English rule for years to come.

This 'Flight of the Earls' marked the first wave of emigration, as the old ruling class fled the new order. Later, in the 17th and 18th centuries, many historic Irish families left, and many of those who did so took advantage of the strong links between Bordeaux – the centre of French wine production – and Ireland, through which much of that wine was being imported into England. These émigrés came to be dubbed Ireland's 'Wine Geese'.

Founded in 1725 by Irishman Thomas Barton, Barton & Guestier is the oldest winehouse in Bordeaux.

In 1725, a certain Thomas Barton of County Fermanagh arrived in Bordeaux and set about becoming one of Europe's most reputable wine brokers, or 'négociants'. French Tom, as he became known, would build a fortune and establish one of Ireland's most enduring 'Wine Geese' dynasties, living long enough to train his grandson Hugh into the family business at the age of 20.

French Tom left his legacy in good hands, and Hugh continued to build the growing Barton empire, until another historical turning-point somewhat sidetracked his plans. As France lurched towards the French Revolution in the late 18th century, Hugh rather inconveniently found himself thrown into prison. Fortunately, with the help of his loyal wife Ann, Hugh managed to evade the guillotine. 'There are lots of great stories about that time,' Lisa enthuses. (Some are less verifiable than others, such as the tale of Ann disguising her husband as a woman to secure his escape. 'But who am I to let the facts get in the way of a good story?' she adds with a mischievous wink.) What we do know is that the couple took refuge from France's Reign of Terror in Hugh's birth country of Ireland, where he fell in love with and purchased an idyllic piece of land hugging the River Liffey at Straffan in County Kildare.

The Bartons would later resume residence in France, where Hugh's friend Daniel Guestier had been managing his affairs in his absence. In post-revolutionary France, non-nationals were barred from owning land, but the partnership between Barton and Guestier allowed Hugh to continue building his business. He was so successful that the Barton & Guestier brand continues to thrive to this day, and his family remain proud owners of the prestigious Château Langoa and Château Léoville-Barton, which were bought by Hugh in 1821 and 1826 respectively.

However, Hugh never forgot that slice of Irish countryside in a lush green corner of County Kildare. In 1830, he returned to Straffan to build his very own Irish château, and the remains of Hugh Barton and his wife Ann are buried in the local Straffan graveyard.

LISA O'DOHERTY SOMMELIER

Thankfully, Hugh's legacy did not die with him. A certain Anthony Barton was born at Straffan House in 1930, and Lisa has heard first-hand reports of a handsome young Anthony setting many a local Kildare heart aflutter with his 1940s film star looks. Today, Sir Anthony Barton is the charming octogenarian at the helm of Château Léoville-Barton in Saint-Julien, whose wines command a lot of respect in the wine world for both their quality and value. They fetch a fine (but fair) price on the hotel's list today, where they nestle amongst the collection of Bordeaux Crus Classés, next to the likes of Châteaux Margaux, Lynch-Bages, Cheval Blanc, Haut-Brion and Lafite-Rothschild.

Although the estate at Straffan was sold by the Barton family in 1949, its legacy eventually returned into the wine-loving hands it deserved. When the house came under the stewardship of Dr Smurfit, an Irish businessman and entrepreneur famed for his appreciation of fine Bordeaux wine, an exciting discovery was made. As the Smurfit Jefferson Group set about developing the property into today's magnificent K Club Resort at the cusp of the 1990s, they found a basement storeroom that turned out to be the original vaulted cellar built by Hugh Barton all those years ago.

And what is a wealthy wine connoisseur to do with an empty cellar built by the descendant of one of Ireland's most celebrated Wine Geese? Fill it with the finest wine known to mankind, of course.

The cellar, its legacies and treasures

If you're going to build a world-class luxury country club resort and expect the cream of society to come and stay there, a significant part of redeveloping such a richly historied house and estate will be to stock the vaulted cellar in the manner it deserves.

Thankfully, the Smurfit Jefferson Group had just the man for the job. Didier Fiat was at the top of his game when he joined The K Club in 1991 as resident sommelier. To prove the point, he returned from Rio de Janeiro in 1992 as Bronze Medallist in the World's Best Sommelier Competition.

Didier remained sommelier at The K Club until the early noughties, when he handed over the keys of the cellar to sommelier Lisa O'Doherty, who has overseen the wine management and service at the hotel ever since. The cellar Lisa inherited from her predecessor was by now one of the most famous in the country, at one point containing wine worth up to €1 million in value – although Lisa is quick to point out that the resell value would have been far higher than the cost-price evaluation. However, it was less the value of the wines that The K Club cellar was famed for than the rarity and prestige of some of the iconic and aged wines stored there, including a notable contribution from one of France's most prestigious wineries – Château Pétrus.

Bordeaux's Right Bank, which includes the denominations of St-Émilion and neighbouring Pomerol, and where the blend of Merlot with the region's signature Cabernet Sauvignon makes for a fleshier, more opulent style of wine, was once so underrated that it was not included in the definitive 1855 'Grand Cru' classification of the finest Bordeaux wines. However, the stratospheric rise in the reputation of Château Pétrus from 1945 onwards transformed the denomination of Pomerol into the jewel in the crown of the Right Bank – and arguably of Bordeaux itself, certainly if monetary value is to be your guide.

The K Club's Pétrus collection spans over three decades of vintages, from the mid-1960s up to the mid-1990s, but it is the 1990 vintage – whose racy charms were described by one *Wall Street Journal* wine wag as akin to 'the best one-night stand you ever had' – that takes pride of place in the collection. It also fetches the highest price, at its current wine list price of €9,000.

However, for the most highly valued trophy wine in The K Club cellar we have to leave Bordeaux and head north-east to a region that Lisa describes as both a wine-lover's dream and a never-ending challenge to any wine buff's knowledge. Where an understanding of Bordeaux hinges on the château system, Burgundy revolves around the strict classification of the vineyards themselves. Wine lovers or investors willing to take a punt on a new vintage in Burgundy have a lot of variables to navigate.

Thanks to strict local laws of inheritance, many Burgundian vineyards have multiple owners, each producing wine from their own segment of vines. Some of these owners have really done their homework as to how best to coax those grapes and their juice into the finest of wines; others less so, knowing that the prestige of their plots guarantees a certain degree of sales.

'That what's so fascinating about Burgundy,' explains Lisa, 'that it's not just about knowing the château and the year, as with Bordeaux. It's about knowing the vineyard and – within that vineyard – who you're dealing with.' Lisa's eyes light up. 'And we have the best of the best. We have DRC, or Domaine de la Romanée-Conti, to give it its full name.'

The renowned vineyard of Romanée-Conti was laid down in the 14th century by pioneering monks, who reputedly filtered water through the soil and drank it to determine the minerality. These medieval monks recognised that this plot of land was of Grand Cru quality: that this was the best site for wine-growing, with the best aspect and soil and sunlight.

Unusually for Burgundy, today's Domaine de la Romanée-Conti is a single-owner 'monopole'. It stands at just four acres (tiny compared to Bordeaux's equivalents, where, for example, Pétrus cultivates 28 acres and Lafite an extensive 250 acres) and produces a very limited quantity of between four and seven thousand bottles a year, depending on vintage. Each bottle is individually numbered – including the two sitting in Lisa's beloved cellar.

At a whopping €20,000 a bottle, Lisa admits that her Domaine de la Romanée-Conti 1990 is possibly slightly overpriced – 'though not by much!' – but the honest truth is that, with 25 years under its belt and many years left in it, this is the one wine that Lisa wants to showcase on her list without actually wishing to sell, certainly not yet and possibly never. She did recently sell a bottle at that price, but the last two bottles are going nowhere.

The other wine that has recently come off The Book (which is the fully comprehensive list offered to guests in the dining rooms and bars of the resort) is the oldest in the cellar. Produced in Bordeaux before the young Anthony Barton was born here in Straffan House, the Château Beychevelle 1928 remains in great condition, as indicated by the tell-tale sign that the levels of wine within the bottle are high and the cork is still sound. Besides, Lisa knows firsthand that it is drinking beautifully. The second last bottle of the same vintage was sold recently to three sommeliers from New York, who figured they would never have this opportunity again. And part of Lisa's job as sommelier is to taste every bottle of wine she serves to a customer, so of course she got to taste this rarity.

'It was on at €350, which is how much it was worth. We drank it here in the cellar. I asked them, are you ready? Then cork out, muslin over the glasses (not pretty, but literally you have half an hour and that wine is going to die) – and it was absolutely amazing. It was the colour of our terracotta walls, no red left in it. A beautiful bottle of wine: really soft and silky and gorgeous.'

That's the world of fine wine for you. Because those three sommeliers grasped the opportunity to taste an 86-year-old bottle of Grand Cru Bordeaux, no one else staying at The K Club will ever get to again. The rest of the wines on Lisa's list, however, are there to be drunk. 'We're often applauded for the value of our fine wine, which seems crazy when you're talking about thousands of euro. But we're not in New York. We're in Kildare. And we're competitive.'

Even if your budget doesn't stretch to ordering some of the more precious treasures within these cellars, a tour with Lisa allows you to inspect the dusty old bottles for yourself. Most are stored within walls of terracotta tubes, which, unlike the old wire racks she initially inherited in the cellar, help to protect the labels from wear and tear. Terracotta also prevents mould from growing on the labels, which is useful when humidity is in the high 90s, as it is in the fine wine cellar.

Many of them are stored in 'own wood', within their original individual wooden box, which Lisa describes as the perfect vessel for holding fine wine. Like the terracotta, wooden boxes muffle sound, vibrations and light and they keep the wine on its side. Being porous, wood allows air to circulate, while the temperature within the box is regulated – all factors that demand consideration when storing fine wine. However, Lisa has learned a lot about buying and selling old wine in her time here, so there is another motivation for keeping the wine 'in its own wood', as she explains.

'My dad is passionate about vintage cars. Every now and then he sells one and buys a new one. And it's the same kind of thing with wine: a lot of it is about reinvesting and selling it through, and it's all about provenance, about who we bought it from and who they bought it from. "One careful owner", that's what you're looking for. And one thing you always ask is, is it in its own wood? It's like driving the car out of the forecourt. As soon as you break that box, 10 per cent of the wine's value is gone.'

Not surprisingly, then, the DRC is in its own wood: a really old tatty box, to be precise, which hails from Corney & Barrow wine merchants in London and authenticates the journey that this wine took to get here.

There are so many other treasures down here, and so many stories attached to them. There's the Château

The Art of Pairing Food and Wine

'First of all I'm a great believer in drinking what you like – if you want red wine with fish, have red wine with fish – but if I'm asked about food and wine pairing, it comes down to one thing: you've paid for both, so you should taste both. Neither should overpower the other. And if you pair them well, you'd hope that each would give something to the other.

Also, it's important to remember that it's not the protein you're matching, but rather the strongest flavour, which is usually the sauce. So, at Christmas time, you're looking to match the Brussels sprouts and the cranberries, not the turkey. You also have to think about how something is cooked (for example, poached or steamed chicken or fish demands a delicate match). Acidity is important too, even in red wines with food – you need to have that mouth-water, otherwise it's just flabby.

Matching a wine with curry is incredibly hard. The spices dry out a wine and cause red wine to take on a metallic taste – although Thai food loves aromatic whites like Riesling or Gewürztraminer, even a fruity Sauvignon Blanc. Smoked salmon is tricky too: oily, smoked and fishy flavours are all hard to match, though they say oak loves smoke, so an oak-aged Burgundy makes a great match – a nice Pouilly-Fuissé or Meursault, for that buttery nutty flavour.

But ultimately, as a sommelier, I have to ask not only what are you eating but also what do you like normally? And then I try to steer people towards trying something new – if they like Sauvignon Blanc, I might suggest a Grüner Veltliner or Spanish Albariño, which I'd love to see becoming the next big thing.'

Lisa O'Doherty
The K Club Sommelier

d'Yquem 2003, which is still 'way too young' to make an appearance on the hotel's wine list. (Ask Lisa to tell you about her first sip of the 1983 d'Yquem and watch a professional lady turn swooning groupie. 'I couldn't get over it. I thought, good heavens, that's why it's the best wine in the world.')

There's the vintage port stored in a dedicated dimly lit cellar, some of particularly good value thanks to labelling or bottling quirks. Potential thrills for port lovers include a 1944 Oporto Tawny bottled in 1986, making it somewhat less valuable in investment terms but no less spectacular to drink. Similarly, Lisa suspects that three bottles of 1960 port from Quinto do Noval might in fact be Quinto do Noval Nacionale, which has a conservative market value of €1,000. However, as they're missing the crucial label to confirm their identify, Lisa has them listed at €200 a bottle.

Lastly, there's the last of the Ryder Cup list of obscure, high-end Californian wines sourced especially for the American team, who wanted to have the choice of ordering it should they feel like having a glass with dinner.

For those who really want to have the full wine cellar experience, there's even the option of having a private tasting or wine dinner down here in the rustic surroundings of the original vaulted cellar, but most guests prefer to sample the delights of the carefully curated wine list in the rather more salubrious surroundings of one of the several dining rooms throughout the resort. And with dining choices including the crisp-linened Byerley Turk and the daylight-drenched River Room restaurants, both with stunning views over the landscaped grounds of the estate, who could blame them?

The Book, dining rooms and wine ethos

Even if you don't take one of Lisa's tours, you'd be hard-pressed to come to The K Club for even the briefest of visits and not experience her personal approach to wine. If you don't meet Lisa face-to-face in the River Room or Byerley Turk dining rooms, you'll probably pass her memorial to wines gone but not forgotten in the corridor en route to the Vintage Crop bar. Or you might relish one of several half-bottle white wines she has made available for room service. Even if you don't make it to the main house, you'll enjoy her influence through the wine choices handpicked for weddings and other events, or for the Thai clubhouse restaurant.

But it is in The Book, that master list of all wines available throughout the resort, that The K Club's inclusively exclusive wine ethos is best exemplified – and particularly in the first three pages of it. Fine wine devotees and thrill-seeking voyeurs may choose to fast-forward to page three of The Book, where they can ogle The K Club Iconic Fine Wine Collection, with its collection of Pétrus, DRC, Domaine LeFlaive, Hermitage and Cristal. Lisa is rightly proud of this page, even a little protective of it, as those empty bottles displayed in the corridor testify.

However, Lisa is equally proud of the two pages that precede this heady list, where you'll find The River Room Selected Wines. 'I'm very much a price to quality ratio girl: I believe in giving the customers more than they pay for.' Lisa also believes that a house wine shouldn't just be the cheapest thing you can get your hands on, but rather should say something about you as a house. The Kildare Hotel & Country Club Barton & Guestier Bordeaux Réserve says several things about The K Club. Firstly, this is a Bordeaux house, but also one that rates consistency, loyalty and value for money.

'Barton & Guestier has been our house wine since the day we opened: obviously it has much to do with the historical connection but also I'm really proud of it. We probably pay more for our house wine than any other hotel in this country, but it's a great bottle of wine and it's great by the glass.'

Lisa prefers to categorise wines by style rather than by grape variety or origin ('We're obsessed today with grape variety, but the French believe that a sense of place is more important') and she tends to lean towards wines with a blend of grapes for the extra complexity that offers ('It's like seasoning a wine with another variety'). Listed under 'Light, Fresh, Crisp Whites', the Sauvignon Blanc-led B&G Réserve benefits from the presence of Semillon, which fleshes it out and makes it brilliantly food friendly.

Lisa is also very proud of what sits between the house wines and the investment-level icons. She loves it that her excellent-value Chablis is sourced by a wine supplier who knows her customer very well indeed, being none other than Didier Fiat, who set up Classique Gourmet Wines when he left his post as former K Club sommelier. And she loves telling people about Charles Derain. Charles traded in his formal sommelier's suit for a pair of wellies and transformed himself into a wine-producing importer, several of whose wines now feature on the list at The K Club.

Many of the small but carefully curated selection of non-French wines have a personal significance for Lisa. Being a Bordeaux house allows Lisa to have a bit of fun elsewhere on the list, where she can offer her personal favourites. Her choice of Super Tuscan goes back to her days as sommelier at Dublin's historic Shelbourne hotel, when the Ornellaia from Lodovico Antinori nearly 'took the legs from under me' when she first tasted it. She's been loyal to it ever since.

Having discovered her love for wine while working in Madrid as a model, Lisa has retained a passion for Spanish wines that sees her working on a consultancy basis with the commercial office of the Spanish embassy. She is pleased to have on her list the poster boy of Modern Spain that is the Alvaro Palacios l'Ermita 1995 from Priorat, at €500 a bottle. However, at less than a tenth of that price, the Baron de Ley Rioja Reserva remains her absolute favourite wine on the list.

'I just love it. It would be my ultimate Christmas wine – it's rich and full, old and sensuous, smooth and intense. It's aged in French oak for five years, which is two years more than they need to by law. I like that while the French sell their wine quickly and expect the drinker to age it, the Spanish hold on to it – like their children, who live at home so long! – and they age it for you.'

A superbly versatile food wine, the Baron de Ley often features on the Byerley Turk's tasting menu alongside dishes such as Finbarr Higgins' signature suckling pig. Lisa relishes the opportunity that pairing wine with the tasting menu gives her to talk wine with the customers and perhaps encourage them to try something a little different.

The Coravin

'We Irish don't tend to value dessert wines, but, when people taste something like the Thomas Barton Réserve Sauternes, rumoured to be made from Yquem grapes, matched with the right food they often discover they love it.'

Menu and food knowledge is a key element of wine service at The K Club. Indeed, in her extensive professional role beyond that of sommelier to The K Club, Lisa lectures on the art of food and wine pairing (see panel on page 248 on food and wine pairing). However, Lisa also works closely with Finbarr Higgins. 'A sommelier can't work in isolation. You have to work with your chef.'

That close professional relationship took a little work in itself. 'We're both strong personalities,' Lisa explains, rather delicately. 'I'll never forget the first day I walked into The K Club kitchens. Finbarr's first words to me were "Don't even think of serving Sauternes with my foie gras", which of course is a classic pairing. "My foie gras is too delicate for Sauternes!" That told me!' Lisa rose to the challenge. 'I served it with Coteaux du Layon instead. The Chenin Blanc grape gives an acidity that Sauternes can lack, at a pouring price-point at least.' She was proud of the resulting pairing, but also of the good working relationship that developed between sommelier and chef.

Today that conversation is a two-way street. 'I credit myself with giving him the idea for his pigeon dish, through a conversation about a peanut butter ice cream I had tried at a Dublin restaurant.' Likewise, the enthusiastic endorsement of the Vintage Crop bar manager John Ryan for Dingle Original Gin saw it turning up in one of Finbarr's dishes.

The arrival of the Coravin to The K Club has allowed Lisa huge freedom to play with her offering of wines by the glass. This revolutionary system allows one to pour wine by the glass without pulling the cork: by piercing the cork with a needle, extracting the wine and replacing it with argon gas, which protects against degradation for up to two years. 'We can sell the likes of Léoville-Barton 2006 at €55 a glass, Haut-Batailley 1966 at €65 and even La Tâche 1991 at €1,200!'

Generally, however, Lisa is keen to get the cork and the wine out of the bottle, being passionate about decanting wine, even – if not especially – at house wine level. 'I hate the money-based treatment.' Old wines demand decanting because of their sediment deposits, but young wines in particular will benefit from it, as they need to be opened up. Another reason why Lisa and her team decant all their wines is because their customers love it. It looks good, and it makes people feel special.

'We've served princes, presidents and pop stars,' says Lisa, 'but everyone gets treated the same. For one thing, you never can know exactly who you're serving or what they know or don't know about wine. Some customers just want your discretion: to serve the wines and leave them to enjoy the company they are with. Others will want to hear the story of the wine, and of this estate's surprisingly rich wine legacy.' Thankfully, when it comes to wine at The K Club, there's no end of truly great stories.

A Note on Dessert Wine Pairings from Lisa O'Doherty

Dessert wine is a hard sell and it's such a shame, as I love it and regularly will skip dessert and just have the sticky… So instead of suggesting a wine with each dessert recipe, I'm going to suggest some of my favourites and let you choose. Remember, as a rule of thumb, the wine should always be sweeter than the food.

Sauternes – a very rich full-bodied sticky, with just a hint of putty flavours, very moreish. It is great with rich egg- and cheese-based desserts.

Muscat de Beaumes de Venise – a much cleaner fruitier style, almost grapey. This is lovely with fruit-based desserts.

Pink Muscat – Australia has some very good sweet wines and this is a favourite, almost like strawberries in a glass. It is light and refreshing. Try it with any berry fruit.

Banyuls – a red dessert wine that is fab with any dark chocolate dessert.

Eiswein – very rich, very sweet and very expensive, or at least the good ones are. Keep this wine for a special occasion.

CHAMPAGNE
Veuve Clicquot Ponsardin
BRUT

THE VINTAGE CROP BAR

The bar at the heart of the hotel

The K Club is a destination hotel, one to which the most discerning of guests travel from near and far. And how better to mark your arrival than with a drink at the bar? When you step inside the door of the Vintage Crop – into the moss-green, cocoon-like space with its handsome mahogany bar and its snug leather armchairs – there's no doubt that you've arrived.

The Vintage Crop is where you can begin the journey of your K Club stay, where you can return to digest the day's unfoldings or a sumptuous meal in one of the resort's or the city's restaurants. It's where you can strike up conversation with guests at the next table, or with John and Remi behind the bar, perhaps while you sample some of their favourites from the eye-level shelf of Irish whiskies. Or it's where you can sit in quiet contemplation and nurse a perfect nightcap. It's where you can be yourself, with no airs and graces required.

Vintage Crop

Besides being the beating heart of hotel life, the Vintage Crop is also the link to the land around it. The bar's reaches spill out beyond the walls on to the terrace, with its magnificent view across manicured lawns, past great native Irish oaks and Western red cedars, and down towards the sweep of the River Liffey, which snakes through 550 acres of estate and back out into the Kildare countryside beyond.

Back inside the bar, the walls are adorned with some remarkable testimony to the equestrian tradition of the surrounding county. Indeed, the bar itself is named after Dr Smurfit's great Irish gelding Vintage Crop, famed for winning not only the Jefferson Smurfit Memorial Irish St Leger for two years running (1993, 1994) but also the 1993 Melbourne Gold Cup.

Trained by Dermot Weld, Vintage Crop was the first Irish racehorse to surpass one million pounds in winnings. (His name is very apt, as that sum of money is approximately what was invested in the crop of stellar vintages that make up the fine wine cellar in the basement below.)

He was also the first horse to go from the northern to the southern hemisphere and win in Melbourne, a record which stood until 2002, when another of Dr Smurfit's horses – and Vintage Crop's stable-mate – Media Puzzle, did the same.

Both Melbourne Cup trophies are on glittering display in the Vintage Crop bar today, along with the civic keys to Melbourne city. And, if you look, you'll also spot what John Ryan describes as the 'amazingly small' outfit worn by jockey Mick Kinane during that 1993 Melbourne Cup win. 'I often joke with Mick that he'll never get into that again,' quips John with a wry smile.

The champagne trolley: a cause for celebration

All in all, there are many fine celebrations commemorated within this intimate bar's walls. Which is rather appropriate really, because this is a place where celebration is often the order of the day – whether the cause for celebration be a special anniversary, a successful day on the fairways or with the resident gillie down by the river, or simply the fact of being off-duty in great company.

JOHN RYAN JOB TITLE HERE

And many guests choose to celebrate with a glass of Laurent-Perrier Grand Siècle or its fragrant rosé champagne. Others opt for a bottle from some of the esteemed champagne houses displayed in the fabulous champagne trolley, including a very reasonably priced non-vintage Krug, as well as Dom Pérignon (but of course), Bollinger's Grand Année Rosé 2002 and, the daddy of them all, Louis Roederer's Cristal 2000.

'I love that champagne is coming back,' says John, who is the guardian of the champagne trolley. 'Of course, during the Celtic Tiger years it flew out, but now people are drinking it – not because it is the done thing but because they want to; because they are interested in it.'

The whiskey conundrum: what to drink and how to drink it

If champagne provides a stylish start to your evening here, then surely whiskey offers the perfect ending. You might choose to enjoy yours in an Irish coffee. And, if you do, you're in good hands, John being a champion of the perfect Irish coffee – quite literally, having won awards for his skills. He'll even give a hands-on demonstration to those interested in learning the subtle but eminently useful art of making the perfect Irish coffee. (If there was ever a party trick worth having up your sleeve, this must be it.)

Or you might prefer to wind down with a caffeine-free cocktail, in which case you can choose from one of the classic cocktails that the Vintage Crop specialises in and which John loves to see making a comeback. You won't find any flashy mixologists or show here. Instead you'll find old-school classics being executed with attention to detail and a solid reliance on quality ingredients: the freshest hand-squeezed juices or boutique, small-batch liquor brands.

Order yourself an Old Fashioned, and you'll be asked your choice of whiskey (John would recommend a blended Irish – perhaps one chosen from the entire Jameson family that is on offer, or perhaps an American whiskey such as Woodford Bourne). Fancy a martini? Choose from over two dozen gins and vodkas, including the rowan, heather and fuchsia-infused craft gin from Dingle in the south-west wilds of Ireland.

However, if you were to put yourself totally in John's capable hands, he would probably suggest that you get up close and personal with his extensive list of local whiskies. 'I remember when the selection of Irish whiskey took up a small corner of the bar, which was very much dominated by a Scottish selection,' explains John, who now stocks over forty Irish whiskies, which is nearly half of all the whiskey on offer here today.

'I've seen Irish whiskey take such an amazing journey during my time here and I have really loved sharing that journey with others and opening eyes to the diversity available today. After all, we make the smoothest whiskey going, thanks to its triple distillation. And now, with so many new distilleries coming on board, there's a renaissance in Irish whiskey, and the excitement about it is palpable.'

John's Irish whiskey tastings are a popular activity for corporate visits or for family gatherings, and offer an opportunity to taste samples from each of the main distilleries currently operating in the country. You could compare the charms of a blended Red Breast 15-year-old with those of a Bushmills Single Malt 16-year-old, which is finished in port casks, or contrast the sweet softness of a Midleton Very Rare with the smoky bite of a Connemara Peated Single Malt.

But John's recommended route to understanding the charms of Irish whiskey is to slowly work your way through a few samples over the course of a weekend and, one by one, to savour each as they should be: unrushed, unadulterated and on its own unique terms.

A renowned collection and a personal passion

If a tasting tour of Ireland's finest whiskies is not your style, you might prefer to get John talking about one of his other passions: the hotel's renowned art collection. Or, even better, you could book yourself to go on one of the official art tours that he conducts in the main house.

Some pieces are impossible to miss if you spend any time here, like the riotous 'Blackbird Bathing at Tir na nÓg' in the stunning Yeats Room (dedicated to the great Irish Expressionist), or the towering presence of Sir John Wootton's 'Byerley Turk', one of three founding sires of today's thoroughbred horse-racing brood stock, which keeps watch over the eponymous fine-dining restaurant. There are also a surprising number of quirky little pieces that might catch your eye, should you be paying sufficient attention – or should you have an insider art lover pointing them out to you with infectious enthusiasm.

One of John's favourites sits just outside the bar. A beautiful globe of the world studded with precious stones, it's a quirky piece picked up by Dr Smurfit on his travels. It often stops passers-by in their tracks, and those who do stop invariably have the same response: they give it a spin and ask 'So, where to next?'. It's a tantalising question, to consider where in the world tomorrow might take you. With any luck, that journey will eventually see you return to The K Club, as so many of John's guests have.

Up close and personal

John has been working here for ever, or at least since 1994, and he's learned a thing or two in his time. And so, of course, there's another attraction to sitting up at the Vintage Crop's mahogany bar, besides the eye-level collection of uisce beatha, and that's the man himself – and, specifically, the chance to pick his brains about the many useful things he has stored in it.

These might include where to go for the best steak dinner on a trip up to the big smoke in Dublin, or where exactly Tir na n'Óg is and how one might get there. Or, if it's gossip you're after, he might divulge details of the various ill-fated owners through whose hands the estate passed in the forty-odd years between Barton and Smurfit ownership. (Of these five interim owners, several lost their marriages or their money – and one unfortunate even lost his head!) Of course, being the master of discretion, he'll refrain from gossiping about past guests at The K Club, or at least from naming names. He does have one great story involving a bathful of Dom Perignon, but you'll have to ask the man himself about that.

Several decades on, John is lucky enough to be able to say that he loves his job. He loves the fact that he spends his days surrounded by some of the finest art in the country. He loves the skill he has developed for reading people ('You need to know that they want the next drink before they know themselves"), the showmanship of making cocktails and the theatre of serving hand-rolled Cohiba cigars from the specially commissioned humidor. (This miniature of the hotel was created by Viscount Linley, nephew of the Queen of England, and incorporates woods such as maple, holly, dark sycamore, cedar and mahogany.)

John Ryan has learned a great deal in his time at The K Club, from tasting the most incredible wines and from his visits to the Champagne region or to the two-day course held at the Irish Whiskey Academy in Midleton, County Cork ('What a luxury! That was one of the most rewarding things I've ever done'). Or simply from chatting to his guests about their travels in far-flung and fabulous corners of this world of ours. After all, guests at The K Club tend to be a pretty well-travelled bunch who enjoy the best of the best, and know where to find it.

The Vintage Crop

This cocktail is named after Dr Michael Smurfit's famous Irish gelding Vintage Crop, winner of the 1993 Melbourne Cup and the 1993 and 1994 Jefferson Smurfit Memorial Irish St Leger.

40ml (1½fl oz) Midleton Very Rare whiskey
10ml (½fl oz) Martini Rosso sweet vermouth
10ml (½fl oz) Martini Bianco dry vermouth
dash of orange bitters
2 dashes of Angostura bitters
2 Irish chocolate truffles rolled in gold leaf, to garnish

Fill the mixing glass with ice, add the Midleton Very Rare, Martini Rosso and Bianco and the dashes of Angostura and orange bitters and stir. Run lemon around the rim of a chilled martini glass and dip it in gold leaf to coat the rim. Strain the contents of the mixing glass into the martini glass. Garnish with 2 Irish chocolate truffles rolled in gold leaf on a cocktail stick.

THE K CLUB COCKTAILS

Bramble

One of the great cocktails to emerge from the 1980s is the Bramble, from the renowned English mixologist Dirk Bradsell in Soho in London.

40ml (1½fl oz) Tanqueray gin
20ml (¾fl oz) fresh lemon juice
10ml (½fl oz) sugar syrup (see page 271)
15ml (½fl oz) crème de mûre
6 fresh blackberries or raspberries
2 small straws

Fill an old-fashioned whiskey tumbler with crushed ice and add the Tanqueray gin, fresh lemon juice and sugar syrup. Top up with more crushed ice and pour over the crème de mûre, so that it 'bleeds' down through the crushed ice. Garnish with the fresh berries.

Old-Fashioned

Another American classic from the late 1800s, this creation is credited to a bartender at the Pendennis Club in Louisville, Kentucky.

5ml (¼fl oz) sugar syrup (see page 271)
1 orange slice and 1 maraschino cocktail cherry
3 dashes of Angostura bitters
60ml (2fl oz) Woodford Reserve bourbon

Put the sugar syrup, orange slice, Angostura bitters and cocktail cherries in the bottom of an old-fashioned whiskey tumbler and muddle. Add ice and Woodford Reserve and stir well.

Manhattan

Legend has it that this classic American cocktail was created in 1874 in New York's Manhattan Club in honour of Lady Randolph Churchill, mother of Sir Winston Churchill, and served at a celebration dinner for the Governor of New York.

50ml (2fl oz) Woodford Reserve or Bulleit rye whiskey
25ml (1fl oz) Martini Rosso sweet vermouth
2 dashes of Angostura bitters
3 maraschino cocktail cherries on a cocktail stick, to garnish

Half-fill a mixing glass with ice cubes, add Bourbon, Vermouth and Angostura bitters and stir. Strain into a well-chilled martini glass and garnish with 3 maraschino cocktail cherries on a cocktail stick. Variations of this very famous cocktail include: the Irish Manhattan, which is made using Jameson whiskey instead of bourbon or rye; Rob Roy, which is made using Scotch whiskey; and the Eastern Manhattan, which is made using Suntory Japanese whiskey.

Cosmopolitan

The Cosmopolitan is a classic cocktail, which has had a new lease of life thanks to exposure on popular television programmes.

40ml (1½fl oz) Ketel One vodka
20ml (¾fl oz) Cointreau
20ml (¾fl oz) fresh lime juice
40ml (1½fl oz) cranberry juice
wedge of lime, to garnish

Fill a cocktail shaker with ice, add all the ingredients (except the garnish) and shake well. Strain into a chilled martini glass and garnish with a wedge of fresh lime. If you prefer your Cosmopolitan with a more tart flavour, replace the Cointreau with Triple Sec.

Champagne Cocktail – The London Edition

This wonderfully named cocktail has changed very little in the 150-plus years since it appeared in the first edition of Jerry Thomas's *How to Mix Drinks* (1862).

1 sugar cube
Angostura bitters
30ml (1fl oz) Hennessy cognac
Laurent-Perrier champagne
twist of orange, to garnish

Soak the sugar cube in 2 to 3 dashes of Angostura bitters. Place the soaked sugar cube in a champagne flute and add the cognac. Top up with Laurent-Perrier champagne and garnish with a twist of orange draped over the side of the glass.

French Martini

35ml (1¼fl oz) Ketel One vodka
35ml (1¼fl oz) Chambord raspberry liqueur
71ml (2½fl oz) pineapple juice
3 raspberries on a cocktail stick, to garnish

Fill a cocktail shaker with ice, add all the ingredients (except the garnish) and shake well. Strain into a chilled martini glass and watch as a lovely foamy head appears on the top of the cocktail. Garnish with 3 raspberries speared on a cocktail stick.

Candy Apple Martini

20ml (¾fl oz) Ketel One vodka
15ml Butterscotch Schnapps
20ml (¾fl oz) Apple Schnapps
10ml (½fl oz) fresh lime juice
35ml (1¼fl oz) cranberry juice
wheel slice of red apple, to garnish

Fill a cocktail shaker with ice, add all the ingredients (except the garnish) and shake well. Strain into a well-chilled martini glass and garnish with a nice thin wheel slice of red apple.

Whiskey Sour

The original sour, a classic cocktail dating from the mid 1800s, has inspired many different styles of sour. The key to this balanced cocktail is the use of fresh lemon juice. A fantastic variation on this cocktail is the Amaretto Sour, in which the Maker's Mark bourbon is replaced with Amaretto di Saronno.

50ml (2fl oz) Maker's Mark bourbon
25ml (1fl oz) fresh lemon juice
12.5ml (½fl oz) sugar syrup (see page xxx)
dash of egg white (optional)
slice of lemon and 2 maraschino cocktail cherries, to garnish

Put the Maker's Mark bourbon, fresh lemon juice, sugar syrup and egg white (if using) into a cocktail shaker and shake vigorously so that all the ingredients are blended together. Strain into a well-chilled old-fashioned whiskey tumbler. Garnish with the slice of lemon and cocktail cherries.

The Pink Paradise

15ml (½fl oz) Bacardi Carta Blanca rum
15ml (½fl oz) Malibu
15ml (½fl oz) Amaretto di Saronno
60ml (2fl oz) pineapple juice
60ml (2fl oz) cranberry juice
1 wedge of orange and 2 maraschino cherries, to garnish

Place some ice in a cocktail shaker, add everything except the garnish and shake well. Strain into a well-chilled hurricane glass. Garnish with a wedge of orange and 2 maraschino cocktail cherries.

Kir Royale

dash of crème de cassis
Laurent Perrier champagne

Place a dash of crème de cassis in a champagne flute and top up with Laurent-Perrier Champagne.

Mojito

30ml (1fl oz) fresh lime juice
20ml (¾fl oz) sugar syrup (see page 271)
8 large fresh mint leaves
50ml (2fl oz) Havana Club 3 Years
sprig of fresh mint, to garnish
soda water

Combine the fresh lime juice, sugar syrup and mint leaves in a highball glass and bruise the mint leaves with a muddler to release the essential oils. Add the Havana rum and top up the glass with crushed ice. Stir the ingredients so that the leaves are pulled up through the crushed ice. Garnish with a sprig of fresh mint and top up with a splash of soda water.

Americano

This classic cocktail was introduced by Gaspare Campari, owner of the Caffè Camparino in Milan and distiller of Campari. It was named in honour of the Americans who came to Milan during Prohibition in the USA and who were partial to a nice alcoholic cocktail.

35.5ml (1¼fl oz) Campari
35.5ml (1¼fl oz) sweet vermouth
soda water
1 slice each of orange and lemon

Fill a highball glass with ice, add the Campari and vermouth and top up with soda water. Garnish with a slice each of orange and lemon.

The Story of Irish Whiskey

Recently Irish whiskey has been enjoying a renaissance on the global stage. Never before has there been so much interest in this wonderful Uisce Beatha or Water of Life. Before Prohibition, Irish whiskey was very well established and highly respected in the United States and at home. However, during Prohibiton, the canny Scots moved in, establishing themselves as the tipple of choice, and the term 'Irish' unfortunately became associated with a poor-quality black market spirit. As a result, Irish whiskey sales collapsed and, one by one, the great distilleries closed. By 1948, there were only three distilleries left in the Republic of Ireland and three in Northern Ireland. By 1953, only five survived on the island, mainly supplying the domestic market. These were the Jameson and Powers distilleries of Dublin, Cork Distilleries Company (CDC) of Cork and the Bushmills and Coleraine distilleries in Northern Ireland. Sensing that the writing was on the wall regarding the might of the Scottish distilleries, Jameson, Powers and CDC merged in 1966 to form Irish Distillers Ltd. This date marked the start of the revival of Irish whiskey and lay the foundation stone in Midleton for something very special. Through the Jameson brand, new doors opened for Irish whiskey and exciting things began to happen. After Jack Teeling entered the race and reopened the Cooley Distillery, the Irish Whiskey industry began to dust itself off, once more offering the discerning drinker a diverse array of styles and flavours of top-quality Irish whiskeys to choose from.

Today, in this golden age of Irish whiskies distilling, there are over fifteen distilleries in various stages of production, sales, planning and development. Leading the charge is Irish Distillers, who have recently opened a state-of-the-art distillery in Midleton. William Grant of Scotland have built a brand new distillery in Tullamore and have reopened the old distillery as a visitor centre, while the Old Bushmills Distillery has been acquired by the Mexican Tequila House, Jose Cuervo. Jack Teeling is back with a brand-new distillery in Dublin 8, while the Walsh Distillery in Carlow has brought us The Irishman and Writer's Tears. And we're looking forward to tasting the whiskey offering from the Dingle Distilling Company, who have already brought us delicious gin and vodka, as we await the arrival of their whiskey, currently still being laid down. With so many of the world's major spirit players entering the Irish whiskey market, it can only go from strength to strength.

Connemara Peated Single Malt by Beam Suntory

This single malt whiskey is made entirely with peated malt.

Colour: Yellow gold
Nose: Pungent, smokey (imagine the smell of an open turf fire)
Palate: Mouth-filling, sweet, with enough green fruits to keep the smoke mild
Finish: Dry, toasty, turfy smoke

Bushmills 16 Years Single Malt by Jose Cuervo

This 16-year-old whiskey is matured in bourbon casks and is blended with a slightly smaller amount that is aged in oloroso sherry butts (both are 16 years old). It is then re-casked in port piles for a further 6 to 12 months.

Colour: Deep amber
Nose: One of the most complex fruit aromas in Irish whiskey
Taste: Mouth-filling, tongue-coating, smoothness of juicy summer fruits, tinged with maltiness, spiced and rich bitter toffee kick
Finish: Thick and syrupy, with red fruits and treacle tart

Jameson Gold Reserve by Irish Distillers

Colour: Deep gold
Nose: Fragrant notes of toasted oak with an added dimension of sweet wood from the clever use of unseasoned virgin oak, combined with the aroma of pot still spices and soft sherry fruitiness
Taste: Deep succulent fruit and a touch of nuttiness from the oloroso sherry butts are layered with flavours of the bourbon barrels and vanilla sweetness from virgin oak. Pot still oils and spices combine perfectly with the wood flavours, delivering an exceptionally smooth and complex flavour
Finish: A very long finish with a pleasantly peppery finale

Redbreast 15 Years Old by Irish Distillers

This is the quintessential Irish single pot still small batch whiskey.

Colour: Deep gold
Nose: Full and rich with a complex yet balanced mix of berry fruits and aromatic oils
Taste: Fully round and mellow, with the succulence of fleshy fruit combined with spices and toasted wood
Finish: Long and sophisticated

Midleton Very Rare by Irish Distillers

This blended Irish whiskey is ideal for a very special occasion or celebration.

Colour: Deep gold
Nose: A rich, full pot still character with touches of ripe juicy sultanas, yeasty fruitiness and acacia honey
Taste: A crisp, truly unique taste. A maltiness is first apparent and then the richness of honey, berry fruits and hints of clementines come to the fore
Finish: A very long finish with a pleasantly peppery finale

BASIC RECIPES

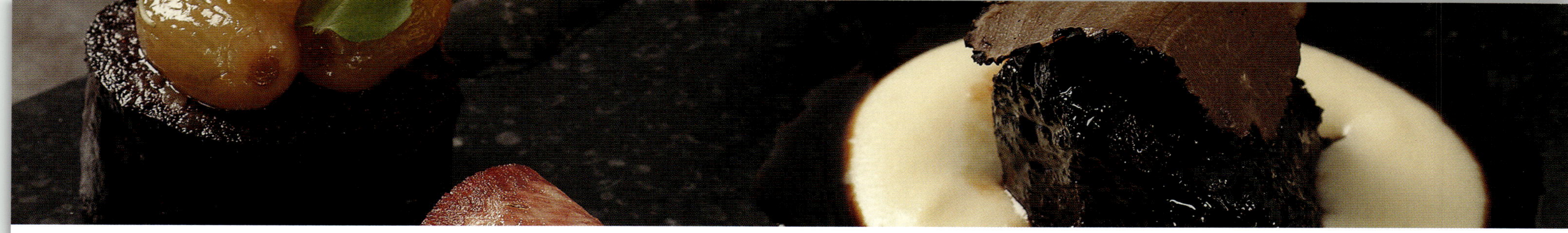

SAVOURY AND SWEET STOCKS

WHITE CHICKEN STOCK

Makes about 3 litres (5¼ pints)

3kg (6–7lb) chicken carcasses
6 litres (10½ pints) water

Using a meat cleaver or similar, chop the carcasses into small pieces to maximise flavour. Place the bones and the water in a large pot and bring to the boil. Remove any fatty scum or impurities that rise to the top. Reduce the heat and leave to simmer on a low heat for 4–6 hours, continuing to remove any scum that rises to the top. Once a good chicken flavour has been achieved, pass the stock through a fine sieve or chinois and cool. When cold, the stock should set like jelly and be clear. Note, we do not use vegetables in this stock, simply chicken and water.

FISH STOCK

2 kg (4½lb) white fish bones (e.g. turbot, halibut, cod, etc.) (If you are including heads, always remove the gills and eyes.)
60ml (2fl oz) Newgrange Gold rapeseed oil
100gm (3½oz) sliced onions
80gm (3oz) sliced fennel bulb
80gm (3oz) chopped leeks, white part only
1 star anise
5gm (¼oz) coriander seeds
4 litres (7 pints) water

Using a meat cleaver or similar, chop the fish bones into quite small pieces to maximise flavour. Pour the oil into a large pot and add the bones. Sweat over a low heat for 10 minutes, then pass through a fine sieve or chinois to remove the fatty impurities. Put the bones back in the pot and add the onions, fennel bulb, leeks, star anise and coriander seeds. Pour in just enough water to cover the bones by 2cm (1in). Put the pot back on the heat and gently bring to the boil, then reduce to simmer for 25 minutes, removing any fatty impurities that rise to the top. Pass the stock through a fine sieve or chinois and allow to cool. When cold, the stock should set like jelly and be clear.

BROWN CHICKEN STOCK

Makes about 3 litres (5¼ pints)

3kg (6½lb) chicken carcasses
200gm (7oz) white onions, roughly chopped
150gm (5oz) carrots, peeled and roughly chopped
100gm (3½oz) leeks, roughly chopped
60gm (2oz) celery, roughly chopped
5 litres (9 pints) white chicken stock
60ml (2fl oz) Newgrange Gold rapeseed oil

Preheat the oven to 180°C. Using a meat cleaver (or similar), chop the carcasses into small pieces to maximise flavour. Put the rapeseed oil in a hot roasting tray, add the chicken bones and vegetables and transfer to the preheated oven. Stir the bones occasionally as they roast and remove from the oven once they are golden brown. Drain off the excess fat and place everything in a large pot. Pour over the white chicken stock and bring to the boil, removing any fatty scum or impurities that rise to the surface. Reduce the heat and leave to simmer on a low heat for 4–6 hours, continuing to remove any scum that rises to the top. Once a good chicken flavour has been achieved, pass the stock through a fine sieve or chinois and cool. When cold, the stock should set like jelly and be clear.

BROWN VEAL OR BEEF STOCK

3kg (6½lb) veal or beef bones
60ml (2fl oz) rapeseed oil
200gm (7oz) white onion, roughly chopped
150gm (5oz) carrots, peeled and roughly chopped
100gm (3½oz) leek, roughly chopped
60gm (2oz) celery, roughly chopped
6 litres (10½ pints) water

Preheat the oven to 180°C. Using a meat cleaver or similar, chop the bones into small pieces to maximise flavour. Place the rapeseed oil in a hot roasting tray, add the veal or beef bones and vegetables and transfer to the oven. Stir the bones occasionally as they roast and remove from the oven once they are golden brown. Drain off excess fat and place everything in a large pot. Pour over the water, bring to the boil and remove any fatty scum or impurities that rise to the top, then reduce the heat and leave to simmer on a low heat for 6–8 hours, continuing to remove any fatty scum or impurities that rise to the top. Once a good meaty flavour has been achieved, pass through a fine sieve or chinois and cool. When cold, the stock should set like jelly and be clear.

MOREL STOCK

Makes 200ml

75gm dried morels
2 shallots, chopped
1 litre white chicken stock

Place all the ingredients in a pot, bring to the boil and reduce over a medium heat until reduced to approximately 200ml. Pass the stock through a fine sieve or chinois and muslin cloth. Cool and refrigerate for use.

BROWN VEAL OR BEEF JUS

Makes about 2 litres (3½ pints)

60ml (2fl oz) Newgrange Gold rapeseed oil
1.6 kg (3½lb) veal or beef trimmings, cut into 2cm (1in) cubes
200gm (7oz) white onions, roughly chopped
150gm (5oz) carrots, peeled and roughly chopped
100gm (3½oz) leeks, roughly chopped
60gm (2oz) celery, roughly chopped
5gm (¼oz) crushed black pepper
2 garlic cloves
1 sprig of fresh thyme
½ sprig of fresh rosemary
3½ litres (6 pints) brown veal or beef stock

Preheat the oven to 140°C. Place a large, heavy-based frying pan over a high heat and add a little oil. Sear the trimmings in the hot pan in 3 or 4 batches until all the meat is nicely browned (being careful not to overload the pan). Once browned, transfer the meat to kitchen paper to drain off any excess fat, then brown the vegetables in the hot pan and drain. Place the meat, vegetables and herbs in a large pot and add the brown veal or beef stock. Bring slowly to the boil and remove any fatty scum or impurities that rise to the top. Cover with a circle of parchment paper and transfer to the oven. Cook for about 1 hour and 30 minutes, or until the liquid has reduced by 40% and has reached a light sauce consistency. Pass the jus through a fine muslin cloth and sieve. Allow to cool.

Note: We do not add any seasoning in this recipe, as this is a base for sauce-making only.

WHITE MUTTON OR LAMB STOCK

Makes about 3 litres (5¼ pints)

3kg (6½lb) mutton or lamb bones
200gm (7oz) white onions, roughly chopped
150gm (5oz) carrots, peeled and roughly chopped
100gm (3½oz) leeks, roughly chopped
60gm (2oz) celery, roughly chopped
2 sprigs of fresh rosemary
6 litres (10½ pints) water

Using a meat cleaver or similar, chop the bones into small pieces to maximise flavour. Put the mutton (or lamb) bones, vegetables and rosemary into a large pot. Place over a medium-high heat, pour in the water and bring to the boil, removing any fatty scum or impurities that rise to the top. Reduce the heat to low and leave to simmer for 6–8 hours, until you achieve a good meaty flavour. Continue to remove any scum that rises to the surface as the stock is cooking. Pass through a fine sieve or chinois and leave to cool. When cold, the stock should set like jelly and be clear.

VEGETABLE STOCK

10ml rapeseed oil
2 onions, peeled and chopped into large 2cm-thick chunks
1 head of celery, chopped into 2cm-thick pieces
2 large button mushrooms
1 small fennel bulb, chopped into 2cm-thick pieces
6 garlic cloves, smashed
1 bay leaf
1 sprig fresh thyme
80gm flat leaf parsley, roughly chopped
5gm white peppercorns
5 litres water

Heat the rapeseed oil in a pot over a medium heat and add in the rest of the ingredients. Cover with a lid and cook out, stirring occasionally, until the vegetables are beginning to soften. Remove the lid. Add in the water and bring to the boil. Reduce the heat and simmer the stock until reduced by half. Remove any impurities that rise to the top during the cooking with a ladle. Pass the stock through a fine sieve or chinois and muslin cloth. Cool and refrigerate for use.

SPARKLING ELDERFLOWER WINE

650gm (1lb 6oz) granulated sugar
4.5 litres (8 pints) water
1 lemon
20ml (¾fl oz) white wine vinegar
4 heads fresh elderflowers, in full bloom

Add the sugar to a pot with 500ml (just under 1 pint) water and warm it gently until the sugar dissolves. Set aside and pour into a large plastic container when cool. Cut the lemon into quarters, squeeze out the juice (discard the juice) and place the rinds in the sugar and water mixture. Add the vinegar and remaining water and finally the elderflower heads. Cover the container with parchment paper and cling film and leave to steep for 4 days. A mouldy crust will form on the top. Remove this with a spoon and then strain the liquid through a fine sieve and a double layer of muslin cloth. Pour into glass bottles with strong lids and store for 6–10 days. To check if the wine is ready, it should fizz when you open the bottle cap. After ten days, make sure to store the bottles in a cold environment or they will be in danger of exploding.

SUGAR SYRUP

Makes about 500ml (approximately 1 pint)

500gm (1lb 1oz) caster sugar
500ml (just under 1 pint) water
1 vanilla pod, split in half lengthways

Place the ingredients in a pot and bring up to a strong simmer. Remove from the heat and leave to cool. Refrigerate until required.

DRESSINGS AND MAYONNAISE

BALSAMIC DRESSING

100ml (3½fl oz) 12-year-old Villa Manodori balsamic vinegar, or similar
300ml (10½fl oz) Newgrange Gold rapeseed oil
salt and freshly milled black pepper

Mix the balsamic vinegar and oil together and season with salt and milled black pepper to taste.

CITRUS DRESSING

250ml (9fl oz) fresh orange juice
125ml (4fl oz) fresh pink grapefruit juice
250ml (9fl oz) Newgrange Gold rapeseed oil
salt and freshly milled white pepper

Pass the fresh juices through a fine sieve. Place in a small pot over a high heat and boil until reduced down to 250ml (9fl oz). Set aside to cool. Whisk in the oil and season with salt and milled white pepper.

FRESH MAYONNAISE

Makes about 800ml (approximately 1½ pints)

6 free-range egg yolks
1 tbsp Dijon mustard
350ml (12fl oz) Newgrange Gold rapeseed oil
350ml (12fl oz) sunflower oil
squeeze of fresh lemon Juice
salt and pepper

Whisk the egg yolks and Dijon mustard to ribbon stage. Continue to whisk and slowly pour in the oils until they are completely emulsified. Finish with a little lemon juice and season with salt and pepper to taste. Store in an airtight container in the fridge and use within 2 days.

PLAIN SALAD DRESSING

40ml (1½fl oz) white wine vinegar
5gm (¼oz) Dijon mustard
40ml (1½fl oz) olive oil
125ml (4fl oz) sunflower oil
20ml (¾fl oz) walnut oil
20ml (¾fl oz) hazelnut oil
salt and freshly milled white pepper

Whisk the white wine vinegar and mustard together. Add the oils, season with salt and milled white pepper and whisk to combine.

BUTTER AND FLAVOURED OILS

CLARIFIED BUTTER

Makes 80ml (3fl oz)

200gm (7oz) Avonmore unsalted butter

Place the unsalted butter in a pot and bring to the boil. Remove from the heat and allow to settle (all the clear butter will rise to the top and a whitish liquid will sink to the bottom). Using a small ladle, remove the clear butter by skimming with the ladle until all that is left is the white liquid. Store the clear, clarified butter in an airtight container and refrigerate until required.

COUNTRY BUTTER

Makes about 2.5kg (5lb 8oz) butter

5 litres (approximately 9 pints) Avonmore cream
20gm (¾oz) salt

Leave the cream to sit at room temperature for 2–3 days until it sours. Place the cream in a mixing bowl and, using a paddle attachment, mix the cream on a very low speed until the cream curdles. Do not use a high speed or the butter will be too white in colour. The slower you mix, the better, as this will achieve a nice yellow butter colour. Strain the butter through a sieve to separate the buttermilk from the butter. Take the butter and return it to the mixing bowl. Add the salt and mix for a further 5 minutes, to help remove any excess buttermilk. Strain off the remaining buttermilk. Place the butter on a marble top or board and knead it well to remove any last drops of liquid. Finally, roll the butter in parchment paper and refrigerate to set it.

GARDEN SAGE OIL

250gm (9oz) fresh sage leaves
170ml (6fl oz) sunflower oil

Blanch the sage leaves in boiling, salted water for 10 seconds and then cool down immediately in iced water. Drain the leaves and squeeze them in a cloth to remove any excess water. Place the sage and oil in a HotmixPRO blender (or similar) and blitz on high for 5 minutes. Pass through a fine chinois or sieve and store in a bottle with an airtight lid. This oil will keep in the fridge for up to 3 months.

BASIL OIL

100gm (3½oz) fresh basil leaves
50gm (2oz) baby spinach
150ml (5fl oz) sunflower oil
100ml (3½fl oz) Newgrange Gold rapeseed oil

Blanch the fresh basil and spinach leaves very quickly in boiling, salted water for 10 seconds. Drain and squeeze to remove excess water. Place the blanched basil and baby spinach leaves in a HotmixPRO blender (or similar) with the oils and blitz on high for 5 minutes. Pass the mixture through a fine chinois or sieve and allow to infuse for 24 hours. This oil will keep in the fridge for up to 3 months.

WILD GARLIC OIL

100gm (3½oz) fresh wild garlic leaves, washed
50gm (2oz) baby spinach
150ml (5fl oz) sunflower oil
100ml (3½fl oz) Newgrange Gold rapeseed oil

Blanch the wild garlic and spinach in a pot of boiling, salted water for 10 seconds. Drain the leaves and squeeze them in a cloth to remove any excess water. Place the wild garlic and spinach in a HotmixPRO blender (or similar) with the oils and blitz on high for 5 minutes. Pass the mixture through a fine chinois and allow to infuse for 24 hours. This oil will keep in the fridge for up to 3 months.

CURRY OIL

30gm (1oz) ras el hanout
5gm (¼oz) ground turmeric
2 curry leaves, crushed
1 lime leaf, crushed
150ml (5fl oz) sunflower oil
90ml (3fl oz) Newgrange Gold rapeseed oil

Gently heat the leaves and spices in a dry pot; do not allow them to overheat or burn. Add the oils and allow to warm slightly until the temperature of the oil reaches 80°C. Transfer to an airtight container with a lid and allow to stand for 24 hours. Strain through a fine chinois or sieve and muslin cloth and allow to infuse for 2 days before use. This oil will keep in the fridge for up to 3 months.

CORIANDER OIL

100gm (3½oz) fresh coriander leaves
50gm (2oz) baby spinach
150ml (5fl oz) sunflower oil
100ml (3½fl oz) Newgrange Gold rapeseed oil

Blanch the coriander leaves and spinach in a pot of boiling, salted water for 10 seconds. Drain the leaves and squeeze them in a cloth to remove any excess water. Place the coriander and spinach in a HotmixPRO blender (or similar) with the oils and blitz on high for 5 minutes. Pass the mixture through a fine chinois and allow to infuse for 24 hours. This oil will keep in the fridge for up to 3 months.

PARSLEY OIL

100gm (3½oz) fresh parsley leaves
50gm (2oz) baby spinach
150ml (5fl oz) sunflower oil
100ml (3½fl oz) Newgrange Gold rapeseed oil

Blanch the parsley and spinach in a pot of boiling, salted water for 10 seconds. Drain the leaves and squeeze them in a cloth to remove any excess water. Place the parsley and spinach in a HotmixPRO blender (or similar) with the oils and blitz on high for 5 minutes. Pass the mixture through a fine chinois and allow to infuse for 24 hours. This oil will keep in the fridge for up to 3 months.

FENNEL SEED OIL

25gm (1oz) fennel seeds
50ml (2fl oz) Newgrange Gold rapeseed oil

Toast the fennel seeds in a dry pan over a medium heat for 1–2 minutes to release the flavour. Add the rapeseed oil and return to the heat. Bring up to 160°C and then remove from the heat and allow to cool. Allow to infuse for 2 days before use. This oil will keep in the fridge for up to 3 months.

CHUTNEYS AND PRESERVES

PRESERVED BABY ARTICHOKES

10 baby artichokes
5gm (¼oz) ascorbic acid
200ml (7fl oz) water

Peel the artichokes with a small knife. Place them in a sterilised Kilner jar (or similar) with the ascorbic acid and water. Close the lid and transfer the jar to the steamer and steam for 15 minutes. Allow to cool and then refrigerate. Store for at least 1 month before using.

Note: These preserved baby artichokes will last for up to 3 months unopened. Once opened, store in the fridge and use within 3 days.

TOMATO CHUTNEY

70gm (2½oz) brown sugar
60ml (2fl oz) malt vinegar
10gm (½oz) fresh coriander stalks
50gm (2oz) Avonmore unsalted butter
125gm (4½oz) white onions, chopped
500gm (17oz) tomato concasse (the tomatoes should be blanched, deseeded, peeled and chopped small)

Caramelise the brown sugar in a pan. Deglaze with the vinegar and coriander stalks to make a gastrique reduction and set aside. In a separate pan, sweat the onions in the unsalted butter until they are soft and translucent but not coloured. Add the sautéed onions and chopped tomatoes to the gastrique reduction. Cook over a high heat until 80% of the liquid is gone. Transfer to a sterilised Kilner Jar. Close the lid and place the jar in a steamer for 15 minutes. Store for at least 1 month before using.

Note: This tomato chutney will last for up to 6 months unopened. Once opened, store in the fridge and use within 3 days.

PRESERVED MIRABELLE PLUMS

1 thick bourbon vanilla pod
600ml (21fl oz) water
200ml (7fl oz) caster sugar
1kg (2lb 3oz) fresh mirabelle plums, washed thoroughly

Split the vanilla pod in half lengthways and place it in a pot with the water and sugar. Bring up to the boil and then allow to cool. Place the plums in a large sterilised Kilner jar and cover with the cooled vanilla syrup. Close the lid and place the jar in a steamer for 15 minutes. Leave to cool and store in the fridge. Store for at least 1 month before using.

Note: These preserved plums will last for up to 12 months unopened. Once opened, store in the fridge and use within 3 days.

APPLE CHUTNEY

60g (2oz) brown sugar
50ml (2fl oz) cider vinegar
10ml (½fl oz) Calvados
juice of 3 fresh limes
6 cloves
1 cinnamon stick
1 tsp ground cumin
1.5kg (3lb 5oz) Granny Smith apples, peeled, cored and sliced

Place all the ingredients, except the sliced apple, in a pot and bring to the boil. When the liquid is boiling, add the apples and cook until just soft. Transfer the chutney to a sterilised Kilner jar, close the lid and place in a steamer for 15 minutes. Store in the fridge for at least 1 week before using.

Note: This apple chutney will last for up to 6 months unopened. Once opened, store in the fridge and use within 3 days.

PRESERVED GARDEN PEARS

4 whole garden pears, peeled and cored
500ml (17fl oz) sugar syrup (see page 271)

Place the pears in a pot, cover with the syrup and set over a low heat to simmer gently until just soft. Transfer to a large sterilised Kilner jar, making sure the pears are covered in the syrup. Close the lid and place the jar in a steamer for 15 minutes. Store in the fridge for at least 3 months before using.

Note: These preserved pears will last for up to 6 months unopened. Once opened, store in the fridge and use within 3 days.

STRAFFAN RED RHUBARB COMPOTE

4kg (9lb) Straffan Red rhubarb, chopped
400ml (14fl oz) grenadine
200gm (7oz) caster sugar

Place the rhubarb and grenadine in a pot and cook over a medium heat until it has stewed right down and is just dry. Add the sugar and cook for another 10 minutes. Taste and check for bitterness; if it needs more sugar, add a little at a time, but leave the compote tasting slightly sharp.

MANGO AND VANILLA CHUTNEY

2 ripe mangoes, peeled and diced
30ml (1fl oz) malt vinegar
15gm (½oz) sugar
¼ fresh vanilla pod, cut in half and seeds removed

To make the chutney, place the sugar in a small pot and cook to a light caramel. Add the malt vinegar, mix to combine and then add the vanilla. Next add the mango and cook until the mixture softens and forms a chutney consistency. Transfer to a sterilised Kilner jar and place in a steamer for 15 minutes to seal. Preserve for at least 1 month before using.

BREAD

BRIOCHE

Makes 4 loaves

1kg (2lb 3oz) strong flour
100gm (3½oz) caster sugar
20gm (¾oz) salt
55gm (2oz) fresh yeast
200gm (7oz) free-range egg yolks
400ml (14fl oz) water
400gm (14oz) Avonmore unsalted butter, chilled and cut into cubes
egg wash, to brush

Grease 4 brioche loaf tins (19cm x 9cm x 5cm; 7½in x 3½in x 2in). Mix all the dry ingredients and yeast together in a mixer. Add the egg yolks and water. Mix for about 15 minutes, until you achieve a firm but soft dough. Let the dough rest for 30 minutes. Now add the cold butter and mix until just combined, being careful not to over-mix the dough. Cover the bowl with cling film and leave to prove in a warm place until the dough has doubled in size.

Divide the dough into four even pieces and place each one in a greased loaf tin. Cover once more with cling film and leave to prove until aerated and doubled in size once more. Preheat the oven to 170°C. Brush the brioches with a light egg wash and bake in the preheated oven for 45 minutes.

Note: To make baby brioche rolls, divide the dough into 25gm (1oz) pieces and roll into round shapes. Place the balls into well-greased tart moulds and follow the same proving procedure as above. Bake at 170°C for about 15 minutes.

RYE AND SUNFLOWER SEED BREAD

Makes 4 loaves

460gm (1lb 2oz) rye flour
680gm (1lb 8oz) strong flour
100gm (3½oz) spelt flour
15gm (½oz) sea salt
50gm (2oz) sunflower seeds
15gm (½oz) muscovado sugar
50gm (2oz) fresh yeast
680ml (24fl oz) Avonmore milk
egg wash, to brush

Grease 4 loaf tins (19cm x 9cm x 5cm; 7½in x 3½in x 2in). Mix the flours, sea salt and sunflower seeds together in a mixer with a spade (or dough hook) attachment. In a separate bowl, mix the muscovado sugar, yeast and milk together. Add the wet mix into the dry mix and work together until you achieve a nice shiny dough. Cover with cling film and leave to prove in a warm place until the dough has doubled in size. Divide the dough into four even pieces and place each one in a greased loaf tin. Cover once more with cling film and leave to prove until aerated and doubled in size once more. Preheat the oven to 180°C. Brush the loaves with a light egg wash and bake in the preheated oven for 45 minutes.

WHITE SODA BREAD

400gm (14oz) self-raising flour
400ml (14fl oz) buttermilk (retained from country butter recipe on page 272)
pinch of salt

Preheat the oven to 180°C. Mix all the ingredients together in a bowl and very gently knead to form a wet dough. Line a baking sheet with a Silpat or similar non-stick mat and transfer to the oven to cook for 30 minutes. Remove from the oven, wrap in a clean tea towel and allow to cool.

BASIL AND TOMATO BREAD

Makes 4 loaves

1125gm (2lb 8oz) strong flour
35gm (1¼oz) salt
75gm (2½oz) caster sugar
65gm (2½oz) tomato paste
65gm (2½oz) fresh yeast
250gm (9oz) sundried tomatoes, diced
50gm (2oz) fresh basil, chopped
700ml (24fl oz) water
egg wash, to brush

Grease 4 loaf tins, each measuring 19cm x 9cm x 5cm (7½in x 3½in x 2in). Put all the ingredients in a mixer and set to mix for 20 minutes, until the dough is nice and shiny; this should be a very soft dough. Cover the bowl with cling film and set aside somewhere warm to prove until the dough has doubled in size. Divide the dough into four even pieces and place each one in a greased loaf tin. Cover once more with cling film and leave to prove until aerated and doubled in size once more. Preheat the oven to 180°C. Brush the loaves with a light egg wash and bake in the oven for 45 minutes.

CHOCOLATE STICKS

135ml (4¾fl oz) sugar syrup (see page 271)
80gm (3oz) cocoa powder
45ml (1½fl oz) liquid glucose

Preheat the oven to 160°C. Place all the ingredients in a mixing bowl and whisk to form a paste. Transfer to a disposable piping bag and snip a 2mm (1⁄10in) hole in the end. Line a baking sheet with a Silpat or similar non-stick mat and pipe the paste in straight lines the full length of the mat. Transfer to the oven for 4 minutes. Remove and cut the chocolate sticks into 12cm (4½in) lengths and store in an airtight container until ready to serve.

WILD GARLIC BREAD

Makes 4 loaves

1kg (2lb 3oz) T55 flour
30gm (1oz) fresh yeast
30gm (1oz) salt
500ml (17fl oz) water
120gm (4oz) wild garlic leaves, finely chopped
egg wash, to brush

Grease 4 loaf tins, each measuring 19cm x 9cm x 5cm (7½in x 3½in x 2in). Place all the dry ingredients in a mixer and mix briefly to combine, then add the water and mix for about 20 minutes to achieve a soft shiny dough. Cover the bowl with cling film and set aside somewhere warm to prove until the dough has doubled in size. Divide the dough into four even pieces and place each one in a greased loaf tin. Cover with cling film and leave to prove until aerated and doubled in size once more. Preheat the oven to 170°C. Brush the loaves with a light egg wash and bake in the preheated oven for 15 minutes.

VANILLA ICE CREAM

4 bourbon vanilla pods
1 litre Avonmore milk
200gm free-range eggs yolks
150gm caster sugar
200ml Avonmore cream

Mix the free-range egg yolks together in a bowl. Boil the milk in a pot and pour 200ml into the egg mix. Then add the egg mix back into the hot milk and whisk well. Cook over a low heat for 2 minutes. Pass through a fine chinois or sieve and allow to cool down. Pour the mix into a Rowser beaker and freeze and then blitz in the Rowser when needed or churn the mix in an ice cream machine for 20 minutes and then freeze.

BROWN SODA BREAD

Makes 4 loaves

725gm (1lb 9oz) plain flour
475gm (1lb) wholemeal flour
185gm (6½oz) wheat bran
25gm (1oz) bicarbonate of soda (bread soda)
30gm (1oz) salt
10gm (½oz) caster sugar
110gm (4oz) Avonmore unsalted butter
50gm (2oz) free-range egg yolks
1275ml (2¼ pints) Avonmore buttermilk

Preheat the oven to 200°C. Grease 4 loaf tins, each measuring 19cm x 9cm x 5cm (7½in x 3½in x 2in). Mix all the dry ingredients and butter together. In a separate bowl, mix together the egg yolks and buttermilk. Add the wet mix into the dry mix and bring together by hand to form a dough. Divide the dough into four even pieces and place each one in a greased loaf tin. Transfer to the hot oven and bake for 1 hour 20 minutes. Remove the loaves from the tins. Turn the oven down to 180°C and return the loaves to the oven for a further 40 minutes. Remove from the oven and wrap the loaves in a tea towel to cool.

SWEET SPICED BREAD

Makes 1 loaf

455gm (1lb) plain flour
60gm (2oz) dark rye flour
2½ tsp baking soda
1½ tsp ground cinnamon
1½ tsp ground ginger
½ tsp salt
¼ tsp fresh grated nutmeg
¼ tsp ground cloves
¼ tsp ground black pepper
½ tsp ground aniseed
55gm (2oz) Avonmore unsalted butter, at room temperature
1 large free-range egg
340gm (12oz) honey
zest of 1 large orange
240ml (8½fl oz) water

Preheat the oven to 180°C. Sieve all the dry ingredients together. In a separate bowl, mix the soft butter, egg, honey and orange zest together. Add the water and mix well to combine. Add one-third of the dry ingredient mix and mix well, add another third and mix well and finally add the last third and mix well. Grease a loaf tin measuring 19cm x 9cm x 5cm (7½in x 3½in x 2in) with unsalted butter, dust with flour, shake off excess flour and pour the bread mix into the tin. Bake in the oven for 60 minutes. The top of the bread will darken, but that is fine. Remove from the oven and allow to cool in the tin for 10 minutes, then tip the bread out to cool on a wire rack.

PREPARING WHOLE LOBSTER

I have found that killing and breaking down a lobster quickly produces the most tender and succulent results. This process does not call for dropping the lobster into boiling water. It demands quick and efficient killing and breaking down of the shellfish, along with patience in the cooking process. We have found that, even though a lobster may be dead, its muscles need to stop seizing before it is cooked in order to prepare a succulent dish. Brining helps to season the lobster while also cleaning the flesh and tenderising the meat.

brine for 4 lobsters
15 litres (25 pints) water
750gm (1lb 8oz) salt

FOR THE LOBSTER

4 lobsters

THE BRINE

In a large pot combine the salt and the water. The salt will take some time to dissolve and quite a bit of stirring, but be patient, it will dissolve. Once the salt is dissolved, divide the brine into three containers: one large enough to hold the lobster tails (with brine), one to hold the claws and legs (with brine) and one to hold the heads of the lobsters (with brine).

THE LOBSTER

Place a live lobster on the cutting board. Take an oyster knife and plunge it into the lobster's shell between and directly behind the eyes. Twist the oyster knife a half turn and remove it. This procedure destroys the lobster's brain, killing it instantly. Remove the tail from the body. If any dark green roe is apparent, remove it and retain. Repeat with the remaining lobsters. Place the tails in the container with the brine as prepared above and refrigerate for two hours.

Remove the claws and the knuckles from the lobster bodies. Separate the knuckle joint from the claws. Leave the flesh in the shells. When the claws and knuckles are all separated, place them in the container of brine and refrigerate for two hours.

This brining process will help to clean the lobster and draw out the hemolymph, which runs through its body. As the muscles continue to contract, the hemolymph and brine exchange places. The salt denatures the surface proteins of the lobster and the proteins in the hemolymph. This allows for the lobster to be cooked without developing much albumen coagulation on the outside of the flesh. Furthermore, the brine seasons the meat and makes for a flavourful lobster.

After one hour, remove the lobster bodies from the brine and rinse them in cold water.

After two hours, remove the tails, claws and knuckles from the brine and rinse in cold water. Refrigerate overnight. The reason for waiting to cook the lobster is that the lobster muscle fibres only stop contracting after 24 hours. If we cook the lobster when the muscle fibres have stopped contracting, the flesh will be more tender and succulent.

Place a large pot of water on the hob to boil. Since every part of the lobster is a different size and has a different muscle fibre structure, each needs a different cooking time. Blanch the lobster parts in boiling water to cook the lobster just long enough to be able to remove the flesh from its shell. The knuckles and the legs are the exception, as they are just cooked through after blanching and can still be reheated.

To prepare lobster tails for carpaccio (uncooked): To prepare the lobster tails, grasp the shell in the middle and squeeze while pulling the shell away. Slowly ease the tail out and the lobster's digestive tract should come with it. Repeat with the other tails. If the tail does not come all the way out, it may be removed after blanching the tails. Peel back the shell and then carefully pull the lobster out of its shell. Cool quickly by placing the tail in a pan or bowl set in a bath of iced water. Repeat the shell removal process with the other tails.

To prepare cooked lobster tails: Place the tails in a vacuum-pack bag and seal. Place in a waterbath set to 65°C. Place a needle probe in one of the tails and cook until the probe reaches 60°C.

To cook the crusher (larger) claws, place them in the boiling water for 4 minutes. Remove, drain and place on a cutting board. When the claws are cool enough to handle, hold them horizontally on the board with the rounded side of the claw facing up. Hold the claw by its pincers. Use the back of a heavy knife to crack the edge of the claw, keeping the knife perpendicular to the claw. After the first crack is made in the claw, lay the claw flat on the cutting board and use the back of the knife to follow the crack line so that a crack runs right around the claw. Pick up the claw by the rounded side and grasp the straighter smaller portion of the claw. Snap this smaller piece 45° in either direction to loosen it from the claw itself. Use a kitchen towel to remove the cracked-off bottom of the claw and free the flesh. Gently pull the small claw tip out of the remaining claw. This will free the flesh of the claw and pull out the central cartilage from inside the claw. Place the cleaned claw in the pan set in iced water.

To cook the knuckles, place them in the boiling water for 3 minutes, then remove them from the water and put them on the cutting board. When the knuckles are cool enough to handle, use a pair of scissors to cut through the shell and release the knuckles. To cut the knuckles, lay them on the cutting board with the bendable joint facing up. Follow the edges on either side of the knuckle and cut away the plate of shell. Gently pull the knuckle out of the shell. As you pull the knuckle out, the cartilage that runs through it will come out as well. Place the cleaned knuckle in the pan set in iced water. Repeat this procedure with the remaining knuckles.

INDEX

T

V

W

Y